BULLYING
IN THE WORKPLACE

BULLYING
IN THE
WORKPLACE

An occupational hazard

HELENE RICHARDS • SHEILA FREEMAN

HarperCollins*Publishers*

HarperCollins*Publishers*

First published in Australia in 2002
by HarperCollins*Publishers* Pty Limited
ABN 36 009 913 517
A member of the HarperCollins*Publishers* (Australia) Pty Limited Group
www.harpercollins.com.au

HarperCollins*Publishers*
25 Ryde Road, Pymble, Sydney NSW 2073, Australia
31 View Road, Glenfield, Auckland 10, New Zealand
77–85 Fulham Palace Road, London W6 8JB, United Kingdom
Hazelton Lanes, 55 Avenue Road, Suite 2900, Toronto, Ontario M5R 3L2
and 1995 Markham Road, Scarborough, Ontario M1B 5M8 Canada
10 East 53rd Street, New York NY 10022, USA

Richards, Helene, 1949– .
   Bullying in the workplace: an occupational hazard.
   ISBN 0 7322 7424 9.
   1. Bullying in the workplace. 2. Conflict management.
   I. Freeman, Sheila, 1948– . II. Title.
331.133

Cover and internal design by Luke Causby, HarperCollins Design Studio
Printed and bound in Australia by Griffin Press on 79gsm Bulky Paperback White

5 4 3 2 1   02 03 04 05

CONTENTS

Acknowledgments   vii

Introduction   ix

PART 1

THE BULLY

Chapter 1   Workplace bullying   3

Chapter 2   Bullies — their profiles   19

Chapter 3   Why bullies bully   35

THE VICTIM

Chapter 4   'It was only a joke!'   44

Chapter 5   'Why me?'   53

Chapter 6   Bad for your health   60

THE WORKPLACE

Chapter 7   Business bears the cost   74

Chapter 8   Co-workers and bystanders   88

Chapter 9   Employers' 'duty of care'   94

MAKING A COMPLAINT

Chapter 10   Victims — choices to make   106

Chapter 11   Unions — help or hindrance?   122

Chapter 12   Legal options   129

PART 2

THE AFTERMATH

Chapter 13   The bully — is there another way?   143

Chapter 14   Survivors — leaving the past behind   151

Chapter 15   Employers — where to from here?   164

VOICES OF EXPERIENCE

Chapter 16   Personal journeys   180
Chapter 17   What the practitioners say   198
Chapter 18   The employer view   227

Conclusion   247

Appendix A Australia: tackling workplace bullying   251

Appendix B Australian laws relevant to workplace
                violence, harassment and discrimination   256

Appendix C Where to get help   258

Appendix D Human Synergistics information sheet:
                impact of management style on staff
                behaviour   263

Bibliography   268

Endnotes   271

ACKNOWLEDGMENTS

We owe a debt of gratitude to the following people: Terry Amey, Paul Azzopardi, Amanda Barker, Julie-Anne Bennett, Judith Cooke, Jim Glaspole, Barbara Gurry, Carl Marsich, Philip Merifield, Stephanie Merifield, Susan Miller, David Morarty, John O'Reilly, Michael Peacock, Jane Rylance, Patsy Toop, Jill Wood and Jo-Anne Zappia, and to the many professionals who preferred not to be named but very generously gave us their insights into different aspects of bullying. We are also grateful to Annie and Greg, the Crown Hotel, Newstead, for meals and chat and to Evelyn, Collins Bookstore, Altona Gate, for her encouragement.

Special thanks to Cathy Jenkins, HarperCollins, for her professionalism and ready availability, and to all those who shared their stories with us, even though it meant reliving a time of great trauma. Most of you did not want to be acknowledged by name, and we have respected your wishes. You know who you are and we thank you.

As individuals, we wish to thank special people.

Helene — I thank Colin for his encouragement, forbearance, incisive comments and assistance with editing; Sarah, Sean and Callum for their patience and willingness to endure domestic chaos; and my extended family and friends for putting up with my lack of chat, availability and sociability over the past few months.

Sheila — I thank Jeff for his continuous love and support, particularly during the last few difficult years, and for his cooking, washing and ironing; Claire for being patient when she rang from overseas and I couldn't talk as I was too busy with 'the book'; Christopher and Stuart who agreed to go out for so many meals; Helene, Terry and Barbara for their belief in me, their support and encouragement; Bev for allowing me to sit in her lounge and drink coffee; my ex-colleagues for their unstinting support; Scooter and Molly for keeping me sane.

We are extremely grateful to David Williamson and Currency Press for permission to use sections of *Charitable Intent*.

Charitable Intent is the third of a trilogy of 'community conferencing' plays (the first was *Face to Face* and the second *A Conversation*). This complex and topical play looks at workplace tensions in the not-for-profit sector.

The characters are:

Jack (the conciliator/facilitator)

Amanda (long-term employee, program manager and primary victim of bullying)

Brian (chair, board of management)

Stella (long-term employee and Amanda's only supporter, Stella worked as financial controller until she was switched to researching for Bryony)

Tamsyn (human resources manager)

Cassie (previously Stella's assistant, Cassie took over Stella's job)

Giulia (head of public relations and marketing)

Bryony (chief executive officer)

Apart from Jack, the players are employed by a charitable organisation called 'Enabling and Caring', which assists the intellectually and physically impaired. Two and a half years previously, Bryony took over as CEO. Bullying in the workplace is the major focus of *Charitable Intent*. The play, a story of victimisation and ruthless personal ambition, focuses on a workplace mediation conference that attempts to resolve tensions caused by Bryony's efforts to reform what she regards as outdated work practices.

Disclaimer: Some case studies are taken verbatim from taped interviews, some are condensed versions of stories told to us in interviews, some have been written by the victims themselves, and some are compilations of cases told to us. Because of confidentiality issues, all names have been changed and any identifying information removed.

INTRODUCTION

All Human Beings are born free and equal in dignity and rights ... No one should be subjected to arbitrary interference with his privacy, family, correspondence, nor to attacks upon his honour and reputation. Every one has protection of the law against such interference or attacks.

Articles 1 and 12 Universal Declaration of Human Rights 1948

Bullying. What do we think of when we hear this word? For most of us, it conjures up images of the schoolyard — taunts and fist fights, stolen lunches, trashed lockers, groups of girls sniggering and pointing; we have all been victims or witnesses of school bullying, and may even have participated in it. We have read shocking stories of apprentices being tortured by older workmates, and military recruits being brutalised. Fortunately, times have changed. Australian schools now have policies that attempt to prevent or minimise bullying; children are taught that such behaviour is unacceptable, and that, if bullying does occur, there will be serious consequences for the perpetrators. The Australian Defence Forces have adopted similar policies and, hopefully, fines and criminal convictions handed down against employers in recent cases of workplace violence will deter others from continuing traditional workplace cruelty to young employees.

Despite this growing awareness, bullying remains widespread in our society. Why? Is it because some school bullies continue their aggressive behaviour into adulthood? Is it because, in some areas, we accept bullying as part of the Australian culture? For example, it is condoned, and even encouraged, in our adversarial legal and political systems, in stricter parenting styles and in sport (sledging, verbal abuse, standover tactics, 'behind the play' attacks). The bullying style of certain media personalities and programs is even considered 'entertainment' (as in the aggressive responses of some talkback radio hosts to callers and the pugnacious nature of reality-TV game shows).

The prevalence of bullying in Australian workplaces has recently become an open issue for governments, trade unions and employers. In the past decade, there has been a significant rise in the number of reports of workplace bullying, with a 1998 Morgan poll[1] indicating that 46 per cent of Australian employees have been verbally abused or physically assaulted by a co-worker or manager, 31 per cent have suffered verbal abuse from a manager and 35 per cent from a co-worker, and 50 per cent of employees have experienced verbal abuse by members of the public.[2] A 2001 VicHealth survey found that 91 per cent of Victorians had been intimidated, teased, belittled, or verbally or physically abused to the extent that they could no longer tolerate it.[3] A 2000 ACTU anti-bullying Occupational Health and Safety campaign surveying over 3000 participants revealed that almost 70 per cent of respondents were bullied by a manager or supervisor, but in only 18 per cent of these cases was something done to stop the mistreatment.[4] Recent research and studies show similar levels of workplace bullying in the United States and the United Kingdom.

What the statistics don't show is the catastrophic effect of bullying on its victims. A hostile work environment can lead to depression, prolonged duress stress disorder (PDSD), mental and/or physical breakdown, financial problems, marital conflict, divorce and even suicide. Let's face it, many Australians spend more time at work than they do at home and their families get the time left over from their working day. When the victim's employment is terminated, either voluntarily or involuntarily, as a result of bullying, the job loss is an additional trauma, especially for those people who equate themselves with their jobs. Losing such a major part of their lives cuts to the core, leaving behind scars which, in most cases, are as raw many years later as they were when the job loss occurred, and which never quite heal. Sadly, victims are often not believed and receive little support from colleagues and employers, with their distress attributed to a lack in themselves rather than a problem within the workplace. Survivors of bullying recall the insidious erosion of self-esteem, their confidence in their own abilities and their belief that 'the good guy wins in the end'.

We decided to write this book because we know from personal experience that workplace bullying is traumatic and painful and that it has long-lasting effects. The more we researched, the more complexities we found. There are so many layers that need to be taken into consideration — the victim, the perpetrator, the co-workers, the employer, the victim's background, the perpetrator's background and personality, and outside forces which may impact on the situation. We have tried to present the overall picture in a way that is practical, comprehensive and easy to read. We summarise the different types of workplace bully, the effects of bullying on employees and employers, the rights of employees and employers, legal avenues for victims, and more.

Workplace bullying is certainly not a black-and-white situation. We found that some people who accuse others of bullying are often guilty of that behaviour themselves, so employers need to ensure that those accused of bullying receive justice. As well as helping victims, this book will be a useful resource for employers, human resource managers, employees, counsellors, secondary and higher education lecturers and students, GPs, psychologists and therapists.

We use the word 'victim' in the text to denote the abused worker, though many researchers avoid that word because it has connotations of vulnerability and helplessness. We prefer plain language — victims *are* vulnerable and helpless in the beginning but, with support and acknowledgment of their trauma, they can take charge of their lives once again and begin the healing process. Occasionally, we have had to use 'him' or 'he' when referring to the bully and the victim; this was done for ease of writing and reading only and should *not* be taken as an indication that we assume all bullies and victims are male.

Our methodology? We *talked* to people. We spoke to our friends, relatives and professional contacts, who then referred us to their contacts, and so it went on. In supermarkets, coffee shops, hotels, restaurants, offices, just a mention of the topic brought forth story after story, from workers, other customers and passers-by, of their own experiences of mistreatment and those of colleagues, family members or friends. We estimate that approximately 50 per cent had had some experience of workplace bullying, as victims or witnesses, and one in four had experienced long-term systemic abuse. We were overwhelmed by the number of people willing to speak to us even though, for many, this meant reliving the experience and revisiting a time of extreme stress. Some survivors of workplace bullying have written their personal journeys in the hope that other victims will read their stories and realise that they are not alone, the bullying was not their fault, they can get through it and will emerge stronger, safe and able to get on with their lives.

We also interviewed or had feedback from employers (large and small businesses), health professionals and human resource practitioners.

This is not an academic text. It is more of a victim impact statement, showing the catastrophic effect of bullying. Case studies —

stories of bewilderment, pain, despair and survival — are used extensively to give these victims a voice, in the hope that perpetrators and employers can truly understand the damage that bullying does. The more stories we heard, the more we began to grasp the enormity of the problem. When we understood how many people's lives had been damaged — in some cases, destroyed — we felt a sense of outrage. In our politically correct society, how has this been allowed to happen, and how has it been allowed to continue, virtually unchecked?

PART 1

CHAPTER 1

Workplace bullying

A threat is basically a means for establishing a bargaining position by inducing fear in the subject. When a threat is used, it should always be implied that the subject himself is to blame by using words such as 'You leave me no other choice but to...' He should never be told to comply, 'or else!'

CIA Human Resources Manual, for Latin America, recently declassified, 1997.

We are all capable of behaving like bullies. As a society, Australians have come to expect instant gratification. Advances in technology have given us fast food, microwave meals in minutes and computers on which we can work from a vast geographical distance, pay bills, e-mail friends overseas, even have cyber sex. As a consequence, we are not used to waiting for what we want. When queues are long or our telephone call is put 'on hold', frustration goads us into abusing the bank teller, the supermarket checkout person, or the call-centre operator. Which of us has not been guilty of rudeness in such circumstances?

These sorts of aggravation, combined with high levels of general stress caused by other factors, such as overwork, fatigue, lack of job security and financial or relationship problems, have led to an upsurge in episodes such as spectator violence and umpire abuse at sporting events, and incidents of 'urban rage syndrome',[5] such as road rage. However, such outbursts, if they are one-off incidents and of which we later feel ashamed, do not make us bullies. Bullying is a game of power and control usually played by psychologically damaged people.

What is workplace bullying?

There are hundreds of different definitions of workplace bullying or abuse, some far more complex than others. We define bullying generally as a *repeated pattern of unprovoked, unwelcome hostile behaviour that intentionally inflicts, or attempts to inflict, injury, hurt, humiliation or discomfort*. Workplace bullying has other components.

- It occurs in a situation where there is **an imbalance of power**, which can be real or perceived. This 'misuse of relative power ... can arise in many areas: size, seniority, authority, control of resources other people need, or social influence',[6] it can be a difference in personality (one person is more dominant and forceful than the other) or in command of language (one person has a sharper tongue or a quicker wit than another). Though bullying more commonly occurs from a higher level down, it can also take place 'horizontally' (between employees at the same level) or upwardly (directed by a lower level employee towards a supervisor or manager).

- There may be **a single perpetrator or a group of bullies**. With a group, there is usually a ringleader, with others condoning the conduct or behaving similarly, often because they wish to avoid becoming the next victim.
- The abusive behaviour **usually gets worse over time** and is able to continue long term because victims and witnesses are afraid to retaliate or confront the bully.
- Bullying often **begins or intensifies as a result of change** in the workplace, for example, the arrival of a new manager, or a new colleague who is competent or has superior social skills.
- Bullying is **often condoned by upper management** and written off as 'tough management', a personality clash or an attitude problem.
- Most victims of bullying suffer from loss of self-esteem, chronic stress and other serious **physical and mental health problems**, which have a further detrimental impact on their relationships with partners, families, friends and colleagues.

In a workplace situation, some conflict and interpersonal difficulties are inevitable simply as a result of normal human interaction, but many of these can be dealt with through in-house mediation or, if the problem can't be solved internally, through the appropriate industrial relations channels. There are few avenues able to successfully resolve workplace bullying situations.

There are two basic types of workplace bullying:

1. Physical

Physical bullies physically pressure or assault their victims in some way, for example, touching, pushing, hitting, kicking or worse. This is more commonly a masculine behaviour, used to improve one's status or to appear macho in front of workmates. The bully thinks, 'It's just a joke, we're having fun, I'm not really hurting anyone' and, in the majority of cases, such as Damien's below, no one does get hurt. Sometimes, however, the joke goes too far and turns into outright criminal assault, such as extremes of the traditional rituals that tradesmen often inflict on apprentices.[7] These bullies are easy to identify and in most countries there is legislation to contain this form of bullying.

When I was seventeen, I commenced an electrical apprenticeship with a large company that worked on construction sites. On my first day the site foreman jokingly told me to watch out for the boys, as every new apprentice goes through an initiation. I didn't think much of it, until lunchtime when I went into the site shed and one of the guys offered me a seat. I sat down, then suddenly I was on the ground, with everyone laughing at me. The chair's legs had been cut so that they would collapse.

Thinking this must have been my initiation, I laughed with them. But after that, just about every day, I was bullied in various ways. I particularly remember two events. The first happened when I was working on top of a ladder. One of the guys started shaking it and I nearly fell. I am afraid of heights and was nearly crying with terror; when they eventually stopped, I got down and threw up in the bushes. I felt so bad that I had to go home. From then on they called me a 'wimp'. The second thing, which really got to me, was when three of the guys actually nailed me to a wall with a nail gun. They grabbed me, held me up against the timber wall, shot the nails through my shirt and overalls, and then they left me there for more than two hours. I tried to tell the foreman but he said, 'They do it to everyone, just laugh it off.' My bullying didn't stop until another apprentice was taken on twelve months later.

(Damien, 23, electrician)

Some physical bullying behaviours, such as assault (including indecent assault), may be criminal offences; the police should be contacted in these circumstances.

2. Pyschological

Psychological bullies use subtle, underhand strategies to undermine their victims, mentally and emotionally. More devious and calculating than physical bullying, psychological bullying includes verbal abuse, such as taunts, name-calling, hurtful personal remarks, malicious teasing, the subtle undermining of performance and competence by strategies such as isolation, humiliation, excessive supervision, denial of leave and so on. Psychological bullies are the most common in the workplace but also the most difficult to identify and expose because either there are no witnesses to their behaviour or it is done under the guise of 'humour' or 'tough management'. With psychological bullying, it is the steady build-up of small incidents, rather than major incidents, that wears the victim down.

Physical bullying is another term for workplace violence and, because justice is available through the criminal system in cases of workplace violence (and through anti-discrimination or equal opportunity laws in cases of harassment and discrimination[8]), we will not be addressing these issues. Instead, this book concentrates on psychological bullying, which is more damaging to the victim's mental and emotional wellbeing, yet is not an offence under any current legislation unless it escalates into physical violence.

CASE STUDY

There was never anything I could put my finger on, or really complain about. Her put-downs were so subtle, so clever, and delivered with such a sweet smile, that only I noticed. I used to feel ill whenever she came near me, dreading the next concealed knife-thrust into my self-esteem. My friends at work thought she was really nice and said I was imagining things.

(Freda, 44, sales assistant)

Can you give more examples of the strategies used by psychological bullies?

We list below some of the behaviours that constitute psychological bullying. Remember, to be considered bullying, these behaviours need to be *repeated over time and intentionally hurtful*, not just a one-off occurrence.

- **Attacks on work performance**: nit picking; trivial fault-finding; constant unjustified criticism of work; distorted or fabricated allegations of underperformance or incompetence with no acknowledgment of achievements; responsibility increased but authority removed; unrealistic goals or deadlines; unachievable performance measures; goals changed without consultation or notice; unnecessarily strict supervision or excessive monitoring of performance; verbal and/or written warnings that lack basis or substance; unfair or manipulative complaints to management; isolating or ignoring; denial of adequate resources, training or attendance at work-related conferences; removal of work, leaving virtually nothing to do; blocking applications for promotion.
- **Belittling movements**: eye rolling; eyebrow lifting; heavy sighs; finger gestures; shoulder shrugging; arm waving.
- **Denial or manipulation of leave**: having requests for annual leave denied; having leave cancelled despite prior approval; having leave interrupted by constant work-related telephone calls.

> AMANDA: My annual leave application was turned down and scheduled for the middle of winter.
> TAMSYN: I did the best I could for you Amanda, but not everyone can go on leave in summer.

- **Emotional attacks**: made to feel guilty, think you have 'lost the plot' or are going mad; your attitude or personality blamed for work problems; the impression of you held by colleagues manipulated adversely.

- **Forced departure**: manipulated into reluctant resignation; targeted for redundancy or 'restructuring'; made to accept early retirement or departure due to ill health.

- **Isolation**: ignored or ostracised within the workplace or at team meetings; given the silent treatment; communicated with via memorandums, e-mails or Post-it notes left on desk; different treatment, that is, given less flexibility or leeway than other staff.

- **Sabotage**: intentional exclusion from essential information, tools or systems; tampering with work equipment; provision of misinformation, later explained as your misinterpretation; unfair allocation of shifts; not kept informed of workplace developments; having work or ideas stolen, plagiarised or copied, with the bully taking credit for it; meetings called when you are unavailable; colleagues 'requested' (under perceived threat to their positions) to manufacture written complaints about you.

- **Threats of dismissal**: unjustified disciplinary action on fabricated charges or flimsy excuses leading to threats of dismissal; invitations to 'meetings' which, in reality, are disciplinary hearings; denied representation at internal grievance meetings because the bully fears that a union representative or mediator will expose his bullying.

AMANDA: Tamsyn said it was last chance time for me. I either had to make a big effort to adapt to the new corporate culture or clear my desk and get out. I said I had no intention of getting out.
JACK: What happened then?
AMANDA: The bad times started in earnest.

- **Too much work**: an overload of work, raising the risk of mistakes being made and/or tasks not being completed on time; expectation of long working hours.

- **Undermining**: having decisions overruled; not having a clear job description (a deliberate strategy to make role unclear); devaluation of role (important and interesting tasks taken away and replaced with menial tasks such as photocopying and filing).
- **Verbal attacks**: shouting; temper tantrums; irrational outbursts; threats; spiteful teasing; insults; continued deliberate use of offensive language; spreading malicious gossip or lies; ridicule; humiliating or patronising comments made in front of others; constant name-calling, for example, 'psycho', 'loser,' 'waste of space'.

Louise's story below is a typical example of psychological bullying.

CASE STUDY

I had been working for a large electrical company in administration for over ten years, and got on really well with my immediate manager, often acting in her position when she was on leave. When she left, the new manager seemed to take an instant dislike to me. I don't know why. I had always received excellent appraisals and had successfully completed a review of our administration processes for which I received commendations from the Director. It's hard to remember exactly when it started, but odd things began to happen — documents would go missing off my desk, important telephone messages were not passed on and, in two instances, I acted on misinformation and was totally embarrassed. I was the most experienced in the office area as I had worked there the longest, but as soon as this new manager came she excluded me from everything she possibly could. She would completely bypass me and ask other staff members for their opinions and gain their involvement. My position was 'restructured' and I went from a responsible position to doing the jobs the junior used to do. I finally built up the courage to ask the manager what I had done wrong. She patronisingly commented that sometimes it was difficult for people to adjust to change, and suggested that I needed to be more flexible and not so sensitive. Everything she did was so subtle and calculated. She was even overheard accepting praise for work I had done. I have never felt so helpless in my life. She would call me into her room saying that she needed to talk to me about my 'attitude' at work. She was a professional bully!

(Louise, 43, administrator)

Some people accuse others of bullying when, in fact, they are the ones doing the bullying by manipulating co-workers into 'ganging up' against the victim.

I went in with high hopes and expectations. I'm a good manager, and my staff and colleagues have always responded well to me in previous jobs, so I had no reason to believe this one would be different. But I was shut out, sidelined, from the very beginning. My approaches to staff were met with blank faces. They were polite but never said more than the bare minimum; there were no smiles. My instructions were ignored and work was done the old way. The blanket response was, 'That's the way we've always done it.' They were like puppets and I soon realised who was controlling them. Isabel had somehow got them on side before I started — it was never going to work. Isabel had been acting manager before I arrived and felt that I was in 'her job', that I had unfairly ousted her. Messages from higher up were not given to me, I missed meetings and appointments (an important client waited almost forty minutes for me because I was 'double-booked' and no one told me he was there). It was made impossible for me to perform competently and the last straw was when, after I told her I knew what she was up to, she went to the CEO and accused me of bullying her. She was an astute operator with enormous physical appeal, very good-looking, very 'sweet', softly spoken, and so charismatic that everyone believed her. Fortunately, I had recorded every incident of sabotage, with the time, dates and the name of the person I knew or suspected had done it. There was an inquiry and Isabel and two of her more active cronies eventually left. But so did I. I had endured the bullying for twelve months and, for me, the place was tainted.

(Miriam, 41, general manager)

What are the differences between bullying, workplace violence, discrimination and harassment?

These are all unacceptable abusive behaviours that can occur in a workplace and, because they can overlap, it is often difficult to decide which category the behaviour fits. Obviously, though, when violence or bullying has a particular focus, such as race or gender, it presents as racial or sexual discrimination or harassment. We have tried to summarise the essential differences below.

Workplace violence

Workplace violence can be physical or non-physical. **Physical violence** includes behaviours such as pushing, shoving, punching, kicking, unwelcome sexual touching and sexual assault; **non-physical violence** includes verbal abuse, intimidation and threatening behaviour. Common victims of workplace violence are found 'in industries where people work alone and handle cash, such as taxi drivers, service station attendants and late night retail outlet operators'.[9] Shift workers, such as police, security guards, pizza deliverers and public transport employees, are also vulnerable.

Workplace violence is different to bullying in the following ways.

- **Workplace violence** may be a one-off, random occurrence (for example, from a dissatisfied customer or client) and is often triggered by alcohol or drugs; **psychological bullying** is calculated, carried out repeatedly and over time.
- **Violence at work** is usually open, in front of witnesses; most **psychological bullying** is done 'on the quiet', without witnesses, or in such a subtle manner than onlookers do not notice.
- Some forms of **workplace violence**, such as physical or sexual assault, are clearly criminal acts, which can be dealt with by the courts; there is no legislation that *specifically* covers **bullying** and litigation is rarely settled to the satisfaction of the victim (with most pulling out of the WorkCover process before it gets in to the court system).
- **Victims of violence** usually report it; **victims of bullying** hesitate to report their experiences because often the bullying is covert and the damage is psychological.

The most important difference, however, is that **violence** is infrequent whereas **psychological bullying** is more prevalent: it is often a daily occurrence for victims and is estimated to affect 25 per cent of the workforce.[10] Media headlines[11] about workplace violence tend to distract attention from the less obvious forms of bullying, even though they have an equally devastating effect on the lives of victims.

Discrimination

Discrimination can be direct or indirect. **Direct discrimination** is when one person is treated less favourably than another because of gender, race, ethnic origin, religion or disability. **Indirect discrimination** is where there is a requirement or rule which is the same for all but has an unequal effect on a particular group, for example, the high wall that all potential Victoria Police recruits were once expected to scale, discriminated against women because of their smaller body size and strength (the wall has since been removed). Australian anti-discrimination laws (Federal, State and Territory) already protect employees from various forms of discrimination (see Appendix B).

Harassment

Harassment is unwanted, unwelcome, offensive and intrusive behaviour, which may range from unpleasant comments to physical violence. If the behaviour relates to gender or sexual orientation, for example, suggestive comments or jokes, leering or unwelcome touching, it is termed **sexual harassment**; if it relates to skin colour, race or cultural background, it is termed **racial harassment**. If the harassment consists of following, watching, recurring unsolicited contact or gifts, it is termed stalking. The Commonwealth Sex Discrimination Act makes it unlawful to sexually harass another person, and all States and Territories have laws prohibiting sexual harassment (see Appendix B).

Because of the level of complexity in trying to differentiate between bullying and harassment — bullies do harass but harassment stands on its own — we have used Fatimah's story below to show where the bullying 'crosses the line' into discrimination and harassment.

CASE STUDY

I was working in a small office taking customer orders at the front counter. I loved my job and the people I was working with. Because I am Muslim, I always wear a headscarf, and this was accepted by the other staff. After I had been there for about eight months, a new staff member was taken on as my immediate manager. He seemed quite nice until one day, quite out of the blue, he called me 'hanky head'.* I was hurt, but didn't say anything as I thought it was a joke. But it wasn't.

He kept on saying it, then the rest of the staff picked it up. He would pick on me all the time, saying I wasn't taking enough calls, or taking down the wrong orders.** Then he took me away from the counter, saying customers would not want to deal with me 'dressed like that'.*** He hid me away in the store room. He said if I stopped wearing my headscarf, I could return to the front office.** I started to hate going to work, but I had to, as I needed the money to feed my family.

My manager then started coming up behind me, standing very close, putting his hand on my shoulder and trying to blow in my ear. Wherever I went in the office, he would follow me, trying to get me in a corner.****

In the end I couldn't take it any more, I was getting depressed and crying every day. So I left. I wish now that I had confronted him, or put in a complaint against him.

(Fatimah, 33, office worker)

* RACIAL HARASSMENT ** BULLYING *** RACIAL DISCRIMINATION **** SEXUAL HARASSMENT

How prevalent is bullying?

With no national statistics available on workplace bullying in Australia, the Beyond Bullying Association, using international research, estimated that between 400,000 and 2 million Australians would be bullied in 2001 and between 2.5 and 5 million will experience bullying at some point in their careers.[12] A survey conduced by the South Australian Working Women's Centre in 1997[13] found that over half of the respondents had been bullied over the last three months, and more than 80 per cent indicated that others were being bullied at work. In October 2000, Gary Collis, the South Australian Employee Ombudsman, said: 'Bullying has become endemic. My office sees it from small business to government agencies, from shop assistants to executives and professionals. One has to see it to recognise the pain and trauma ... One of the problems is the rewarding of bullies by promotion.'[14]

Of course, the full extent of bullying in Australia is unknown as many cases are not reported by victims. They may simply be reluctant to 'dob', may be fearful of losing their jobs, may not want to appear weak or unable to cope or may simply accept it as part of their working environment.

Reduction in trade union membership may be one reason for the increase in workplace bullying as bullies feel freer to abuse because they are aware of the lack of union support and assistance for their victims.

Who are the bullies?

Workplace bullies can be employers, managers, supervisors, individual work colleagues or groups of work colleagues. They are found in all walks of life, even amongst the clergy.

> He was running a small suburban parish at the time — and running scared of a superior cleric with a vicious tongue. So abusive were the tirades ... that [he took] Valium to help him cope ... 'It's like the battered-wife syndrome ... I kept thinking I must have contributed to the situation.'[15]

In some instances the bully can be the workplace itself when an autocratic organisation has an entrenched culture of long working hours or where staff are told what to do and not permitted any personal initiatives (see 'Organisational or corporate bullying', page 26-29, Chapter 2). Indications from other literature and data are that between 75 and 80 per cent of bullies are managers.[16] 'Managers, principals and chief executive officers are rarely brought to account. Yet, they are not only responsible for bullying in the ranks — too often they are the bullies.'[17]

Bullying does not appear to be gender specific — both women and men bully, and both men and women suffer from bullying. However, if we accept from the above statistics that those in positions of authority are more likely to be guilty of bullying, then it follows that bullies are more likely to be male, not because they are innately bad people but simply because there are more males in positions of authority. Others might take the opposing view — that there would be more female bullies — because the more 'female' professions are prone to bullying, that is teaching,[18] nursing[19], health and community services.[20]

Why has workplace bullying only recently become a major issue?

While bullies have always existed, it is only recently that physical violence and discrimination in the workplace have been clearly identified as unacceptable behaviours by a national implementation of legal deterrents (see Appendix B). Ironically, this may have instigated an increase in bullying behaviour, that is, with open harassment, discrimination and physical violence now against the law, abusers have been forced to 'go underground' and to use covert aggressive strategies, like the psychological bullying behaviours listed previously.

Another reason for bullying being 'outed' recently may be that, as legal avenues to redress harassment and discrimination are used successfully, workers are becoming aware that abusive behaviour can be stopped, and so are more willing to report bullying and take action.

Employers, too, have come to realise that workplace bullying has to be contained because of the financial implications for them (such as increased WorkCover premiums). In recent years, significant financial damages have been awarded to employees who have suffered as a result of bullying — for example, $350,000 in Victoria,[21] $549,220.83[22] and $270,791.98 in Queensland.[23]

Media reports of results of surveys on bullying (such as the ACTU survey in 2000, the VicHealth survey in 2001) and reports of the cost to taxpayers of escalating stress claims (many as a result of bullying) have brought bullying to the attention of the general public.

How is Australia tackling this issue?

Governments, trade unions, employers, universities and community groups are beginning to understand the significant impact workplace bullying is having on Australian industry and to acknowledge a need to find methods to prevent and control the problem. Various publications and studies on this subject, as well as government initiatives, are outlined in Appendix A.

Where do human rights begin? In small places, close to home: the neighbourhood; the school or college; the factory, farm or office. Such are the places where every man, woman and child seeks equal justice, equal opportunity, equal dignity without discrimination. Unless these rights have meaning there, they have little meaning anywhere.

Eleanor Roosevelt

CHAPTER 2

Bullies — their profiles

And once all the men and women who want a reasonable life are taken out, that leaves the psychopaths, sociopaths and narrow-minded thugs. Anyone, in short, who is so obsessed with power they'll work 16 hours a day.

Eva Cox, University of Technology, Sydney, quoted in
'What (working) women want', by Denise Ryan, *Age*, 2 August 2001

'You can't tell a book by its cover.' How many times have we heard this or said it ourselves? This saying is very true when applied to bullies. There is no obvious bullying 'type' and you certainly cannot recognise them by their appearance. They can be good-looking, short, tall, fat, thin, with or without a beard — the delicate blonde with the baby-blue eyes is just as capable of bullying as the muscle-bound macho man.

There has been a lot of work done around the world to build up profiles of workplace bullies, but there is no universal terminology. Different researchers have given different names to the same type of bully, and some are so imaginative — 'Two-Headed Snake',[24] 'Screaming Mimi',[25] 'Corporate Hyena'[26] and so on — that they give a visual picture of some of the obvious bullying traits.

What are the different types of psychological bully?

We summarise the most widely recognised types below. However, please treat this as a guide only. Even though we have slotted them into specific groupings, many bullies will not fit neatly into one category. They will adopt whatever tactics are necessary to attain their goals and so may use behaviours that cross several categories.

1. Chronic or serial bullying

This is the most common type. The problems of many dysfunctional companies can often be traced to a chronic bully who has victimised a succession of employees with the aim of 'eliminating and destroying' them. Chronic bullying usually starts slowly and then escalates rapidly, as in Alice's case below.

CASE STUDY

It started with nit-picking, rude comments about my appearance, demoralising remarks made about me to others, encouraging them to do the same, and then it 'hotted up'. I can see now he was building up to a climax. It was like I was being stripped of my assets — access to a phone was taken away, my comfortable chair was replaced with a hard chair from the cafeteria, I was removed from my bright, airy office to a dark, much smaller office, and then all of a sudden I was out the door!

(Alice, 43, payroll officer)

The traits of chronic bullies are:

- **A 'split' or dual personality.** They are calculating, devious and vindictive in private but in public present as friendly and pleasant.

Their 'nice' façade is so convincing that they are able to fool their bosses, clients, management boards and tribunals, and victims are rarely believed by others because the bully has charmed them.

Everyone liked the new supervisor. She seemed interested in all of us, asked about our families and our hobbies, saying she liked to get to know what made us 'tick', and the bosses obviously thought she was great. After about two months, though, her attitude towards me started to change. At first it was just a coolness — her smile and charm were no longer directed at me. Then, she began criticising everything I did, and I knew she was talking about me to everyone else — they'd stop talking when I entered the office. Then, a few months later, at a team meeting, she tore strips off me in front of my colleagues, saying she had tried, and been 'very, very patient' with me, but I was not performing at my co-workers' standard and I could no longer expect a free ride. I turned to the others for support, but they couldn't wait to back her up, saying how tolerant she had been, that she had been protecting me until now, that I didn't seem to grasp basic essentials. I couldn't believe this attack, so I abruptly left the meeting. That evening I was so depressed that I went to see a friend, who is a psychologist. She said my supervisor sounded like a bully who wanted to get rid of me.

(Lorraine, 39, sales)

BRYONY: Don't try and act the innocent, Tamsyn. You wanted her out of there as much as I did ... you came bounding into my office with a huge grin on your face and said, 'We've got her.'

TAMSYN: OK. I became part of the game. It was like school again. All the 'in' group victimizing the outcast. It's insidious with someone like Bryony around. Even Stella joined in eventually.

BULLIES — THEIR PROFILES

- **Hypocritical.** In contrast to their actual behaviour and treatment of others, chronic bullies portray themselves as caring and thoughtful, even to their victims. 'I am only thinking of you,' the bully might say, before delivering a devastating criticism. This is obviously confusing for the victims, making them feel that there must be something wrong with them. Chronic bullies also give preferential treatment to some workers.

She had her favourites who got the plum jobs. She had long morning tea 'meetings' with them every day, from which the rest of us were excluded. Her cronies were allowed long lunches, sometimes took half-hour breaks to have a cigarette, left work early almost every day, and she said nothing. The rest of us were hauled over the coals if we were only a few minutes late for work.

(Sandra, 24, bank worker)

- **Accomplished liars.** They are highly skilled in the art of lying and, when called to account, lie so plausibly that they get away with their actions.
- Glib and superficial chameleons. They are glib and superficial 'Yes-men' who 'suck up' to others, and are able to say, with great skill, what others want to hear, that is, they are able to be all things to all people. Their social and people skills are a veneer only — there is no depth once you probe beneath the surface.
- **Control freaks.** They are arrogant and self-righteous, and need to be in control of every aspect of their lives, whether it be at work, at home with their families or socialising in the wider community. They believe they are always right, do not like anyone to question their decisions and do not delegate work or share information because they see that as losing control.

He was very domineering and it was his way or no way. He had to control everything and the atmosphere in the office was very tense. He was nice as pie to his bosses and the customers but treated me like dirt. He thought he was wonderful and if anything went wrong blamed everyone but himself. I was frightened of him and my work suffered.

(Rosemary, 19, receptionist)

- **Devoid of emotion.** They are inhumane, emotionally untrustworthy and lack empathy.

My mother rang to say that my father had been rushed to hospital after an accident. When I explained to my supervisor, Hazel, that I had to leave work, she made the appropriate noises but, in the next breath, told me that she expected me to make up lost time. My father was in a critical condition for some time. Hazel's only concern was that the work schedule didn't suffer and she expected me to come in at night and weekends to complete my hours. She kept saying things like, 'Well, if you don't want to work, there are plenty who do.' Even when Dad died, she made a big deal about me having the whole day off for his funeral.

(Denis, 29, postal worker)

- **Inflated ego.** They are narcissistic and delude themselves into believing that they are very good at their work and blame everyone but themselves for mistakes. However, they are also very sensitive to criticism, often misinterpreting what is said as negative comments about them.

Because we are not psychologists or psychiatrists, we do not 'label' bullies with any personality disorder. However, more qualified researchers have no such qualms. Tim Field, author of *Bully in*

Sight, believes that the characteristics of chronic or serial bullies mimic those present in people with narcissistic personality disorder (NPD), the symptoms of which are: a grandiose sense of self-importance; a desire for constant admiration; fixations of unlimited success and power, beauty or ideal love; a belief that he or she is 'extraordinary' and should only associate with influential or important people or be associated with high status institutions; unreasonable expectations of favourable treatment or immediate compliance with his or her expectations; exploitative interpersonal behaviour, that is taking advantage of others to achieve own ends; lack of empathy regarding the feelings of others; envy of others; arrogance.[27] Tim also believes that the majority of chronic or serial bullies have psychopathic characteristics,[28] and he is not alone in this belief.

John Clark, a University of Sydney psychologist, believes that up to 5 per cent of the population are psychopaths who have the same psychological make-up as killers, the only difference being they can 'hide their psychopathic tendencies behind the front of a respectable white collar job'. They show 'a pervasive pattern of disregard for and violation of the rights of others [and] a number of them are ticking time-bombs waiting to go off'.[29]

Robert Hare, Professor of Psychology at the University of Vancouver, says that psychopaths 'use superficial charm, manipulation, intimidation, and violence to control others and satisfy their own selfish needs. They lack conscience and feelings for others, cold-bloodedly take what they want and do as they please, violating social norms and expectations without the slightest guilt or regret.'[30]

These descriptions sound remarkably similar to some victims' descriptions of the people who bullied them. Most readers will encounter at least one person with the profile of the chronic bully during their working lives.

2. Opportunistic bullying

Many bullies are simply opportunists, who climb the ladder at work by successfully interpreting the workplace culture and noting the prevailing pattern of promotion. Their competitive nature means that they will step over anyone who gets in their way, manipulating circumstances to eliminate their rivals. Unlike the chronic bully, opportunistic bullies are able to leave their bullying at work and behave normally in their private lives.

Marcia and I had a lot in common and had been good friends since we began working together straight from university. One of our supervisors was leaving in six weeks and told us that we were both being considered for promotion to her position. Soon afterwards, things started to go wrong at work. Important files were misplaced, I missed several meetings because they weren't in my diary (Marcia swore she told me about them), customers complained that I didn't ring them back (again, Marcia said she left messages on my desk). She talked over me at meetings, took sole credit for work we'd done together and generally made me look like an idiot in front of the bosses. It was only when she got the promotion that I realised how she'd manipulated my 'incompetency'.

(Fiona, 25, market research)

3. Self-preserving bullying

In a competitive 'every-man-for-himself' environment, some people will bully because they see it as the only way to protect their jobs against a perceived threat, for example, an older, less-educated manager defending himself against a younger, better-qualified person, or a newcomer to a workplace feeling the need to get rid of a long-standing employee who knows the business inside-out and could show up the newcomer's weaknesses.

4. 'Sergeant major' bullying

Another type of bully — probably the least harmful — is the 'sergeant major', who runs the company like a battalion, expects instant obedience and does not require creativity or initiative from the staff. The person may have a military background and is the type of whom people say, 'His bark is worse than his bite.' There is usually no malice in this type of bullying.

CASE STUDY

I went straight to the company from school and couldn't believe how everyone jumped to attention when the boss spoke. They would stand up when he entered the room and would tremble if he gave them a tongue-lashing. He was a real tyrant — they were all afraid of him. I remember when I asked for a raise to bring me up to the same salary as the other [male] clerks, he said, 'We'll have none of that women's lib nonsense here, Miss Crowley. You'll get a rise when I say so and not before.'

(Maureen, 20, clerk)

5. Organisational or corporate bullying

Organisational or corporate bullies are employers who make unreasonable demands of their employees, knowing that people need their jobs. The size of the workplace is irrelevant; this form of bullying can take place in small businesses as well as large corporations. Some examples are:

• Employees are expected to work longer hours than they are paid for as that is the prevailing work culture (companies that model their businesses on American and Japanese work cultures are particular culprits here); anyone who does not conform is ostracised, sidelined or dismissed. This practice seems to be prevalent in the IT industry; despite good wages, the reality is that many IT professionals are being exploited.

I found out early on that no one left the office on the dot of five — in fact, anyone leaving before six-thirty was called in for an 'informal discussion' the next day and quizzed about his workload. There was competition to be the last one there. It was as though we were outstaying each other, like a grim sit-in situation. It became farcical in the end because no bosses were there to see who was left.

(Joel, 33, project management)

Inhumane eighteen-hour day, six-day weeks are long-accepted working conditions for doctors and lawyers fresh from university. 'There are countless anecdotal "horror stories" . . . of young lawyers . . . being exploited and pressured to work inhuman hours for which they receive no time off in lieu, nor overtime payments.'[31]

- Companies can inflict emotional damage on employees by poorly handled retrenchment or downsizing.

It left a horrible taste in everyone's mouths. She was trying so hard not to cry that she couldn't talk when I spoke to her. I gave her a hug and could feel her whole body shaking. The whole thing was so badly handled, and the rest of us started to wonder who would be next. Most started looking for other jobs straight away. We didn't want to be associated with a company that condoned their workers being treated with such contempt.

(Irene, 40, telephone sales)

- Sick workers continue to work in order to prove their loyalty or worth because there is a prevailing belief that really dedicated staff would not get sick.
- Employees suffering from stress or mental health conditions caused by the workplace find themselves 'restructured' out of their jobs because their conditions are seen as a sign of weakness or may cost the company financially if a stress claim is made in the future.

- Employees are forced to 'up-sell' to clients, that is try to sell an additional item after an initial sale has been made, with a certain percentage of successful up-sales expected of each staff member. (If you fall below this percentage, you can be asked to attend compulsory 'retraining'.) It has always been a practice at McDonald's stores, but is becoming increasingly common, for example, at service stations and in hairdressing salons. Even bank tellers push the bank's electronic and Internet banking services as an alternative to their 'face-to-face' services. Australians are generally unreceptive to this type of pressure and the bank employees are copping the backlash.

> *The standard line is to say: 'If I wanted it I would have bloody asked for it.' But you get a lot worse than that. Some people mimic you in a sarcastic voice, some people get abusive ... It certainly causes plenty of friction.*
>
> **(Brett, service station employee)[32]**

- Employee anxiety and insecurity are high because of workplace practices such as 'behind-closed-door' conversations, checking on employees' whereabouts, listening in to telephone conversations,[33] tracking or reading employee e-mail without their knowledge, constant talk about cutbacks or retrenchment.

> *Launching the results of a national survey of call-centre workers, Ms Burrow, President of the Australian Council of Trade Unions, told employers to listen to their staff. Intensive operator monitoring, substandard work environments and poor training and support are causing unacceptably high levels of stress amongst call-centre workers ...[34]*

- Employees are asked to accept short-term contracts instead of full-time permanent positions. Because of high unemployment, job applicants feel they have no choice but to accept below-award wages, even though this is illegal. Some employers may deliberately hire contractors over permanent employees, not because they are better or more efficient workers, but because the contract system gives employers more power and control. Bullies thrive when companies opt for outsourcing and short-term contracts because contractors feel no sense of belonging in the workplace and no real connection with, or loyalty towards, other employees.

> *In the service and retail sectors ... negotiation consists of slapping an individual contract on the table and saying, 'If you want the job, sign there ...' Ten-hour shifts are normal and 12 hours common, with no specified breaks, as is working up to 13 days a fortnight on broken rosters.*
>
> (Alan Holgate, Mooroolbark, Letters, *Age,* 31 July 2001)

- Employers take advantage of those who are vulnerable to exploitation and pay below-the-poverty line wages, for example, to university students who need casual work, outworkers (migrants who cannot speak English) and young, eager pilots who flying schools pay only for the time they are actually flying.

> *I know he doesn't pay me enough — $6 an hour — but I'd been looking for work for ages and he was the only one willing to take me on. He lets me pick and choose my shifts and I need that flexibility.*
>
> (Craig, 20, medical student)

Organisational bullying can start because of external factors, such as economic downturn, budget cuts or shareholder expectations of high profits.

6. Client bullying (sometimes called **pressure bullying**)

This type of bullying is prevalent in the service industries and occurs when momentary stress causes consumers to 'lose it'; they become frustrated, angry and short-tempered because of a perceived lack of service, and may shout or swear or even assault the victim. Increasingly, teachers are being bullied, and even assaulted, by parents and students; nurses by patients; social workers by clients. Bank tellers are abused on a daily basis by customers as a result of long queues, broken ATMs, bank charges and closing branches. Though workers in service industries are bullied by different people, the abuse is a constant factor in their working lives and has the same stressful effect as being bullied by one perpetrator.

Most of us 'lose our cool' from time to time and such incidents seem to be increasing rapidly, as shown by the rise of 'rage' incidents — road rage, computer rage, parking-space rage, queue-jumper rage and so on. Usually, however, when our stress levels return to normal, we will apologise and, hopefully, will handle the next such incident with more grace. It may not be so easy, however, for the telephone technician, the call-centre operator, the checkout person or the bank teller to forget what, for them, are regular, everyday occurrences.

CASE STUDY

I am regularly bullied by customers. One day I had repaired this guy's washing machine but he refused to pay the bill. I disabled his machine and said I wouldn't fix it again until he paid. He locked me in the house and started shoving me around, threatening to call in his mates to 'do me over'. Eventually his wife talked him into letting me go. I told the boss and thought a flag would go on the customer's file to mark him as aggressive and difficult, but in a few days I was told to call there again. When I refused and explained again what had happened, the call was passed on to another technician and the same thing happened to him.

(Mike, 48, parts and service technician)

7. Group/gang bullying (also called **mobbing**)

A group of bullies is often led by a chronic bully. Extrovert chronic bullies will be in front of their gangs, possibly screaming and yelling, making them easily identifiable (and also easy to put on tape or video to use as proof). Introverted chronic bullies generally initiate the attack and then stay in the background, making them harder to identify. Group bullying is common in workplaces where bullying is an accepted part of the culture.

Some members of the gang will bully because they get pleasure from it and enjoy being part of a powerful group, protected by the leader. Others may just want to fit in with the dominant clique, or join in because they are frightened of becoming victims themselves if they don't take part. With group bullying, if the planned attack goes wrong, one group member may end up becoming a scapegoat; angry victims will be persuaded to take their revenge on the scapegoat while the leader watches from a safe distance.

8. Pair bullying

This is when the chronic bully forms a strategic alliance with a colleague or subordinate to obtain power and control. One might bully while the other observes quietly; contrary to appearances, it is likely that the more active person is being manipulated by the passive partner. Also, the manipulated partner might be the 'mouthpiece' for the chronic bully, espousing the bully's 'good points' within the workplace and denigrating the chosen victim.

9. Secondary bullying

Secondary bullying happens when:

- people working with a chronic bully copy what they see as the established pattern of behaviour and also bully the victim
- a colleague of a bullied worker is coerced (for example, by threats of withdrawal of promotion or redundancy, or fear of

becoming a victim) into fabricating written complaints against the bullied worker to back up the bully

- a victim is pressured by rehabilitation providers (such as WorkCover, insurance companies and employers) to return to work as soon as possible, even though the bully is still there or the workplace culture remains the same, thus forcing the victim to choose between returning to the stressful situation and aggravating the trauma or resigning from the job.

10. Financial bullying

We have identified three forms of financial bullying. As secondary bullying, it occurs when a bullied worker is forced into the courts because the employer refuses to accept the WorkCover claim and so drags out the case (see April's story on page 181–4).

Financial bullying can commence in the Industrial Relations Commission in an unfair dismissal hearing where each person pays their own costs. Once again, the case is drawn out, in some instances to six days, which, at an approximate cost of $1500 per day, comes to $9000, which has to be paid by the victim. Employers rely on the fact that most victims do not have the financial resources to cover such amounts.

Financial bullying also occurs when government funding is slashed (for example, to universities and hospitals) and individual departments are expected to function with unworkable budgets. The resultant slow destruction of workers' health (and the inadequate service to clients) was dramatically illustrated in the ABC documentary, 'Facing the Music'.[35]

11. Cyber bullying (sometimes called cyberstalking)

Cyber bullying is the inappropriate use of e-mail and the Internet to send aggressive or abusive messages. Because bullies lack communication skills, these impersonal forms of communication are ideal tools for causing conflict without personal involvement. With computers now readily available in most workplaces, this form of bullying is becoming increasingly common.

CASE STUDY

He used to e-mail daily reprimands to me, with copies to my colleagues — little things like, 'Your visits to the bathroom are excessive — five times yesterday', or, 'You were five minutes late returning from lunch.' It was embarrassing. As far as I know, he didn't do this to anyone else. Why couldn't he tell me off to my face?

(Roma, 44, receptionist)

A public servant received 95 e-mails in a day from a supervisor demanding details of a budget she did not know she had to prepare.

(Peter Morley, 'Bullies cop a beating', *Sunday Mail*, 10 June 2001)

Another recently identified form of cyber bullying is mobile phone bullying, that is the sending of abusive text messages.[36]

We have limited our definitions of bullying to the above eleven types because we feel that they cover the general spectrum of behaviour. However, researchers in the UK and the USA identify many more types, such as vicarious bullies, regulation bullies, residual bullies, accidental bullies, substance-abusing bullies.

Do men and women bully differently?

There may be slight differences in the way men and women bully. Our anecdotal evidence indicates that female bullies sometimes manipulate malleable males into doing their bullying for them, and personable bullies of both sexes (though more often female) use flirtation to get out of trouble with a manager or to persuade colleagues to follow their lead.

Also, because in general males are more physically aggressive and action-oriented, they are more likely to be perpetrators of workplace violence. Women, on the other hand, are more inclined to think before they act and so are more likely to be better than men at the subtle and devious practices of psychological bullying.

Interestingly, in the USA a 'charm school' has commenced for 'America's most frightening women business executives'. Called Bully Broads, the school teaches humility, how to stop scaring colleagues, and 'anti-assertiveness' to women who are 'intimidating and aggressive and arrogant to a degree and just not very pleasant to work with' (at a cost per bully of $A29,000!).[37]

Overall, however, we would say that, with regard to bullying techniques, there seems to be very little difference between the genders.

I've also worked with some misogynist troglodytes who obviously learned the art of people management from the writings on the wall in their caves.

Anne Fussell, Executive Editor, *Courier Mail*

CHAPTER 3

Why bullies bully

If someone tells you he is going to make a 'realistic decision', you immediately understand that he has resolved to something bad.

Mary McCarthy

During our interviews with victims, the following questions came up again and again: 'How could he do that to me?', 'She could see how upset I was but she just smiled and drove the knife in even further. Doesn't she have any compassion?', 'What did I do to provoke him?', 'Why does she hate me so much?', 'How could someone do that to another person?', 'She seemed to genuinely believe I was paranoid. Why couldn't she see that she was persecuting me?' These same questions have occupied researchers for many years and they have developed various theories in response.

How do people become bullies?

Why do some people develop aggressive tendencies? Is it a question of 'nature or nurture'? Are people born that way or are they 'made' because of their conditioning or their life experiences? The most widely accepted theory is that bullying tendencies are part of a general antisocial pattern that begins early in life and, 'unless checked at a similarly early stage, develop beyond control'.[38] It is certainly highly likely that children grow into damaged adults because of mishandling by, or inappropriate care from, their families and schools. Psychologist John Clarke from the University of Sydney says that 'a combination of biological and environmental factors ... conspire to produce this person that feels insecure about themselves ... They feel inadequate, they have a low self-esteem right through from childhood and, to compensate for this, the only way they can feel in control of their own life is to control and destroy other people ... physically killing them, or psychologically destroying them at work.'[39]

We outline below possible explanations for how bullying might have become a pattern of behaviour for some people.

Inadequate socialisation

It is generally accepted that we learn our basic patterns of life and approaches to the world in childhood, and the emotional characteristics of bullies — lack of compassion, inability to share or cooperate, poor social and communication skills — may point to a failure to fully develop in these areas.

Bullying behaviour can be identified even at kindergarten level, and some children continue this behaviour through their school years into adulthood. School and workplace bullies share particular behaviour and personality traits — above-average aggressive behaviour patterns, the desire to dominate peers, the need to always be in control, an inability to feel remorse and a refusal to take responsibility for their behaviour; they are immature individuals who bully primarily for the same reason — to hide their own weaknesses and insecurities. They lack empathy, 'that vital quality that lets us perceive another person's feelings, take them seriously and modify our own conduct in response to what we see. Under any circumstances, an absence of empathy is dangerous. If, for example, I am unmoved by what you feel and your life means nothing to me, then I will be capable of behaving towards you in any way that might give me fleeting pleasure (I might humiliate you in a meeting, or tease you, or fail to give you the help you need).'[40]

To acquire advanced social and communication skills, positive self-esteem and a respect for other's rights as well as their own, children need to grow up in loving families where 'there is balanced interaction between family members — discussion, confrontation and negotiation, agreement and resolution, general banter and encouragement.'[41] In this environment, because their own emotions and opinions are respected, they learn to respect the emotions and opinions of other people and how to manage interpersonal relationships; because clear and appropriate guidelines or limits are imposed on their behaviour, they know exactly what they can or can't do and so learn self-control. 'If they break the rules, they know that there will be consequences for the unacceptable behaviour.'[42] For example, if a child makes a mess, that child is made to clean it up; if the child hurts someone, physically or emotionally, an apology is expected.

A bully, on the other hand, may have grown up in an environment where interpersonal skills were not acquired nor a willingness to take responsibility for his or her actions. Another way of describing this is to say that a bully lacks 'emotional intelligence'. This relatively new measure was coined from the title of Daniel Goleman's book, *Emotional Intelligence*, [43] and can be summarised as the ability to interpret our own emotions and to understand the complex emotional languages of other people. Emotional intelligence is our measure of self-awareness, empathy, insight, resilience, persistence and 'social deftness'. Emotionally intelligent people are able to take responsibility for their mistakes and can recover from disappointments reasonably undamaged. They understand their impact on others and adjust their behaviour accordingly; for example, they know when a joke is inappropriate or a comment will upset or disturb another person.

The results of research conducted in America over some forty years, released in 1997, revealed that children who were considered 'most aggressive at the age of eight ... when studied at the age of 30 ... demonstrated significantly higher rates of abuse within relationships and [retained] the pattern of antisocial behaviour ... Many of these individuals were regarded in the workplace as aggressive, disrupting and had a history of abusing others both physically and mentally.'[44]

There is a new school of thought that considers that 'terrorists, dictators and dysfunctional leaders are not born, but raised', that is, that large-scale tyrants such as Hitler, Stalin, Milosevic, Osama Bin Laden and Saddam Hussein are the result of being bullied, beaten, humiliated and/or neglected in childhood.[45] Workplace bullies are petty tyrants, on a scale far removed from these infamous men, but it is possible that the underlying reason for their inclination towards oppression is the same. Swiss psychologist Alice Miller says that hatred 'is a possible consequence of the rage and despair ... felt by a child who has been neglected and mistreated'.[46]

Inappropriate discipline in childhood

Some researchers believe that physical punishment of children, such as smacking, teaches them that it is acceptable to vent anger through violence: 'coercive discipline ... humiliation and sarcasm, really aggressive looks, behaviours which relentlessly make children feel awful about themselves, are ... damaging.'[47] To develop a good conscience and empathy, and to become adults able to take responsibility for doing right, children 'need parents who ... reason in terms that children can understand, and praise ... what they do well ... Non-coercive punishments grounded within a loving relationship produce adults ... able to take responsibility for doing right.'[48]

Weak or inadequate disciplinary measures may also encourage bullying behaviours. If an attention-seeking child finds that aggressive behaviour, such as fighting with siblings or intimidating schoolmates, gains the notice of a parent or teacher and the 'respect' of peers, that child will continue that behaviour because the reward, that is, attention, continues. The child doesn't care whether it is positive or negative, as long as it keeps coming.

Poor role models

Children learn more by observing their parents' or primary caregivers' behaviour rather than listening to what they say. If a parent loses his temper easily or abuses others on an everyday basis, the child considers that the accepted standard of behaviour. How many of us have cringed at weekend sporting events when we hear parents loudly abusing their own or other children: 'You idiot', 'You stupid moron', 'You're useless', and so on? If one parent is aggressive towards the other parent, if the parenting style is one of such control that the child feels powerless, if a child is physically or sexually abused — in such circumstances and with such role models, children do not learn to respect themselves or others, and having no self-respect or respect for other people is a characteristic of the bully. Parents who encourage their children to be 'tough', to stand up for themselves — the 'boys don't cry' attitude — can also adversely affect their children's emotional development.

Time-poor parents

When both parents work in demanding jobs, family time can become a low priority. Children are expected to 'fit in' around the parents' working lives, and technology often fills the gap. If the television is used as a babysitter, that is where children will learn about life. If they spend hours in front of a computer, it may be difficult for them to learn to interact with real people.

Violence overload

Another theory about aggressive behaviour is that children who watch many hours of violent television tend to grow up to be aggressive adults. They are 'entertained' by blockbuster movies, which usually involve mass destruction, dozens of people killed in gruesome ways, and blood and gore by the bucketful. Is it any wonder that some can become immune to the feelings of others? If they play violent games endlessly on their Nintendo or Playstation, their emotional response to murder and mayhem can 'shut down' as death is just part of the game. Exposure to so much violence can reduce childrens' ability to empathise with, and be sensitive to, the pain of others, and can give them the message that it's OK to use force to deal with problems.

Victims become bullies

Another theory is that some bullies were bullied themselves and have responded by bullying others to regain or retain their sense of power.

Personality disorder

Some researchers feel that bullies have serious psychological disorders. Bullies lack empathy, and certainly such a lack is one sign of a sociopathic personality. Sociopaths are generally cold-blooded, amoral and remorseless, although they can sometimes present as charming, convincing and confident — as we said previously, victims of bullying are easily able to relate this description to their bullies. 'According to [Sydney psychotherapist Robin] Grill, some corporate bosses and politicians are little more than government sanctioned psychopaths. 'Some people become violent in the way society legitimises. A lot of what happens in business and politics is very violent and disruptive.'[49]

Seizing the moment

Realistically, many bullies may simply be clever opportunists who divert attention from their own inadequate performance by making others appear incompetent, thus achieving promotion or retaining their jobs.

Hiding a basic insecurity

Despite their confident and often arrogant façade, most bullies are insecure, with low self-confidence and low self-esteem, and a degree of paranoia that stems from their fear of exposure. Because their inadequacies make them unable to fulfil their job requirements competently, they fear their incompetence being revealed. They have difficulty in delegating work and sharing information, which they see as a loss of control, and their bullying is motivated by jealousy and envy of more competent or more popular workers.

Anecdotal evidence from our interviewees indicated that, in some instances, male bullies had partners who were in more powerful and more financially rewarding work positions. A possible deduction from this is that they feel inadequate as a result of their home situation and so bully to assert their power and control in the work situation.

Power game

Some people will bully simply because they can. They have a degree of power over others and they like the feeling they receive from being able to give orders or manipulate others.

The modern workplace

A general increase in the pace and pressure of work can cause inadequate managers to bully subordinates. Work has become 'increasingly specialised and outsourced, which alienates people from each other and destroys a feeling of belonging in the workplace. People [are] working harder than ever but feeling deprived ... One common response is rage, either turned in upon itself in the form of depression, or outward in rageful outbursts against work colleagues.'[50] Corporate restructures can mean that employees have to do the same amount of work with less people or less resources; these changes also increase the opportunities for bullies or 'bring out the bully' in some people. Those who bully may be being bullied from above, pressured to complete work within impossible timelines, and are so overworked and stressed themselves that their frustration boils over into abuse and harassment of others.

Entrenched culture

The atmospheres of institutionalised workplaces with rigid hierarchies, very structured systems and entrenched attitudes and traditions, such as the defence forces, police and universities, can encourage bullying; this culture is changing slowly, however, as the 'old guard' progressively leave.

Do bullies always know what they are doing?

We believe so, except in those rare instances where, because of pressure from autocratic superiors, poor organisational skills and lack of competence, an overloaded and highly stressed manager may use bullying tactics as a means of getting the work done, without being aware of the impact this kind of behaviour is having. However, if a bully is not aware of what he or she is doing, that bully should not be in a position of power.

We believe that chronic bullies are able to make conscious choices with regard to their behaviour in most circumstances. The stories told to us by victims revealed that there are certain scenarios in which it is obvious that the bullying behaviour was deliberate and pre-planned.

- There is a promotion looming; the bully needs to have a competitor 'eliminated'.
- The CEO wants to restructure and tries to 'force' the victim to leave so the organisation does not have to make a redundancy payment.
- An enterprise bargaining agreement is on the table; the organisation wants to 'restructure' or outsource before this is signed so entitlements do not have to be paid.
- The victim has been in the workplace too long and knows too much of the 'history' of the organisation.
- Because half of the staff have joined the union, a 'hit list' is drawn up to 'eradicate the troublemakers'.
- The victim asks 'awkward' questions, or challenges the organisation.

In most cases, the reaction of victims is so obvious — shock, tears, shaking, migraines, many days away from work — that the bully cannot deny that the bullying behaviour is affecting them. *Bullies must be forced to take responsibility for their actions.*

What's done to children, they will do to society.

Karl Menninger

CHAPTER 4

'It was only a joke!'

If you treat people right they will treat you right — ninety per cent of the time.

Franklin D. Roosevelt

Workplaces are made up of people who might not have anything in common except their place of employment, so naturally there will be difficult or tense moments where a degree of patience and tolerance is needed, when it is wise to follow old adages such as 'Silence is golden' and 'Patience is a virtue'. You might excuse abusive behaviour for some time before the truth finally dawns — you are being bullied.

How can I tell if I am being bullied?

Bullying exists if there is intentional persistent, offensive, abusive, intimidating, malicious or insulting behaviour, an abuse of power, or unfair punishment, which undermines your self-confidence and makes you feel upset, threatened, humiliated, vulnerable and highly stressed. As we have said before, isolated incidents of aggressive behaviour, while to be condemned, should not be described as bullying. In the workplace environment there can be conflicts and interpersonal difficulties, many of which are industrial relations issues that should be dealt with through the appropriate industrial relations channels. Only behaviour that is systematic, ongoing and deliberately hurtful should be regarded as bullying. This can range from the obvious (actual physical harm) to the far more subtle, for example, a dishonest style of dealing with people and issues, such as the 'two-faced' person who pretends to be nice while sabotaging you, or makes nasty, rude, hostile remarks directly to you (behind closed doors) while putting on a pleasant face for others.

She had them all fooled. She'd make 'witty' comments, starting off with, 'I say this because I care about you', or 'I'm telling you this for your own good' or 'I mean this in the nicest possible way', and then say something malicious about my clothing ('your suburban Mum look'), my hair ('Did you cut your own hair again?'), my make-up ('Did you use a trowel to put on your make-up this morning, dear?'), or my dress sense ('There must have been a black-out and she dressed in the dark.'). Ads for Jenny Craig and Weight Watchers were left on my desk. Most days I ended up in tears. The others didn't understand — they thought she was being nice.

(Nicole, 33, insurance officer)

If you are unsure if your boss or supervisor or co-worker may have crossed the line between bad behaviour and bullying, ask yourself the following questions.

- Does this person already have a reputation for bullying behaviour?

- Has your mental or physical health been affected by this person's behaviour towards you?
- Are you the subject of damaging gossip or innuendo?
- Are you on the receiving end of regular verbal abuse, put-downs, insults or obscene or threatening gestures, or attempts to humiliate or belittle you in front of other staff, clients or customers?
- Are you being ignored, isolated from work activities, excluded from information or being over-monitored in your workplace?
- Are your efforts being constantly undervalued or your work regularly criticised unjustifiably?
- Is this person claiming credit for your work or ideas?
- Does this person repeatedly give you impossible tasks, set unrealistic deadlines for work, or pressure you to work longer hours?
- Are Post-it notes left on your desk or your work instructions being sent by e-mail so that no face-to-face discussions take place?
- Have you been demoted, had responsibility taken away, had your telephone removed from your desk, been moved from your office or had your work circumstances similarly changed without any warning or consultation?
- Are your work guidelines being constantly changed?
- Are your applications for leave or promotion being refused or has already approved leave been abruptly cancelled?
- Is your work performance being deliberately sabotaged or impeded?

If you answer 'yes' to several of these questions, you are probably being bullied or, at the very least, the behaviour is inappropriate in the workplace. Remember, behaviour does not need to be violent to be considered bullying — it can be as simple as a continued negative response to your contributions in meetings (such as sighs, eye rolling, condescending comments), continual hovering over you, ignoring you or constant accusations of incompetence. *As long as it is persistent and prolonged in nature, and consciously done, it is bullying behaviour.* If the behaviour is affecting your work performance, your personal relationships, your self-esteem or your physical or mental wellbeing, you are being bullied.

If the behaviour is only occasional, triggered by a difference of opinion between you and the offender, or by opposing working styles, it is not bullying. No job is free from stress. We can't work in isolation, and we can't insist on working only with compatible people. Workplaces are made up of people of different skills, ages, levels of education, background and ethnic origin, and we have to accept that we will not get on with everyone. Difficult or obnoxious personalities, whether supervisors, co-workers, customers or clients, are an unavoidable part of working life and to a certain degree we have to tolerate such people.

Some of our interviewees suggested that females are more likely to interpret certain behaviours as bullying.

CASE STUDY

Gives me the shits, frankly, that I have to waste my time on all this political correctness, when I'm so busy. Women are too sensitive. Give me men any day. I make no bones about it, I am tough to work for. I'm the boss, I tell them what to do. If I shout at them, the men take it on the chin and will still have a beer with me after work. But the women . . . they turn on the waterworks.

(Clive, 65, hotel manager)

Where do I draw the line?

If you make your distress obvious, often the offender's response will be along the following lines: 'It was only a joke.'/'You're being over-sensitive.'/'Don't you have a sense of humour?'/'It was just a bit of fun.'/'You've gotta be tough in this game.'/'Learn to take it, or else!' (implied threat)/'You're really paranoid, you know that?'/'You're reading something into this which just isn't there.'/'Why don't you grow up!' In other words, *it's your fault.* That's the bully's way — blame the victim. *You* are the one at fault. *You* are the one who lacks a sense of humour.

[A] city councillor ... said bullying was recognised as one of the reasons so few women stood for local government ... 'We often have an empty gallery and that's when the behaviour deteriorates. There are insults, insinuations — sometimes couched in terms of humour — but you can feel the sting.'[51]

To assess whether the behaviour is bullying, you need to make an 'intention and interpretation' assessment.

Intention: The joker who deliberately sets out to hurt you, and continues with the behaviour despite your distress, is a bully. *Bullies intend to hurt and repeat their behaviour over time.*

Interpretation: A comment that one person finds highly amusing and harmless can be hurtful or offensive to another. Humour is a very personal thing. Though sometimes caustic, such jokes play a vital part in bridging differences. If we can laugh at the barriers between us, they lose their power to divide. So don't rush off to the union with a complaint. First, document the incidents and think about them carefully. Ask yourself: Could I be over-reacting? Were those criticisms valid, even though harshly delivered? Does this person just have an unfortunate manner?

Sometimes a joker may not know when to stop. He received a laugh the first time, liked the reaction and kept the joke running, selfishly enjoying the response from his peers without considering your feelings. Some people try to hide their personal inadequacy and lack of people skills behind humour without realising they are being cruel. However, teasing and jokes are only fun if both parties involved agree that they are fun. When particular behaviour has an ongoing negative effect on your professional or personal life, it is time to take a stand.

Am I being oversensitive?

No. Bullies often get away with their conduct by making victims feel it's their fault, that they are being hypersensitive or paranoid. Under the pretence of friendship or humour, they make damaging or insulting or inappropriate remarks. Remember: if someone's conduct hurts or offends you and the attacker does not stop after a personal approach, *you are being bullied*.

Remind yourself: You have the right to be treated with respect and dignity.

> AMANDA: Little jibes all the time. Little so-called 'jokes'... Every day there'd be another 'fat' joke or comment ... [like] the time you read the article in the paper — very loudly — about the woman who was forced to buy two plane tickets because she couldn't fit into one seat.
> CASSIE: It was funny. It wasn't directed at you.
> AMANDA: Then I wonder why everyone kept laughing for about three minutes then glancing across at me ... And the day Giulia read out that list of the ten worst dressed women in the world, and Cassie said, 'They should have looked harder.' Glancing at me with a smirk.

Should I stand up to the bully?

Standing up to a bully can be daunting, particularly if the bullying — and the consequent build-up of your stress levels and loss of your self-esteem — has been going on for some time. Employees who are unduly shy, lack education or learning ability, have a physical disability or sensory impairment, are known to be unwilling to complain. You may even blame yourself for the abuse. Remember, you have the right to be treated with respect and dignity, and to work in an atmosphere free from aggression and fear.

It is most likely that your attempt to reason with the bully will be unsuccessful but, if you feel the need to clear the air, take time to think about your approach. If the bully is a colleague or co-worker, you should be able to face the person and express your point of view. Avoid appearing aggressive by focusing on the unacceptable behaviour rather than attacking the person. Don't stand over the bully as this will make him/her feel intimidated. Communicate at eye level, explaining calmly how the incidents are affecting you. Try not to dissolve into tears or otherwise show your distress; this will make you appear weak and vulnerable and the bully will feel confident of having got you where he/she wants you.

If the person bullying you is your supervisor or boss, state that the behaviour is having a detrimental effect on your work performance and you would like it to stop.

It is possible (though not likely) that the 'bully' is blind to the effect his behaviour has on you and, once this is brought to his attention, that behaviour will end. Marnie's case (below) is unusual.

<table>
<tr><td>CASE STUDY</td><td>*I stood up to her and she backed off. I couldn't believe it was so easy. If only I had done it months ago. She started on another girl then, but I said, 'Leave her alone or I'll report you.' You wouldn't believe how different the atmosphere is now.*

(Marnie, 28, nurse)</td></tr>
</table>

If the person apologises because he genuinely did not realise the consequences of his actions and the behaviour stops, try to put it behind you. His actions were clumsy or stupid or selfish, but the degree of hurt was unintended. Move on.

Our own experiences and our research reveal that it is rarely possible to stop a workplace bully with a personal approach. Most bullies do not care how their victims feel. In the overwhelming majority of cases, the bully will become defensive, refuse to accept your grievance and try to put the blame on you by belittling your work or complaining about your attitude in an attempt to humiliate you in front of your witness. Standing up to a bully, in fact, usually only antagonises him further.

He just looked at me blankly, as though I was an annoying insect. With a superior look on his face, he said, 'Eric, you have always been an extremely difficult person. This latest behaviour — manufacturing a complaint against me — is intolerable. Your attitude needs to change substantially if you wish to remain in your position. If you don't like how management works here, you have the option of finding alternative employment.'

(Eric, 36, IT consultant)

Though your attempt to reconcile has not succeeded, this effort could stand you in good stead if you later pursue a formal complaint.

What if the behaviour continues?

Many victims accept bullying for a variety of reasons: they need the job; they love their work; the workplace is convenient to home (that is, minimal travel to and from work); they are close to retirement age and know they will not be able to get another job — the reasons are many.

Other victims will leave as soon as they can, or seemingly accept the bullying but start applying for other positions, trying to keep on the 'right' side of the bully in order to receive a 'good' reference when they go. The problem is that the bully will then turn his attention to the next victim, causing a rapid turnover of staff over time and depriving the organisation of years of experience and training. If more victims were prepared to report bullies, to stand up to them and take their fight to court, more importance would be placed on workplace bullying as a genuine health and safety issue.

Your options with regard to taking action against the bully are outlined in Chapters 10 to 12.

Never be bullied into silence. Never allow yourself to be made a victim. Accept no one's definition of your life; define yourself.

Harvey Fierstein

CHAPTER 5

'Why me?'

People don't ever seem to realise that doing what's right is no guarantee against misfortune.

William McFee

Bullies do not bully everyone in a workplace and appear to 'hone in' on specific people. Do they have 'selection criteria'? What is it about a particular person that makes him a 'suitable' choice?

Why did the bully pick on me?

Anyone who has suffered at the hands of a bully asks the question, 'Why me? Am I aggressive? Do I speak out too much at meetings? Am I too negative? Am I going mad?' In most instances the answer is no. Usually, the bully targets people for one or more of the following reasons.

You were in the wrong place at the wrong time. Some bullies are obsessive and compulsive — they *need* victims — and you were there. If your bully has been at the workplace for some time, think back. Has there been a continuous turnover of staff, and if so why? They may have left for other employment, of course, but they may have been bullied, which means you are just one in a long succession of victims.

You are more competent than the bully, with a more extensive knowledge of how the organisation functions; the bully perceives you as a threat so seeks to control and then eliminate you. He uses covert tactics, such as sly character assassination, spreading rumours, piling on of work, giving unrealistic deadlines and stealing the credit for work well done.

> AMANDA: You didn't give me enough time.
> BRYONY: The time frame was tight, but certainly not impossible.
> AMANDA: It was totally impossible.

You are more popular with colleagues, board members, co-workers or clients than the bully. Bullies target people who are good looking, creative, innovative, quick-witted, competent, high achievers, highly qualified, successful or have highly developed social skills. The bully knows he can never have these qualities and his behaviour is generated by insecurity and jealousy, as well as fear that their incompetence will be revealed.

Your colleagues respect you. You are always helpful, and generous in sharing your knowledge and experience; you are the person your colleagues come to with problems, both professional or personal. Bullies like to think of themselves as leaders, so again, the motive is jealousy and the aim is to isolate you.

You are conscientious and dependable and have a high degree of integrity, which you will not compromise. Such characteristics are found in whistleblowers.

You are vulnerable. You have an area of susceptibility, which the bully is able to identify and exploit (for example, you are unusually sensitive, a perfectionist, a single parent, desperate to keep your job, caring for a sick or aged relative, paying off a mortgage, supporting children through school or university, going through separation, divorce or bereavement, close to retirement age, have a criminal record, and so on).

You have been bullied before.

You are dispensable. You are seen as too old, you are not proficient in modern technology, you don't fit the 'trendy' image of the company or your position is too costly.

You are independent and not part of any clique.

You refuse to become a corporate clone. You question decisions and work methods and are viewed as a troublemaker.

You are in your first job, eager to please, unaware of your rights and vulnerable to exploitation.

You are new to a workplace that has an entrenched culture and you work differently.

You have traits that are considered weaknesses. You have difficulty saying no, are unusually gullible or naive, have a tendency to be indecisive, self-deprecating or approval-seeking, constantly apologise even if not guilty of anything, are non-confrontational, will do anything for peace and quiet — to the bully, these qualities indicate submission, so it is likely that the bully will invade your personal space by standing too close, hovering over your shoulder reading your computer screen, touching you in a controlling way, all the while knowing that you are unlikely to confront him. Bullies rely on people being too frightened or intimidated to report them.

You internalise any feelings of anger and frustration, rather than expressing them.

You are an active, vocal union member.

Did I do something to start the bullying?

Once the bully's victim (you) has been selected, either something you do, or an external factor, will trigger the bullying process. It could be one of the following.

- The previous victim leaves and there is a void that the bully needs to fill.
- The company is reorganised; the bully's activities are able to be hidden in the resultant chaos.
- A new manager is appointed who feels that you pose a threat, particularly if you had applied for, or been acting in, the manager's position.

STELLA: When she couldn't fire Mandy, plan two was to make her life so hellish she'd be forced to resign.
BRYONY: Stella, this is a total fantasy of yours. I certainly wasn't happy with either of you and said so directly and calmly, but there was certainly never any concerted campaign to get rid of you. Please credit me with a little bit of decency and professionalism.

- The bully becomes more insecure when your competent job performance threatens to expose his or her lack of efficiency.
- For some reason you become the centre of attention (for example, win a bravery award, appear on television, become engaged), thus taking attention away from the bully, who feels cheated.
- You draw the bully's attention by supporting a bullied colleague.
- You refuse to obey an order from the bully because it breaches company regulations, is illegal or unethical.

- You 'blow the whistle' on embezzlement, malpractice or a breach of occupational health and safety regulations.
- You become a union representative.
- You stood your ground when the bully tried to intimidate you.
- You are promoted or upgraded.

Is it my fault?

Most definitely not! Your manager, even your colleagues, may say it is your fault. Don't get 'sucked in' to believing this.

<table>
<tr>
<td>CASE STUDY</td>
<td>I stopped communicating in staff meetings or, worse still, was unable to find the word I was looking for. Or my words would come out in a jumble leaving me feeling that I wanted to crawl under the table. I felt such an idiot, with everyone looking at me strangely. I remember thinking, 'She's right. I'm out of my depth here. I should leave.'</td>
</tr>
</table>

(Matthew, 30, administrator)

Bullies want their victims to blame themselves. The intention of the bully is to make you feel insecure, in need of a psychiatrist, think you are having a nervous breakdown or feel totally inadequate in your position even though you have held it successfully for a number of years. Depending on your age and gender, comments may be made that you are menopausal, experiencing premenstrual tension or going through a mid-life crisis. The implication is that your hormones are making you behave strangely or erratically; in other words, *your behaviour is the problem*. Don't believe this — you are the innocent party, and did nothing to deserve this sadistic, destructive treatment. Remember, it is *never* the victim's fault — bullies are responsible for their own conduct.

TAMSYN: And just for the record, Amanda's no more paranoid than I am. Bryony came to see me and asked my advice on how to make her life as uncomfortable as possible.
BRYONY: Brian, this is total hysteria. Amanda was underperforming. The board wouldn't let me fire her. What alternative did I have but to nudge her in that direction?

Can I do anything about it?

The bullying will not stop unless you take action, so you will have to make some decisions. You have the following options:

a   do nothing and put up with it
b   take sick leave while you consider your position
c   make a voluntary decision to leave, or
d   fight for your rights by making a complaint; possible results of this are:

- the issue is investigated and resolved, and the bullying stops
- your complaint is ignored by the employer, in which case you have the choice of:
  - asking the union for assistance
  - taking your complaint to the Industrial Relations Tribunal
  - taking legal action privately
- the employer contests, in which case either:
  - the issue will be dismissed
  - you will be dismissed
  - you will be made redundant.

These options are covered in detail in Chapters 10, 11 and 12.

The easiest and healthiest solution for the victim is to leave the job. Unfortunately, it does not solve the problem, as the bully will simply move on to another victim. The reason so few people report their mistreatment is that they think no one will believe them.

If possible, as soon as the abuse starts, you should keep records (see Chapter 10). The number of incidents and their regularity will almost certainly reveal a pattern of bullying which will be useful when you do come to make an official complaint.

A tough lesson in life that one has to learn is that not everybody wishes you well.

Dan Rather

CHAPTER 6

Bad for
your health

Whatever doesn't kill you makes you stronger.

Old saying

It can be difficult for outsiders to understand the profound effects, both physical and psychological, that bullying can have on victims. They feel powerless, as if they have lost control over all aspects of their lives, and begin to show symptoms of excessive stress. We have used extracts from case studies extensively in this chapter to demonstrate how victims felt during the time they were being bullied. During our interviews, people would say the same things over and over: 'I didn't want to get up in the morning', 'I hated going to work', and 'I thought I was going mad.'

What are the effects of bullying on the victim?

As a result of the excessive demands and pressures inflicted by the bully, victims can experience any or all of the following:

- emotional health problems, such as loss of confidence, low self-esteem, severe anxiety, stress, panic attacks
- behavioural effects, such as heavier smoking, excessive drinking, overeating, drug-taking
- physical health problems, such as dry mouth, facial tics, hand tremors, skin disorders, asthma, high blood pressure, heart disease, reduced immunity to infection, bowel problems, excessive sweating.

Every person is unique and will react to bullying in different ways — some will internalise the damage, becoming quiet, irritable and having mood swings, some will lose concentration at work and start making mistakes or having accidents, some will become tearful, nervous, depressed, others will become physically ill, with stress-related rashes, neck and shoulder pain, nausea, insomnia, stomach and bowel problems. In severe cases, stress resulting from workplace bullying can lead to depression, mental and physical breakdown, financial problems, family breakdown, relationship problems, even suicide.

The psychological health effects include 'feelings of helplessness and isolation, withdrawal, fear of being labelled a troublemaker, fear of dismissal or loss of job promotion opportunities, fear of being transferred to dead-end or mundane jobs, anxiety, feelings of self-blame, suicide, stress, nervous breakdown, depression, loss of appetite, eating disorders, reliance on medication, increased drinking, smoking, insomnia, fatigue, lack of concentration, headaches, nausea, backaches, stomach aches, infections and other illnesses, ill health or early retirement due to stress related illness, low morale, low self-esteem, poor job performance, absenteeism, physical violence to others, and additional impacts on victims' family life and relationships.'[52]

> AMANDA: It turned me into the office madwoman — well and truly.
> STELLA: And the quality of your work was going steadily down.
> AMANDA: I was depressed, for God's sake. Some days I was just sitting at my desk with tears pouring out. If it hadn't have been for the terror of the thought of living on unemployment benefits I would've given in much sooner.

The healthiest and least damaged people are the ones who walked away early, for whom the loss of the job was not a big issue because they knew they could get another job.

CASE STUDY

When I stopped enjoying my work because he was being such a pig, I thought, 'Stuff him! I'll go back to temping.' And I walked out.

(Lynne, 25, secretary)

CASE STUDY

I wanted to go to sleep and not wake up. I felt depressed and afraid to leave my house. I became so antisocial that my friends gave up on me.

(Sara, 26, teacher)

CASE STUDY

I sat at home feeling miserable and eating for comfort. I got fat, and that depressed me more. I didn't see my friends because I didn't want them to see me looking so bad.

(Megan, 30, sales assistant)

I had a physical and mental breakdown — a persistent skin rash, absolutely no energy. Everything was grey. There was no colour or joy in my life and I could barely raise a smile. I lost hope for the future. My wife left me.

(Stuart, 48, financial services)

My hopes for my career, the security you take for granted, were rudely taken away. I felt vulnerable and ... violated, I suppose. Some people will think that word is a bit over the top, but that's how it felt to me.

(Matthew, 48, administrator)

I began to have panic attacks. I was scared to death, and thought I was going crazy.

(Lena, 32, nurse)

I was a wreck. I had to take pills to get to sleep, I was smoking like a chimney, and my hair began to fall out. I was at breaking point so my doctor put me on antidepressants. My family started telling me to take my 'happy pills'.

(Mark, 24, council worker)

It was my dream job. I remember how happy I was when I started work. I felt on top of the world, and couldn't believe how quickly that happiness changed to absolute despair. My motivation and commitment to the job declined to the point where I had to leave. I haven't found work since. It was the boss who bullied me — I can't give her name as a referee, can I?

(Bernadette, 20, beauty therapist)

In most cases, the effects of bullying creep up so slowly that the victim does not associate them with the bullying for some time.

I suddenly started having migraines so severe that I was confined to bed. I put them down to trying to do too much in a short time. The migraines came more often, I was having neck and shoulder pain, I became depressed and, one day, when I wanted to hide under the bedclothes rather than go to work, I realised that all my problems were caused by what was happening to me there.

(Paula, aged 42)

Isolation from workmates is a common effect of bullying, that is, going to lunch and tea breaks by yourself and not attending after-work social occasions. This isolation may come from colleagues who distance themselves from your situation, or may be self-inflicted (some victims become a little paranoid, not knowing who they can trust). Though this isolation may be your choice, it will still add to your overall distress. Remember, by cutting yourself off from potential supporters or witnesses, you are playing into the bully's hands.

Verbal and emotional abuse undermines your self-confidence. Your morale and productivity drop, you begin to have stress-related symptoms and you find yourself fabricating reasons to stay away from work, taking excessive sick leave or wanting to quit to escape from the bully.

Insomnia is a very common effect of bullying. You go over and over particular incidents or words in your head and this overactivity prevents you from relaxing into slumber. Sleep deprivation is an acknowledged form of torture and causes enormous strain on your physical and mental health. The consequent daytime drowsiness and reduction in attention span can cause work-related accidents, which can be dangerous not only for you but also for your workmates.

The worst effects of bullying are post traumatic stress disorder (PTSD) and prolonged duress stress disorder (PDSD). One overseas study of workplace bullying reported that three-quarters of victims of long-term bullying showed symptoms of PTSD, including 65 per cent where the actual bullying had stopped five years previously.[53]

What is prolonged duress stress disorder (PDSD)?

Unlike PTSD, a condition more commonly associated with war refugees, war veterans and victims of torture, prolonged duress stress disorder is not yet a recognised diagnosis. Post traumatic stress disorder can result from a one-off incident, such as the terrorist attacks on the US in September 2001. PDSD, on the other hand, is caused by a series of incidents, as in psychological bullying, over a length of time that can vary from weeks, months and, in some cases, years. The trigger for PDSD can be anything — a word, a name, an action, a glimpse of someone who resembles the bully, a similar item of clothing to something worn by the bully — that prompts an adverse response or flashback. Even ordinary words, taken and used in certain contexts, can be very powerful and destructive. For example, a victim whose bullying consisted of continual use of the word 'behaviour' with a negative connotation, as in 'You need to be counselled about your inappropriate and aggressive behaviour', may come to hate that word, and every time the word is used, it 'triggers' memories of all the psychological bullying incidents. These flashbacks can continue for many years after the events have stopped.

CASE STUDY

I was travelling on a train to the city and the man sitting next to me was reading the business pages of a newspaper. I found myself looking at a photograph of my ex-boss, the woman who made my life hell before forcing me to leave. Memories flooded in of all the things she did and said, and I immediately burst into loud, uncontrollable tears. All the other passengers were staring at me but I just could not stop. I was overwhelmed by an enormous sense of loss, grieving for a job I'd left more than five years previously.

(Angela, 57, ex-teacher)

Why am I feeling like this?

When we feel threatened or helpless, our bodies respond with an automatic 'fight or flight' response, lifting our level of the hormone cortisol to prepare us for battle. This can cause some uncomfortable physical symptoms.

My doctor sent me to a physiotherapist, who said, 'Your shoulders look like street humps! The worst I have ever seen!'

(Jeff, 44, accountant)

For short-term relief, you can try the following simple remedies.

Symptoms	Remedy
Nausea, stomach cramps, bloating, stomach irritation	Eat regular, nutritious meals with the right balance of fibre, fresh fruit and vegetables.
Rapid, heavy breathing, accelerated heart rate, increased perspiration, elevated blood pressure	Rhythmic, deep breathing — inhale fully, filling your lungs with oxygen, then exhale slowly.
Aches and pains in the neck, shoulders, legs or lower back	Exercise regularly to loosen the muscles. Don't sit at a machine or computer for hours on end — stop and stretch every twenty minutes. If you can afford it, have a massage focusing on the problem area.
Sleep problems — insomnia and/or nightmares	Avoid caffeine from mid afternoon, don't eat after 8 p.m., relax in a warm bath before bed, read a few pages of a book or magazine, drift off as you listen to a relaxation tape.

I was not sleeping well and, when sleep did come, it brought nightmares, either flashes of horrific violence or scenarios about work. I was finding it impossible to fit my workload into my day, forcing me to take work home. My supervisor kept asking me, in front of the rest of our team, 'What on earth do you do all day?' I was having difficulty getting out of bed in the morning, and was so tired all the time that I wondered if I could be suffering from chronic fatigue syndrome. One day I started screaming at our storeman at work for no apparent reason, and that was what my supervisor had been waiting for. He issued a warning in regard to my 'behaviour'. That was when the depression really set in, and I asked myself, 'Why am I feeling like this?'

(Lorraine, 38, office worker)

Lorraine is not alone. She is feeling some of the short-term and long-term effects of bullying. Victims lose so much in bullying situations, not just their jobs, but also a sense of trust and security.

I found out that a particular group of colleagues was spreading malicious rumours about me. I approached them one day to have it out with them. They would not talk to me, and became so aggressive towards others who did that gradually I was isolated. I felt alienated and disheartened by the lack of support from colleagues in my section who I had considered to be my friends.

(Sara, 26, teacher)

Sara felt shock at being on the receiving end of the bullies' treatment and betrayal because of the lack of support from colleagues. Like most victims, she began to blame herself.

I wondered what I had done to deserve the nastiness and spite and began to doubt myself. I became anxious and troubled, and replayed the incidents over and over in my head. I'd ask myself, 'What did I do to make this happen? What could I have done differently?'

(Sara, 26, teacher)

For Deidre, quoted below, the worst aspect of her bullying was the feeling that she'd lost control and revealed her vulnerability.

I found myself talking ten to the dozen but not explaining anything properly, particularly in staff meetings. My supervisor would make out that I was suffering from a mental condition and put me down in front of my colleagues. My self-esteem was at an all-time low. My workmates would stop talking when I passed, and when they did speak to me, it was only to say things like, 'Are you feeling OK?', 'Maybe it's time to take it a bit easy'. 'Have you thought about working part-time?', or 'You need to seek counselling.' They were the last things I wanted to hear! When you are in a caring position in the community, there are always urgent clients waiting, needing you to sort out their problems. I would think, 'I can't sort out my own life, let alone worry about theirs!' I'd promise to do a set amount of work in a prescribed time, knowing full well I'd be unable to meet the deadlines.

All of a sudden, everyone was asking me for the work I'd promised, the telephone wouldn't stop ringing, and I was too frightened to answer it. I put my head down on the desk and started crying. I have always been the type of person who hates to show vulnerability, so this was the worst stage for me, particularly because my supervisor heard me crying. He came into my office, with most of the staff following him in.

(Deidre, 43, social worker)

Deidre's experience is very common. She was targeted because she had worked with the organisation for many years, had been acting in the higher position for some time before the new supervisor was appointed, was highly competent and very popular. The bully wanted her out because he perceived her as a threat to his career ambitions.

Depression is a common result of bullying.

The depression was the most unpleasant thing I have ever experienced. It was as though my senses had shut down. I could not imagine I would ever feel happy again. There was no hope, no feelings at all really, not even sadness or anger. Just ... nothing.

(Grace, 42, real estate sales)

Depression can diminish your enjoyment of work, sleep, food, music and social interaction; it can interfere with all aspects of your life. Don't ignore the signs until it is too late. Many a person has thought of committing or has committed suicide due to workplace bullying.

I was shattered. Losing my job really wrecked me. My wife took the kids and left, I couldn't get a permanent job, and I drifted around, drinking more than I should've, getting high. Finally tried to kill myself, though I don't remember doing it. I was staying in a boarding house at the time and another resident found me hanging in the bathroom. Had to see a psychiatrist after that and it was the best thing that could've happened. Sorted me out, she did. I'm good now, but I went through hell first.

(Barry, 57, unemployed)

I'm still at a low ebb. It's a day-to-day thing. Sometimes you think, 'I don't want to get up this morning', and sometimes you think, 'I don't want to wake up at all'. Some days are just black voids.

(Andrew, 28, on WorkCover)

He just drove away in the car and gassed himself. He was found the next morning ... I kept asking myself 'Why?' We had three beautiful children, our relationship was OK — though he had been working really long hours — but I had no idea he was so desperate. After his funeral, a few people from his work came up to me and said things like, 'I feel so bad that I didn't stand up for him', and 'He was made a scapegoat'. When I asked questions, I found out that he'd been victimised at work for months. I hope the bastards realise that this is all their fault. Why didn't he talk to me?

(Lia, 37)

I felt totally shattered. Sucked dry. As though all my energy had been drained out of me. I'd lie awake for hours then finally fall asleep, only to have awful dreams. I didn't want to get up in the morning. I'd get heart palpitations, I'd sweat profusely, I'd feel nauseous just lying there thinking about going to work. Then I didn't want to wake up at all. I never actually took anything, but if someone had offered me a suicide pill, a way out ...

(Mark, 22, on WorkCover)

You can relieve the symptoms of depression, moderate or severe, with medication and therapy, so you should seek medical assistance. We recommend that you find a psychologist or counsellor who has experience working with victims of bullying.

How else will the bullying affect me?

Your social life and relationships with family and friends will change. At first, you may try to hide your problems by not talking 'work' at home. If you think of yourself as a strong person, you may feel that, by revealing vulnerability, you are admitting to failure and that no one will seek your opinion or assistance any more as you have 'lost the plot'.

If you are in a relationship, it will be affected. The changes will be subtle in the beginning. You may be too tired or exhausted for sex, and your partner won't understand; you need to explain your work situation to your partner and ask for understanding and patience. Stress and depression can cause your libido to suffer. If the bullying continues for a number of years, your partner, because of concern for you, may also show signs of depression, and other health problems, such as high blood pressure and insomnia. The extent of the impact on your relationship will depend on a number of factors: how long you have been together, the strength of your bond and how much — and for how long — your partner is prepared to share your suffering.

In addition to getting the cold shoulder, I was belittled in meetings if I tried to give my point of view. Case information I needed was withheld from me and I was made to appear inefficient in front of my clients. My confidence and self-esteem plummeted. What was happening to me was so subtle and devious that it was difficult for me to pinpoint the behaviour and explain my feelings to others. I felt confused, even paranoid, because their behaviour was so unpredictable and irrational. I used up all my emotional and mental resources trying to figure out what was going on and how to defend myself, and had nothing left to give at home. My partner and I split up.

(Duncan, 33, case manager, insurance industry)

If you are known to have a strong personality, others may automatically assume you contributed to the situation because they do not see you as the 'victim' type. Even your partner may blame you, saying, 'It must have been your fault. What did you do?' This more commonly happens where the victim is female. It gets back to the saying, 'Men are assertive, women are aggressive.' You must remember, and keep telling yourself, 'I am not aggressive, I am a victim of a bully, who is threatened by my strength.'

If you are unfit for work, this can cause conflict. Your partner may feel that he or she is 'slaving away all day, while you go out and drink cappuccino'. Remember, the bullying impacts on your partner also, so you both need to be patient and understanding.

Your stress will also impact on your children. They will be aware of tension, and you may be more irritable than usual, with no energy to play, help with their homework or take them out at weekends. If they are old enough to understand, explain that you are having problems at work. If you wish to go into detail, school-aged children will understand the concept of bullying — bullying is a big issue in schools and behaviour expectations are clearly defined to pupils. If the bullying forces you out of work, try to allay their fears about financial problems.

I told the children that I would be home for a while as I'd lost my job. What broke my heart was when the youngest asked, 'But Mummy, who will give us the money to buy the food?'

(Amelia, 33, community worker)

You will need support from friends at this stressful time. It will be therapeutic for you to pour out your troubles to them. However, don't strain the friendship by overdoing it.

She talked of it endlessly, repeating herself over and over again. I listened patiently, as it seemed to help. Perhaps I overdid the understanding, though, because it seemed she couldn't get through a day without unburdening her troubles on me. I began to dread the ringing of the phone and the doorbell, and — I'm ashamed to say this — sometimes I didn't answer them because I just couldn't bear to hear the whole thing again.

(Linda, 63)

If you don't have that special friend or colleague with whom you can discuss your feelings, it may be time to ask yourself: 'Do I need counselling? Should I apply for WorkCover?'

Can bullying affect me financially?

This will depend on how far the bully is allowed to go. If you leave your job without finding alternate employment, you will be without income until you find another job. If you are on WorkCover, your payments will drop over time. (WorkCover implications are covered in Chapter 12.) In some circumstances, bullying can have a devastating effect on your financial situation (see April's story on page 181-4.).

If you find you are unable to manage on your reduced income, seek assistance from a financial counsellor (see Appendix C), who will be able to assist you with organising a budget and give you options regarding mortgages, credit cards, personal loans, and so on.

When you get to the end of your rope, tie a knot and hang on.

Franklin D. Roosevelt

CHAPTER 7

Business bears the cost

We are going through a period of increasing unemployment and job insecurity, of full-time work giving way to what might be called contingent work, and increased workplace stress caused by changes in work processes and technology.

Kim Beazley, Labor's promise on leadership and tax, *Age,* 7 August 2001

Workplace bullying is devastating and costly, not only for the bullied employee(s) and their families but also for the company and the country — it is a no-win situation.

What are the costs of workplace bullying?

Bullying costs are both financial and psychological. Recent estimates of financial costs to industry in Australia of workplace bullying have varied between $A3 billion,[54] $12 billion[55] and up to $36 billion a year.[56] These wide-ranging costs include absenteeism, sickness and stress leave, counselling programs, staff turnover, costs of legal advice and support in ensuring court and tribunal actions, compensation payouts, court-contested and mediated cases, early retirement costs and redundancy payouts. However, it is difficult to pinpoint the exact cost of bullying because many of the claims for leave and so on will be made under the general banner of work stress. Companies should note the financial consequences of 'turning a blind eye' to workplace bullying.

> CASSIE: The impact . . . has been huge.
> People don't like us, don't trust us, and our net income
> has fallen by something like 19 per cent.
> BRIAN: We'll either have to cancel some of our programs or
> go into massive debt.

Who pays?

Individual workplaces will bear the main costs, directly or indirectly, because bullying impacts on workplaces in any or all of the following ways:

Increased leave — Bullied staff will initially use up their sick leave and holidays rather than go to work in a noxious environment, and will then progress to medically authorised stress leave.

Reduced efficiency and productivity — Bullying is neither an effective nor efficient way of working. A bully may initially terrify workers into being productive in the short term, but over time can reduce the productivity of victims by at least 50 per cent and of other employexes (co-workers of victims) by as much as 33 per cent.[57]

Low morale and high turnover — Staff will become disenchanted with the company if the abusive behaviour is allowed to continue, any loyalty and commitment previously felt for the company will be lost and this will be reflected in their behaviour. Workers will dodge work that might focus the bully's attention on them, will become resentful and apathetic, their creativity and work performance will diminish and they will tend to look for work elsewhere.

Staff time — Time spent by other staff addressing bullying incidents, investigating complaints and attending grievance procedures is time taken away from normal duties.

Poor industrial relations — Staff and unions may be more ready to complain or take industrial action in an unhappy and stressful work environment.

Cost of litigation — This includes the actual cost of fighting legal action (lawyers' and barristers' fees, settlement costs, appeal costs) taken by bullied employees, as well as the loss of business and reputation because of adverse publicity arising from the legal action.

Lowering of company profits — This is a result not only of low productivity but also of the added expenditure of legal costs.

Higher employer insurance premiums — Workers' compensation payouts on bullying claims or disability benefits will result in higher premiums.

Recruitment and training of replacement staff — Bullying workplaces have a high turnover of staff; employer costs will include the hiring of temporary staff to fill in for bullied staff on leave, or replacing either the victim or the bully, and perhaps other staff who may prefer to find alternate work in a non-hostile environment.

Management skills training — to prevent further bullying.

It is difficult to measure exact financial outlay. Employers should note that the longer they allow bullying to go on, the greater the damage and consequent cost, and the longer it will take to regain the confidence and commitment of staff. In 1999 the Australian Institute of Management (AIM) Chief Executive Officer analysed the total direct costs [of bullying] for a company of 100 employees on an average salary of $35,000 at $175,000 when calculating absenteeism; staff turnover; legal representation; investigation; workers' compensation premiums; and the indirect costs of disruption to the company from incidents of workplace bullying.'[58]

During our research, we asked Megan (aged 36), on a salary of $35,000 a year, who has been on WorkCover for the past twelve months, to outline her approximate fortnightly costs.

Fortnightly wage	$1,346
Psychologist — weekly visits	200
Doctor — fortnightly visits	36
Medication	40
Physiotherapist twice weekly	
(including massage)	150
Travel expenses — car x 28¢ km	200
Fortnightly total	**$1,772**
Multiplied by 26 fortnights =	$46,072 per year per person
$46,072.00 x 10 employees =	$460,720
$46,072.00 x 100 employees =	$4,607,200

(These figures do not include the cost of temporary staff to fill in for employees on WorkCover, the legal or investigation costs, or increased WorkCover premiums.)

Apart from the cost to business, there are also costs — mental, physical and financial — for victims of bullying (see Chapter 6), and an economic cost to taxpayers in social security payments to those who have left their jobs because of bullying and been unable to find other employment. Each State government WorkCover bears the cost of wages and medical expenses.

Why is there such an increase in workplace bullying?

Perhaps this question should be: Is there actually an increase in workplace bullying? As already stated in Chapter 1, there may not, in fact, have been an increase in bullying but rather an increase in the number of people willing to report it.

If there has been an increase in bullying, it may be because of any or all of the reasons suggested below.

Driven by the economic climate towards the end of the twentieth century, the world of work was changed drastically by globalisation, privatisation, deregulation, downsizing and restructuring. In the resultant 'lean and mean' organisations, pressure on employees at all levels to work harder, faster and longer, with less security, has led to work cultures where bullies flourish. Because they want to please their bosses and hold on to their jobs, employees at different levels are working excessive hours in an attempt to manage more responsibility with fewer resources. Burnout is high. Dr Paul Babiak, a New York psychologist, says, 'Not all psychopaths end up in prison. Some climb the corporate ladder swiftly and quite successfully,' and thrive 'in the organisational chaos that typifies many of today's rapidly growing, downsizing, and merging companies ... Companies in rapid growth or re-organisation ... provide the freedom, fluidity, and disorder in which this kind of individual can flourish.'[59]

The rapid growth in part-time, casual and contract work has created a second-class workforce of mainly young people; they are commonly underpaid, unaware of their rights and at the mercy of their employers, too afraid to report work abuse for fear of losing their jobs. An Australian Young Christian Workers survey (of approximately 1400 people, mainly aged 15 to 20) released in August 2001 found that 55 per cent did not know their correct rate of pay, 19 per cent did not receive a pay slip, 33 per cent were working unpaid overtime, 61 per cent worked while they were sick, 47 per cent had not been provided with written conditions of employment and 23 per cent were not informed of workplace health and safety regulations. 'The rising threat of long-term unemployment ensures that casual workers do not rock the boat and often just go along with what is expected without question.'[60]

Many large Australian companies have adopted Japanese and American work cultures where workaholism is applauded, excessive working hours and unpaid overtime are the norm and those who work an eight-hour day are seen to be lacking the right work ethic. Businesses no longer assume that they have a social responsibility to workers, even though, if they are fully occupied meeting the demands of work and family, they will be unable to meet their personal health needs, such as leisure time, exercise, health and fitness.

In some cases, the reduced role of church and community groups (which once acted as support networks for parents and helped to provide children with an ethical framework) may mean that people are now growing up without strong moral values, decent role models and clear-cut standards of behaviour. As adults, they lack people skills and empathy, and do not know how to develop a rapport with others in a work environment.

The introduction of technology has 'depersonalised' work, replacing people with an automated equivalent whenever possible. This has contributed to the increasing occurrence of 'rage' incidents; people want the personal touch — to interact with the person who answers the phone, to be able to ask a living, responsive human being about their bill or credit card or theatre booking. The most bizarre and infuriating 'customer service' is the cinema's coercion of patrons into telephoning an information line and having to press seemingly endless number options in order to find out when and where a film is showing (and paying for the call!).

The dominance of computers also enables bullies to use e-mail to circulate abusive or demoralising messages to colleagues throughout an organisation in seconds, without having to actually vilify the person face-to-face.

Our reliance on computers in the workplace also leads to enormous frustration when the computer crashes, an unsaved document is lost, the Internet is unavailable or the whole system is down.

What are the management styles/workplace structures that encourage bullying?

Reduced to a simple equation, a workplace structure that can lead to bullying behaviour is:

downsizing → *overwork* → *stressed employees* → *intimidation*
+ threatening behaviour = bullying

Everyone connected to a company, from shareholders to consumers, is affected when staff and services are slashed, often without communication or consultation with employees, to maintain profits, and personal customer service is replaced with automated equivalents. Where fewer people have to cope with the same amount of work, managers may be unable to cope and resort to demeaning or devaluing others as a way of getting the work done.

Workers who see their colleagues' jobs disappearing and watch older staff being pressured to retire early or 'restructured' out often suffer from 'survivor guilt' and have to deal with insecurity every day; they lose confidence in, and feel less positive about, the workplace. Such losses cannot be measured on a balance sheet but are real nevertheless. There is evidence that companies pay a high cost from within, in terms of talent and years of experience lost, if they cut their staff too ruthlessly.[61] Employers should be aware that the growing acknowledgment of the existence of workplace bullying and concern at the apparent increase could result in a flood of legal cases.

A 'sick' workplace can be identified by tracing patterns of absenteeism and resignation over several years and noting any increases in the figures for staff turnover, sick leave, stress breakdowns, deaths, early retirements, disciplinary procedures, grievances, dismissals, involvements in industrial tribunals and legal actions.

Some indicators that bullying is likely to occur in a workplace are shown below.

- The boss is an autocrat who allows workers no freedom or creativity, and refuses to delegate
- There is a cutthroat atmosphere, in which employees have to compete against each other for promotion
- Employees are subjected to unattainable deadlines, excessive workloads or supervision
- An organisational change has prompted a fear of redundancy or termination
- There are no clear codes of conduct, no procedures for solving problems
- There is no ongoing training for staff.

What is the difference between bullying and tough management?

There is a discernible difference between bullying and tough management, though traditional hardline management styles can lead to bullying: if management is aggressive, that aggression will flow through to supervisors and workers.

Companies that promote inexperienced people lacking in expertise and people skills risk bullying; those inexperienced managers may equate toughness with competence and resort to treating their staff like a sergeant major training the troops. Training is essential to teach managers ways of being strong without resorting to abuse. Good managers are efficient, capable and able to delegate; bad managers bully.

You need to be strong to get things done. Can't be wishy-washy. Sensitive people get walked on. That's business.

(Dennis, 45, CEO, manufacturing)

Dennis denies absolutely that his hectoring manner could be construed as bullying. As far as he is concerned, he is just doing his job. Bullies may get away with bullying people out of their jobs by claiming to be reorganising for the purposes of 'efficiency'; consequently they are perceived by those above to be strong managers.

Bullies are often inadequate at their own jobs and survive only by stealing the credit for other people's work and making others appear incompetent, that is, by making ridiculing, humiliating or patronising comments about their victims in front of others, not giving their victims information or access to equipment that is essential for completion of work tasks, and so on. Bullying managers will eventually be found out because their poor management skills and abusive behaviour will result in high staff turnover and sick leave, low staff morale and declining productivity and profitability.

Are there particular work cultures where bullying flourishes?

A workplace culture can be defined as the entrenched traditions, customs and expectations of the place, whether it be a large company or within a lone work group of employees with a single supervisor.

It does appear that some areas of employment are more prone to bullying and, in some workplaces, bullying may be so common that it has come to be accepted as normal working practice. For example, trades apprentices have come to expect a certain level of bullying during their training years.

Hospitality/tourism

Chefs are notorious for bullying and over the years the kitchens of many of Australia's best eating places have been contaminated by the tantrums of a childish or tyrannical chef.

I left the restaurant six months before my apprenticeship finished because I'd had enough of prima-donna chefs. Some were drunk as ten men most of the time, some were on drugs, and out of the half-dozen chefs I worked for there was only one I ever had a normal conversation with. The rest would yell and scream, grab me by my arms or shoulders or jacket, push me around the kitchen, dragging me around by the scruff of my neck. I saw them wave knives around threateningly, hit other cooks over the head with brooms, throw tomato sauce bottles at the waitresses if they got an order wrong or meals were sent back ... I hated every second I worked there.

(Gary, 30, chef)

However, this situation has changed in recent years with more chefs owning or part-owning restaurants; it is in their own interests to take a different attitude entirely — a harmonious atmosphere means less staff turnover.

In the travel industry, almost half (49 per cent) of flight attendants regularly deal with aggressive passengers.[62]

Health/hospitals

During the period January 1999 to October 2000, 864 Victorian nurses were verbally abused or physically assaulted. This figure is most likely a gross underestimate, as one researcher found that 75 per cent of assaulted nurses do not report incidents. Nurses most at risk worked in emergency departments or psychiatric hospitals.[63] 'A national survey ... painted a disturbing picture of domineering women bullying each other in a fairly brutal and often petty power play behind the scenes in hospitals.'[64]

Schools

Bullying is perhaps more common between staff in schools than it is between students. The teacher shortage, huge workload, lack of appreciation, political denigration, reduced resources and ever-higher work targets have stressed the profession. The modern teacher has a complex job that incorporates education, parenting, mentoring, research and social work. Teachers are not only expected to teach (and sometimes to teach subjects for which they have no specialist qualifications), they are also expected to share responsibility for children's social education (by time-poor parents who are working long hours), to handle discipline and behaviour problems, and to take on welfare roles (coordinating breakfast programs, buying books for homeless pupils, helping to sort out problems with families, and so on). Add to that the pressures of inadequate funding, inadequate staff and resources, job insecurity, large class sizes, an ever-expanding curriculum, ongoing skills training, work correction, student reports, parent–teacher interviews and after-school activities, and it is understandable that they would suffer high levels of stress.

> *As a primary school teacher I spend just as much of my time being a social worker, psychologist, counsellor, life coach, drug educator and parent supporter as I do teaching the skills required for academic achievement ... Ask teachers how they spend their 12 weeks, and find out about the correcting, reporting, curriculum planning, self-education and professional development that's done in this so-called holiday time.[65]*
>
> *Sometimes children come to school with no lunch, or ... no warm clothes. Some have emotional problems that stem from their families being caught in cycles of drugs, alcohol or poverty. On a few occasions teachers have had to shower and change children before school, taking their dirty clothes home to wash; other times they have made them breakfast or bought them lunch. Last year a child tried to commit suicide.[66]*

The ideal teacher would have a natural empathy with people in general and children in particular, optimism, a sense of humour, be a truly inspirational educator and able to handle all the stressors of the job with ease. Unfortunately, such paragons are rare. As in every other profession, the majority of teachers are capable, flawed human beings who cope very well with the demands of the job. A few, however, will have personality problems or antisocial disorders which render them unable to deal with the pressures, and they will resort to bullying other teachers with accusations of incompetence and so on. Bullying often begins when new teachers are appointed; if they do not fit in with the culture of the school and fail to follow the accepted way of doing things, bullying can result.

Local government

As with all levels of government, intimidatory practices are used by councillors and staff. Bullying is 'recognised as one of the reasons so few women stood for local government and it was an issue confronting all councillors, male or female'. Women councillors around Australia describe 'instances of being bullied and harassed, feeling isolated and unsupported, being inadequately informed about meeting procedures and being excluded from debate by more experienced representatives'.[67] The Community and Public Sector Union has identified 'management practices associated with increased workloads, changing shift rosters and staff shortages', unreasonable work hours and workload expectations as resulting in 'significant increases in workplace stress and assault . . . misuse of management driven performance management systems has also resulted in setting unrealistic targets and a method for screening out "weak links" and placing psychological pressure on individual employees by supervisory management'.[68]

Universities

Like schools, Australian universities are stressful work environments because of insufficient funding, not enough staff and resources, job insecurity for many, long unsociable working hours, and large class sizes. Rapid change has brought in a different set of organisational imperatives and tensions, and different expectations. Funding requirements require academic staff to publish widely and do original research as well as teach and do an ever-increasing amount of administrative work. Staff are undervalued yet have increased workloads due to the use of new technologies in teaching. Older staff have been accused of being 'past it', 'not flexible enough to cope with the changing world', 'resistant to change', 'too old to adapt to a new challenge'. Harassment or bullying may start or intensify during a period of change, for example, with the appointment of a new Head of Department, Dean, general manager or colleague who is strong and competent.

Bullies keep their jobs, despite obvious incompetence, by diverting attention from their lack of ability by blaming other staff or circumstances for their failures.

CASE STUDY

It began when she gave a paper at a conference which pointed out flaws in his research. He was out to get her from then on. He started a campaign of whispers and innuendo. He told people there'd been complaints by students that her lectures were poorly presented, her marking was questionable, that she was not approachable. He made sure that the people he told would pass the message on to the Dean or the head of department. At meetings he always made her seem inefficient or unreasonable, hinted that hormones made her behave irrationally, that she was hysterical, menopausal. Little things, all done so carefully that it wasn't easy to say he was behind it. But he was.

(Alison, 37, lecturer)

The present and, apparently, long-term funding crisis in universities, with its increasing emphasis on a utilitarian approach to research and teaching, has engendered a more corporate and entrepreneurial style of management. This has undermined the old-style collegiality and sense of a 'special' workplace. Universities are more prone to many of the unpalatable fruits of industry and business, including the fostering of a climate conducive to bullying behaviour.

Charities

The voluntary aspect of charitable organisations offers many opportunities to bullies — they are able to obtain senior positions without having to work their way up the ladder; management committees are made up of volunteers eager to help but with limited, if any, management experience or people skills. Smaller charities may not have any policies and procedures on bullying or harassment in place; voluntary workers would be reluctant to institute legal proceedings against a charity; and charities have vulnerable clients who could be easily manipulated, as well as vulnerable volunteers who may be susceptible to bullying because of their commitment to vulnerable clients and to the ethos of the charity. Charity work also gives the narcissistic chronic bully an opportunity to show how 'caring' and 'compassionate' he is.

The voluntary sector's exposure to bullying may be changing now that they have to tender for services they offer, such as employment, housing and healthcare, as a result of which they have been forced to employ staff with the appropriate professional skills to run them as commercial enterprises. Despite this more business-like footing, however, charity groups cannot survive without volunteers. Time and money need to be set aside to ensure that volunteers, particularly those holding key positions, have the people and communication skills required to ensure bullying does not take place.

It's not what you pay a man, but what he costs you that counts.

Will Rogers

CHAPTER 8

Co-workers and bystanders

The bully rules by fear, and thus corrupts those employees too weak to stand up to improper practices and injustices.

Helen Thomson, review of David Williamson's play *Charitable Intent, Age,* 12 October 2001

In most bullying situations, victims find that they are left to cope alone when previously friendly work colleagues 'turn a blind eye' on the bullying behaviour and fail to support the victims.

Why do some co-workers ignore bullying?

Colleagues may be too scared to support the victim in case the bully's attention is turned to them. If the bully is a manager, they may be afraid that they will be 'reorganised' or 'restructured' out of a job, and they need their jobs because of personal or financial commitments.

On the other hand, they may think the victim is at fault — they believe the bully's version of events, or think the victim should be able to stand up for himself. Because the attacks are subtle, or disguised beneath a veneer of humour, they may think the victim is imagining the abusive element. They may accept the bullying as normal behaviour because of an entrenched work culture, or view the bully as a leader and want to be part of the 'in' group. Or they may not know what to do, so do nothing.

The lack of support from co-workers only adds to the distress of victims.

I was most hurt by the malice and vindictiveness shown by my colleagues. I felt betrayed by these people I'd thought of as friends.

(Megan, 45, secretary)

Another explanation for the lack of support is 'groupthink'.[69] George Orwell used this term in his book *1984*, describing groupthink as a group, easily led by an autocratic leader, who focus their efforts on following orders and making their leader happy, and are unaware that they are making a questionable decision. Groupthink is often found on boards of management where a bully either sits on the board or reports to the board that appointed him. A victim who approaches the board for justice will be treated unfavourably as the board will not go against one of their own or one of their choosing. Thus the bully is protected and remains triumphant.

BRIAN: Let me just say again that we appointed Bryony to spearhead change. At least *some* of us on the board felt the working atmosphere had become a tad too cosy under Alan Twomey's leadership, lovely man that he undoubtedly was. A good leader shouldn't be loved. They should be respected. And yes, when necessary, feared.

Some victims do find support from colleagues who, behind closed doors, are prepared to discuss the abusive behaviour. But sadly, when the victim asks them to stand up and be counted, they stand on the other side of the line, right next to the bully.

They began to avoid me. At first, when my manager was ranting and raving, or putting me down in meetings, I would look at my friends for support but they would look away and avoid eye contact. In the staffroom, no one joined me at my table. I began to feel like an outcast. I could feel that some of them were ashamed of their lack of response and, when I tackled Sharon, who I'd thought of as a good friend, she justified her spinelessness by saying she had a duty to her family — she needed her job.

(Judith, 47, accounts clerk)

STELLA: These three know where the power lies. If leader attacks Amanda then Amanda is a dead duck, so the best career move is to fall in behind leader and help her finish the job.
TAMSYN: It was my professional judgement, Stella. You know I can't be bought and sold.
STELLA: I know you couldn't once. But when a bully enters a schoolyard it's a brave soul who takes the victim's side.

Do any victims receive support from co-workers?

In some cases the victim will find some genuine allies, if only because the bullying is not restricted to one victim. With a chronic bully, you may obtain valuable advice from previous victims and support from those in the same situation as yourself. When a number of employees at any one time are subjected to humiliation and mistreatment, acting together to turn the tables on the bully, no matter how unbeatable that bully may appear on the surface, will be far more effective than acting as an individual. It makes bullies nervous to know that there is a strong group of people who are willing to confront them. (However, they should be prepared for the possibility that the bully's behaviour will become even more extreme if there is a threat of being exposed.)

Some of our interviewees felt that their co-workers were somewhat relieved that they had opted to leave the workplace, as this enabled them to go back to some normality, resume a relationship with the bully without feeling any guilt, and pretend that the victim never existed. Some ex-colleagues will choose to blame the departed victim in an attempt to rationalise their own behaviour.

How can I support a bullied colleague?

Anything you do, no matter how small, that demonstrates support for victims, will help to restore their self-confidence and self-esteem, and will be one step further along their road towards recovery. Most victims, however, will be grateful for any support, even if it is just a simple acknowledgment from a colleague that it is not their fault. Verbal support is reassuring and also has some therapeutic value for the victim. Victims need to be able to talk about the situation, debrief and regroup. They will welcome your reassurance that someone else has noticed what is happening, that they are not going crazy.

- **Listen to their fears.** It is important to victims to be able to express all the hurt, anger and bitterness they are feeling. Some victims of bullying have been driven to suicide, so if you suspect your colleague may be suicidal, don't be afraid to ask. They may be desperate to tell someone. If they do admit to having thoughts about killing themselves, ask if they have made a plan. If they admit to doing so, insist they seek counselling urgently.

- **Remain a friend at work and outside the workplace.** Don't isolate them or allow them to isolate themselves. Continue to share tea and lunch breaks. If they take time off work, telephone and let them know they are not forgotten.
- **Don't take any part in the bullying.** Don't listen to gossip or pass on malicious or derogatory information about other people. Words are not harmless and gossip is far from trivial; it is subtle and insidious, and can cause divisiveness, ruin reputations and destroy careers.

If you feel able to 'stand up and be counted', there are more constructive ways you can support your colleague(s). (However, be aware that these options will leave you open to the bully's anger; the bully may then retaliate by victimising you.)

- **Put your support in writing.** Write down any threatening behaviour or psychological intimidation that you have overheard or witnessed, noting the date, time and place of the incident. This will provide unbiased corroboration of the victim's story should a complaint be made later.
- **Spread the word.** Talk to other colleagues, discuss what is happening and try to persuade them to acknowledge that the behaviour is unacceptable and that they should not ignore it or take part in it.
- **Tell someone in authority.** If you are fortunate enough to have someone attached to your organisation who is trained to handle such sensitive situations, such as a human resources manager, chaplain or counsellor, approach one of them and, in complete confidentiality, explain the situation. If there is no such person available and you have a good relationship with anyone else within the organisation at a higher level than the bully, confide in them.

- **Put yourself on the line.** Agree to act as advocate for your colleague or give witness statements to WorkCover investigators or lawyers if requested by the victim.

Why should I get involved?

You should become involved in supporting a bullied colleague because it will help to expose the bully and, hopefully, nip the behaviour in the bud. Don't say, 'It's not my problem.' It may well be your problem if bullying is permitted to spread its tentacles through your workplace. Bullying in the workplace should not be tolerated and exposing it will reduce the incidents and diminish the devastating effect it can have on victims, their families, other employees and the organisation. The effects and costs of bullying have been outlined in earlier chapters. Considering how much destruction, trauma and unnecessary cost they cause for organisations and employees. It is cowardly and unacceptable to give tacit approval to bullying by ignoring it.

Remember, onlookers can make a difference. By not speaking out against injustice, you are condoning it. Apathy allows injustice to prosper.

In Germany, the Nazis first came for the communists and I didn't speak up because I wasn't a communist. Then they came for the Jews, and I did not speak up because I wasn't a Jew. Then they came for the trade unionists and I did not speak up because I was not a trade unionist. Then they came for the Catholics and I was a Protestant so I didn't speak up. Then they came for me ... by that time there was no one to speak up for anyone.

Pastor Niemöller

CHAPTER 9

Employers' 'duty of care'

Good hours, excellent pay, fun place to work, paid training,
mean boss. Oh well, four out of five isn't bad.

Help Wanted ad, Pennsylvania newspaper, 1994

It is difficult for businesses to survive in today's world, with global conglomerates swallowing up smaller companies, a general economic downturn, and so on. Small-business operators are so busy trying to keep their operations afloat — 'operating on the smell of an oily rag' — that it is understandable that they might turn a blind eye to staff problems. Because business generally is no longer so hands-on, an employer may only become aware of workplace abuse when it is long-standing and entrenched, and the frustration of workers has 'boiled over'. By that time, many people may have suffered irreparable damage. It is far better to identify problems at an early stage and solve them through prevention and education programs. We warn employers, large and small, not to leave it too late to put measures in place to tackle bullying. Remember, bullying costs *you* (see Chapter 7).

> JACK: You all are well aware of the reason you're here . . . the workplace atmosphere has become, in the words of almost all of you, 'poisonous'. . . we have a full on conflict which is causing most of you distress, and effecting the efficiency of the whole organization. Conflicts like this often arise out of misperceptions. We often attribute to other people far worse motives than they actually had . . . If we're frank and honest with each other today, we might just be able to unreavel the causes of what's happened around here and get things back to normal.
> BRIAN: That sounds all very hopeful, but what if the bad feelings *aren't* due to 'misunderstandings'?

As an employer, what are my responsibilities and legal obligations with regard to bullying?

We'll tackle your legal obligations first.

Under the relevant State and Commonwealth Government Acts, you are legally obliged to provide a safe and healthy working environment for all employees. Thus, because bullying may endanger the health and safety of workers, you are obligated to ensure that bullying is stopped quickly if it begins or prevented altogether. Every workplace should have an occupational health and safety (OH&S) representative who has the power to insist that bullying behaviour in your organisation stops immediately. If you fail to comply, the OH&S representative can request a WorkCover field officer to investigate; this investigation could result in a fine or even imprisonment for you.

- Under anti-discrimination Acts, you may be found liable if an employee lodges a complaint of discrimination or harassment. This would result in the worker receiving a compensation payment from your organisation.
- Under workplace relations Acts, if a worker is dismissed or forced to resign because of bullying, he may be entitled to lodge an unfair dismissal claim. If the bullying dispute is between an employer and a worker, the victim can lodge a Notice of Industrial Dispute with the Industrial Relations Commission. Workers may also be able to use the grievance procedures of industrial awards in some states in cases of bullying.
- Workers who are psychologically injured as a result of bullying may submit a claim for workers' compensation under their state WorkCover Act.
- Under common law (except in South Australia), if you do not take appropriate precautions to protect an employee from workplace bullying, you may be liable for any physical or psychological injury suffered by that employee.

Second, as an employer, you have certain **responsibilities**.

- No matter who is doing the bullying, it is your responsibility to stop it.
- Your state WorkCover Authority requires you to display a WorkCover poster outlining the employer and employee rights. This poster must be easily accessible to all workers at all times; failure to do this can result in a penalty.

If the employing body is a company employing staff where the total return exceeds $7500 a year, you must pay a premium to your state WorkCover Authority to insure your workers. Any company that does not comply will have to reimburse all costs of the injury to the relevant WorkCover authority.

What are my rights?

Under the various workplace health and safety Acts, you have the right to expect your employees to report bullying behaviour and not to inflict harm on any other employee; they too are legally obliged to contribute to a safe and healthy working environment. If a worker is warned about bullying but continues the behaviour and the victim lodges a WorkCover claim, your WorkCover insurance costs will increase. Some state governments are considering introducing legislation to recover costs from the company if the claim is substantiated. WorkCover may also be able to recover that outlay from the bully. If someone other than yourself or the worker was responsible for your worker's injury, you should advise your WorkCover agent so that the WorkCover Recoveries Unit can investigate.

What should I do if an employee complains of bullying by the manager?

First, don't ignore his complaint and don't view it as a sign of weakness or attribute the problem to a 'personality clash'. Ask if the employee has tried to sort out the situation, but don't force a confrontation with the alleged bully. By the time most victims report bullying, they are at the end of their tether, physically and emotionally.

CASE STUDY

I'm stubborn, and I was determined not to let her get rid of me. I couldn't eat, I couldn't sleep, I was crying for no reason, then I started having panic attacks. At work my heart used to race every time I heard her voice, even if she was right over the other side of the office. That's when my parents made me take a hard look at myself and see what that monster was doing to me. I realised that I had to report her. She denied everything, of course, and my boss said I should 'give it another go'. She got worse, then, and I ended up having to give up the job to keep my sanity and my health. I hated to give in to that bitch, to leave her there and maybe destroy someone else, but it really was the only thing I could do. Now I sleep all night and my appetite's back, I'm in a new job where the people treat me with respect. I'm lucky.

(Allannah, 24, PR)

Allannah's boss was lazy and negligent, and fortunate that Allannah chose to leave and not fight for her rights.

On receipt of the complaint, you should take the following steps.

1 **Find out the details.** You need to interview the employee making the accusation. If the worker not accompanied by an occupational health and safety person or a union delegate, ask if the employee wishes one to be present. At the initial interview, listen carefully to what the employee has to say. Ask how long the alleged behaviour has been going on and if there were any witnesses. Take notes for your records and photocopy any supporting documents, such as e-mails, Post-it notes or minutes of meetings. The alleged victim will most likely be traumatised and you might wish to refer the person to someone in the company for support, perhaps a welfare officer or chaplain, a human resources representative or someone from your employee assistance program.

2 **Speak to the alleged bully and obtain the other side of the story.** Be prepared for an emotionally charged situation. Expect defensiveness and denial of the allegation. The alleged bully may make counter-accusations against the accuser 'aggressive', 'difficult', 'not a team player', 'working outside of boundaries', 'rude and objectionable at meetings', and so on. Once again, take notes, either during the discussion or immediately after; this is too important an issue to leave anything to memory. You may prefer to have a witness present.

Note: It is very important that you remain impartial during your interviews with both parties. Set aside any loyalty you may feel to either the victim or the alleged bully. Even if the accused is a valued manager or personal friend, the rights of both parties must be upheld. Don't necessarily believe all charges of bullying — it is easy for the system to be manipulated. If you are unsure which person is telling the truth, you may be able to decide by reviewing your knowledge of their characters. What have you noticed about them? Is one highly competitive, a control freak, sometimes irrational, or openly aggressive towards the other? Even if you are fairly certain which one is lying, you need to instigate an impartial investigation.

AMANDA: Yes I did. After the Charity Ball Bryony called me into her office and closed the door, then she turned around and just stared at me for what seemed like minutes with a look of total hatred on her face and then let fly with this unbelievable tirade of abuse.
BRYONY: That's another fantasy. In fact I did what managers are supposed to do. I gave Amanda direct and honest feedback about her recent performance.

3 Separate the parties involved while the matter is investigated. Move the accused if there have been other complaints against him; otherwise move the accuser for his own safety. If your business is small and you are unable to transfer either person, the accuser may prefer to take time off work *on full pay*.

4 Gather evidence. You have three options.
   i **Call in an unbiased investigator.** If your company is large enough, you may prefer someone from your human resource section to investigate, or perhaps call in an outside agency.
   ii **Do your own investigation.** Employers in smaller companies may prefer to do the investigation themselves.

Ask other employees if they have noticed, overheard or witnessed any unusual interaction between the two parties. However, be aware that they may not be prepared to disclose anything because they do not want to 'dob', or because they think their jobs are on the line or perhaps fear retaliation. If you have anti-bullying, harassment and discrimination policies in place, follow the set procedure. Remember, any investigation must be thorough, professional and sensitive to the feelings of all concerned.

iii **Consult your risk management department or officer.**

The best option would be to call in a mediator to assess the situation. Mediators have the necessary people skills required to give a completely unbiased opinion, whereas an investigation done by you or other in-house staff could have an unconscious bias, particularly if a 'favourite' manager is the one accused of bullying.

How can I best help the victim?

In these situations, victims need to be reassured that their complaint is being taken seriously and that they have the support of their manager. *Do not take any allegation lightly.*

Advise the victim to consult a general practitioner, if that has not already been done. The GP may prescribe counselling, reduced working hours or sick leave and, if so, will issue the necessary WorkCover certificate and any specialist referrals. A rehabilitation officer will need to be appointed and a return-to-work plan initiated.

What should I do about the bully?

Once the evidence is in and the complaint proven, you will need to decide what to do with the bully. You may decide to instigate disciplinary measures and/or issue a first warning, or fire that person.

> JACK: She's a dead-set bully. Rules by terror everywhere she's been. She reduced her last two organizations to a shambles too.
>
> STELLA: Why didn't the board know that?
>
> JACK: They wrote her marvellous references to get rid of her.

If the bully wishes to stay and agrees to stop the bullying behaviour, you should ensure that training in management and communication skills, and counselling are undertaken. The bully should also have regular evaluation, either done within the company or by an outside consultant. Many business schools now offer courses in management development, working in teams and leadership, that look at how to address different cultures in the workplace (important to any company with a global focus) and will often tailor development courses to the needs of individual companies.

If other employees, for example, those who worked closely with the bully or the victim, have suffered from secondary bullying (see Chapter 2), they may also require counselling or debriefing. It may be advisable to call in a psychologist to talk to the staff, either as a group or individually.

If you feel that the bully is unable to make behaviour changes and you would prefer to terminate his employment, you need advice from a lawyer practising in the area of unfair dismissal. Otherwise you could put the company in a position of having to employ lawyers/barristers to fight an unfair dismissal claim. Alleged bullies must be given an opportunity to defend themselves against the allegations made in relation to their conduct or performance, and appropriate warnings must be given.[70]

The following flowchart outlines the procedures you should follow.

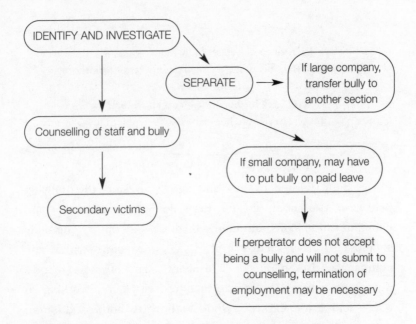

How do I recognise stressed or bullied staff?

To do this, you will need to know your staff well, which may be difficult if you hold a high position in the company. You should look for any obvious changes in behaviour, such as mood swings, anxiety and depression. If a previously outgoing person becomes quiet and withdrawn, if a worker loses their sense of humour or becomes more aggressive than usual, takes a lot of sick leave or suddenly requests holidays, heed the warning signs. Something is not right. This worker has problems, which may be caused by bullying (or may be totally unrelated to work).

What can I do to prevent employees from manipulating the system?

Because psychological bullying damages both the mind and body, it is extremely difficult for a pseudo-victim to carry on the pretence successfully for any length of time. Most victims of psychological bullying are referred to psychologists and psychiatrists, and some are sent to physiotherapists if they have complained about aches and pains in their necks and shoulders; these professionals should be able to assess the degree of stress being suffered.

If there is no evidence to support an allegation of bullying, speak to the accuser's colleagues. If you have a human resources section, seek their help. The 'alleged' victim may feel overworked, undervalued or have issues at home that are unresolved. Full-time employees spend at least one-third of their day at work, and this may be the only place where they can attract the attention they are seeking.

CASE STUDY

When I commenced my new job, I was advised that there was an ongoing problem with a particular member of staff. Due to physical and emotional health problems, she was absent at least one day per week, which meant that other staff had to pick up her workload. If they didn't do the work her way, she'd lose her temper or burst into tears. She was always complaining about petty things — one day she left because someone laughed too loudly and gave her a headache! Tensions were high so I suggested calling all staff together for a meeting to discuss the problems. She immediately felt threatened and said she wanted her union representative present. When the union rep was unable to be there, I decided to cancel the meeting, feeling sure she would not attend in the circumstances. When I advised her of the cancellation, she accused me of trying to bully her, went home and was off 'sick' for more than a week. The next thing I know is that I'm asked to attend a formal mediation meeting with my boss, the union rep and the staff member to discuss her bullying accusation, and was told that I was not to have any contact with her until the matter was resolved.

I felt extremely angry, as I've always bent over backwards to maintain good relations with my staff and, until this present position, been held in high regard by my colleagues. I feel that I have been targeted by this person. The union took her side and did nothing to support the other staff who have been manipulated by her for years; the union is very strong here and the human resources people were quite useless.

I did nothing wrong, but was professionally ostracised as a result. Whatever I say, and whatever the outcome, my reputation has been tainted. Already I am being treated differently. People who were previously friendly now give me the cold shoulder. Staff who've heard only her side of the story are very formal in their interaction with me; even my bosses seem to be wondering if some of what she's saying is true. They obviously believe that old saying, 'There's no smoke without fire'. I don't enjoy going to work at all and wonder if I should resign. But that would be interpreted as an admission of guilt.

(Michael, 50, general manager)

Michael's organisation has handled this situation badly. No new manager should have been put into the position in which he found himself. This issue should have been resolved years before his commencement. Naturally, the alleged victim felt threatened by having to attend a meeting with all present, as anyone would at the prospect of facing a character annihilation. At the mediation meeting a person from Human Resources or an independent mediator should have been in control, not Michael's boss. This meeting put Michael in a humiliating position, that is, his boss 'going over his head' by initiating the mediation without any consultation. The victim had a union delegate for support. Who did Michael have?

Cases like Michael's are more likely to occur in large companies with an impersonal atmosphere where less value is placed on the individual. If employers know their managers and staff, and have a proven track record of a safe working environment, it is very unlikely an employee will try and manipulate the system.

What this case does bring up, however, is that the alleged victim, because of her health problems, may genuinely believe that 'everyone is out to get her' and is not, in her own mind, fabricating the charge. This is a delicate case, which will need highly skilled staff to resolve it.

Hurt people need helping hands, not accusing fingers.

Sign outside Knightsbridge Baptist Church, Leabrook, Adelaide, South Australia

---

CHAPTER 10

Victims — choices to make

We can't stop what happens to us, but we do have a choice about how we react to it. That's the magic of being human.

Sharon Gray, 'Beyond poor me', *Age*, 8 August 2001

Most victims of workplace bullying just want it to stop. They will put up with the abuse for a long time, thinking, 'Perhaps it is just a personality clash, a temporary problem that will go away if I work harder and don't do anything antagonistic.' However, ignoring the mistreatment will not make it go away. In fact, the bully is likely to see your acquiescence as a sign of weakness and the behaviour will probably get worse. There's nothing wrong with choosing to be passive over minor issues, but don't let anyone treat you with disrespect for long. Decide what you will and won't accept. Because trust, stability and mutual respect are very important in a working relationship, you will eventually reach a point where you have had enough and will have to take action.

> CASSIE: We couldn't stand up to her. No one could. She'd go ballistic. You just saw it.

What choices do I have?

You can resign or you can make a complaint. You may be reluctant to complain because you are afraid of being victimised even more or because you feel that you should be strong enough to deal with the situation yourself or perhaps you want desperately to hold on to your job. If you are an older person, you may be less inclined to complain because you were brought up to take troubles 'on the chin', or you may be close to retirement age and don't want to jeopardise your payout.

CASE STUDY

My old boss sold the company and the new bloke makes me out to be a complete idiot. If the job's running behind, he says, 'It's the old codger, he's a bit slow.' His attitude has spread to the others and these young kids ridicule me. I'm the scapegoat for anything that goes wrong, but I just have to put up with it. I've got no choice — my two kids are still at high school. I've done this job for 45 years and could do the work with my eyes shut but he's got me doubting myself. I've lost loads of weight and am a real cranky bastard with my family. At work, my hands shake all the time and I'm afraid I'll cause an accident. He wants me to quit, I know, but he's not going to get rid of me that easy.

(Barry, 65, electrician/linesman)

If you are a younger worker, you are more likely to protest because modern youth are encouraged to stand up for their rights and generally have a more flexible approach to employment — they don't expect their jobs to be long term and are willing to move in and out of employment many times in their working lives. Remember, this is not about conflicting personalities; it is about someone infringing your human rights and denying your dignity. *Nothing justifies bullying.*

If you choose to make a complaint, you will need to plan carefully.

> AMANDA: Stella said that the type of abuse I'd been subjected to was absolutely beyond the pale and I should go straight to human resources and be honest about what had happened to me. Human resources, said Stella, is there to help ovecome difficulties and frictions. So off I went to Tamsyn to report the threats and ask her advice about what to do.
> STELLA: Big mistake.

It's my word against the bully's — how can I prove anything?

Unfortunately, because psychological bullying is usually done one-to-one, without witnesses, or is handled in such a subtle way that only the victim is aware of it, the abuse can be very difficult to prove. It often comes down to your word against the bully's.

To help you prove your case, you need to document everything — what is happening to you, who is doing it and how you felt at the time and afterwards (shaking, tearful, unable to concentrate, and so on). Verbal bullying should be quoted verbatim as much as possible. This documentation is vital if you are going to make a formal complaint; without such supporting evidence, your complaint will be difficult to substantiate. Employers, and especially the bullies themselves, may try to deny there is a problem at all.

Keep a diary. Record all incidents, however trivial. Write down any conversations you have with the bully, colleagues, supervisors or employers relating to your complaint, any telephone calls and the content of those calls, making sure you note the date and time. Some incidents may seem trivial at the time, but put together they form a picture. Keep memorandums, diary notes, hard copies of e-mails, and any Post-it notes (which are often used by the bully as a method of communication to avoid a face-to-face conversation). If you suffer stress, anxiety or other health problems as a result of the bullying, see your doctor and get written confirmation of your medical complaint. Again, record every dizzy spell, every sign of a rash, every time you get neck and shoulder pain, every headache and every sleepless night.

The diary will help you — and anyone who investigates your complaint — to see the overall pattern of the abuse.

Where do I report this problem?

This is the difficult part. If your problem is with a co-worker and you have indicated that you intend to report the matter, you will need to move quickly or the co-worker may get in first and report *you* as being difficult, uncooperative and a bully.

First, find out if your workplace has a policy on bullying. If one exists, read it carefully so that you are fully aware of how these issues should be addressed.

Make an appointment with your manager or supervisor. Do this on a one-to-one basis if the bully is a colleague, as it makes it less formal. (If you bring in a union delegate at this early stage, upper management will need to be informed of this action in writing.)

By now you should have documented the bullying incident/s, as well as the response you received if you made a personal approach to the bully. At your appointment, you should outline your concerns and present your records to your manager or supervisor, who should then proceed along similar lines to those outlined below.

a The manager or supervisor should discuss the incident/s fully with you and obtain full details of any other relevant events or behaviour; you should be specific about what steps you want to be taken — transfer of yourself or the alleged perpetrator, placement of yourself on sick leave until the matter is sorted or disciplinary action for the alleged perpetrator.

b The alleged bully's version should then be obtained.

c The manager or supervisor should then respond to your concerns and, if you are happy with the outcome, finish the matter.

d If you are unhappy with the outcome, a mediator should be engaged to negotiate between you and the alleged perpetrator.

e If the matter is still not resolved to your satisfaction, your grievance should be referred further up the chain of command (this step may not be appropriate in smaller businesses).

If this further procedure fails, the workplace may have to recruit an independent mediator, or you may have to go to your union or the Industrial Relations Commission (see Chapters 11 and 12).

If more than one person is being bullied, complaining as a group will make it very difficult for the bully or your employer to dismiss the complaint.

If the bully is your manager or supervisor, the process should be along similar lines to the above, but your initial approach would be made to someone at a level higher than that of the bully.

What if I work for a small company (less than ten employees), and the owner is the bully?

The majority of companies in Australia are small companies. In a small business, there may be no one to report to: the bully may be the boss, or the victim may know that the person in authority will take the bully's side. If more than one person is being bullied, make a collective complaint. A group complaint is more difficult to dismiss as untrue.

Unfortunately, in this situation (a regular occurrence in the trades and service industry), you have few options. You can stand up to your employer and state that you will not accept that kind of behaviour. However, be aware that, by doing this, you are leaving yourself wide open to be terminated through 'lack of work'. Before taking any action, you should seek guidance from a legal advice centre or an appropriate state agency that handles workplace issues (see Appendix C).

You will probably have no alternative but to leave. If you walk away from your job, however, you will have to find other employment, most likely without a reference.

The best outcome in these circumstances is that you receive a redundancy package with a reference. The worst outcome is if you are forced to issue an unfair dismissal claim against your employer (see Chapter 12). If you are dismissed, check your job description or contract for notice terms to ensure that you are not unfairly dismissed.

If you are a tradesperson or work in the service industry, it is essential to join a union (and, if possible, a strong one).

Note: The current Federal Liberal Government is considering removing the right of employees of small companies to take the employer to the Industrial Relations Commission for unfair dismissal. This will further erode the rights of workers.

How can my family and friends help me?

The people closest to you will play an important part in helping you to cope; their support is essential if you are to come out of this situation in a reasonably healthy mental and physical state. If you are in a relationship, your main support person is most likely to be your partner. As we have said previously in Chapter 6, your relationship can be affected. This will be minimised by sharing the events with your partner without letting it dominate your time together. Talk of other things, go out to dinner or a show. If you are single, this support could come from either a parent or a friend.

I was lucky to have love and support from my husband, my two best friends and my family. Their patience and understanding helped me to realise that all the bitterness and hatred I was carrying was hurting no one but me, and that I should be grateful for all the good things in my life.

(Caroline, 41, nurse)

How can I help myself?

The following factors will have a major impact on the way you cope with this ordeal.

- **Mental attitude.** This will be a key factor in your survival. Don't continue to play the scenes over and over in your head. Push any lingering guilt feelings away.
- **Sharing your feelings.** Don't shut off your feelings or they may erupt later, perhaps manifesting themselves in health problems. Cry if you want to, unlock the tears. You will need somebody to listen while you express your emotions, to assure you that you are not losing control and that you are undergoing a very normal response to a harmful experience. What you let out lessens what is inside you, which must be a good thing. Even years after the bullying, some of our interviewees could talk about how they felt *after* the experience but, when it came to talking about specific incidents, they 'hit the wall'. As one said, 'I just can't go there' (Lena, 32, nurse). She had not had counselling at the time and had internalised her trauma.

- **Warning:** Try not to allow your bullying experience to become an obsession; thinking, eating and reliving it on a daily basis will only cause you further stress and damage your relationships. If friends and family members are subject to constant harangues over an extended period of time, their invitations, telephone calls and visits — and their support — will dry up.

I really did feel for Graham — his situation was awful, but I got sick of listening to him. It was all he could talk about and my sympathy passed its 'use-by' date. I felt bad but I had to drop him — his continual complaints were ruining my social life! Nobody likes a whinger.

(Alec, 27)

It was all he could talk about. We stopped having conversations. Communication was a one-way street — I'd listen to an endless rant from him about how much work he had, how stressed he was, who'd said what to or about him, how he wasn't given enough information to do his job properly — but if I tried to say something about my day, or the kids' problems, I could see he wasn't taking it in. He'd just continue his tirade as if I hadn't spoken at all. When he was made redundant, I thought, well, at least we'll be able to get back to normal family life, but not so. Now all he talks about is how unfairly he was treated and what he should have said or done. I don't really like him much any more and I feel like walking out.

(Katherine, 37)

- **Look after yourself.** It is extremely important to take care of yourself, both emotionally and physically. Make sure that you get enough sleep, or your health and ability to cope will be adversely affected. If you do experience sleep difficulties, try some herbal remedies and don't eat or drink anything after eight in the evening. Relax with a book or music before going to bed. You may find it helpful to read a book about stress management. Relaxation tapes can be very therapeutic, and your psychologist may be able to recommend a particular one.

I was having trouble sleeping and my psychologist recommended a tape by a psychologist/hypnotherapist. The first time I played it I was asleep in five minutes! It was amazing. Now, whenever I have trouble getting to sleep or when I wake up in the middle of the night, I switch on the tape and I'm soon in dreamland again. The only problem is, my husband says he's going to scream if he hears her voice one more time!

(Rosa, 53)

Treat yourself to an occasional massage, learn to say no to anything that is likely to cause extra stress. Take up swimming, either with a friend or by yourself; there is nothing like a few strenuous laps of the pool to release pressure. If you don't swim, why not take lessons? Go for a walk; better still, take the dog for a walk, or your partner. Have time out, go to a coffee shop, have a cappuccino and read a book for half an hour, or phone a friend and invite him/her to do something with you — go to see a film, play a round of golf or have lunch at the local shopping centre.

- **Regular therapy.** If you live alone and have no one to confide in, or if you experience severe physical or emotional effects, you may need professional help to get you through this difficult period. Again, don't bury feelings of resentment, anger or bitterness. Be open and talk about your feelings — your therapist will be able to help you to attain resolution and/or closure of your experience so that the healing process can begin.

I have had enough — should I confront the bully before making an official complaint?

It may be worth trying one more time to settle the problem face to face before you try to stop it through 'official' channels.

If you are in the union and there is a union delegate at your worksite, explain your problem to the delegate. If you don't have a delegate, talk to your occupational health and safety officer. Your ordeal and its emotional and physical effects are health and safety issues; for you, your worksite is unhealthy and toxic.

AMANDA: I felt that Bryony had no more respect for me than she would for a . . . worm. It was a feeling I didn't ever want to have again. I'm human. I need to feel liked and respected. But suddenly I felt as if I'd entered totally new territory. I just wanted to run.
BRYONY: I'm sorry Amanda, but this is just totally hysterical reaction to a routine dressing down.

If the delegate or OH&S officer offers to have 'a quiet word' with the bully, say no — this is forewarning the bully, who is then able to put his case to his superior before you do. Request a meeting in a 'neutral' place, such as a meeting room or someone else's office. If the bully is your manager, avoid meeting in his office where he will be sitting behind a desk or in a higher chair than you. If you feel uncomfortable attending by yourself and have asked a union delegate to be present, advise your manager that you will be accompanied. It is a courtesy and avoids putting him offside if he appears at the meeting and finds a delegate there.

The union delegate is trained to negotiate so let the delegate guide you through the meeting. It will be hard, but try to look your bully in the eye; this will be off-putting for him. If you receive hostile eye contact or body language from the bully, say something (such as, 'Henry, please don't look at me like that') to bring it to the attention of your advocate.

Bullying situations are very difficult and all are different, depending on the culture of the industry and the workplace. If the delegate and occupational health and safety officer are employed by the same company, they may not want to 'rock the boat' too much. Sometimes they have to decide whose 'side' they are on.

If your attempt at resolution fails, you will have to proceed through the official channels.

How do I report the problem?

Every company should have a policy manual that is easily accessible to all employees. (In the majority of companies it's gathering dust on someone's bookshelf.) If you don't know where it is, ask for it. The policy should state the correct procedure to follow. If a dispute cannot be solved by the persons in conflict, the complaining employee has the right to go to the next line of management. If the bully is your manager and you cannot confront him, you need to take your complaint higher up; this may mean approaching the company's chief executive officer (CEO).

Preparing the official complaint

Always put your grievances in writing, to your manager if your complaint concerns a colleague or to the next level of management if your complaint concerns your manager. The easiest form is a memorandum, which could be something like this:

MEMORANDUM

To: Mr Nice Guy

From: Mia Target

Date: 01/04/02

Re: Bullying in the workplace

Over the past three months I have been subjected to ongoing bullying by my manager, Mr Dick Head. His hostile behaviour has included:

1. Humiliating me in team meetings.
2. Removing documents from my desk.
3. Giving unattainable timelines.
4. Ignoring me in the office and at meetings.
5. Wanting to know where I am every minute of the day.
6. Sending e-mails and leaving sticky notes instead of talking to me (I can supply copies of this correspondence if required).

I feel very stressed and intimidated by these actions and wish them to stop immediately. I look forward to discussing this at length with you. I am giving a copy of this memo to Mr Head for his information.

Make sure that you do give a copy of your memorandum to the bully. Leave it on the desk, or in the 'in' tray when the bully is out of the office. Ask a colleague to witness this action so that the bully cannot later deny receiving the memo.

Usually, the bully will not say anything to you on receiving the copy of your complaint. If the bully does contact you by the internal telephone and you have a 'speaker' phone, put it on and turn up the volume so that anyone nearby can hear. If the bully sends you an e-mail, keep a copy. If a meeting with you is requested, or you are ambushed in the office, refuse to speak to the bully unless you have a witness, preferably your union delegate or the OH&S representative. If the bully refuses to have a witness, walk away. If he insists on discussing your complaint then and there, write down the conversation directly afterwards, noting the date, the time, the bully's attitude towards you and how you felt — for example, 'He moved too close to me, invading my "personal space". I felt intimidated and afraid.' 'He was extremely angry, his face was red and the veins were popping out of his neck. I thought he was going to hit me.' 'He was very controlled and said that if I persisted with my complaint, he would see that I never worked again.'

Even if you have not told anyone else in the organisation about your complaint, it will get around fairly quickly. Be prepared for any 'fallout' from colleagues, such as snide comments like, 'If it's too hot in the kitchen, get out,' or 'You're too aggressive in meetings'. If you need to confide in anyone, ensure that you choose the right person. In some cases of bullying, there are two 'camps' — those who side with the bully and those who side with the victim. Victims will receive colleague support only if the bully is not well liked or trusted in other areas of the workplace. In most cases, however, there is no active support for the victim (see Chapter 8).

I was bullied by a feminist of some prominence. Covering a period of months, the conduct climaxed at a meeting ... Discussion turned to the contentious subject. A sharp attack — directed full pelt against the position I held. Declining to ... be bullied into subjection, I stood my ground ... firmly putting my position. I did not intend to back down ... Like a burst balloon came the collapse, the bullying woman drooping off sobbing, into a corner of the room. Now, as one, everyone present — most being victim/survivors of the bully in times past — turned upon ... me who stood my ground — 'How could you?', 'How awful', before turning to comfort that woman in the corner.[71]

It sometimes happens that the victim's or the union's camp has a 'spy', someone who appears friendly and on 'your side', even to the extent of attending union meetings. Your case could be discussed at these meetings and the spy reports straight back to the bully, who then can anticipate any union moves.

What response should I expect?

A written complaint gives the manager or CEO time to become familiar with company policy and make some enquiries. You should expect to receive a response of some kind within 48 hours — a written acknowledgment of receipt of your letter, with an 'I'll get back to you', or a telephone call, e-mail or memorandum requesting an interview.

Undoubtedly, the manager or CEO will speak with the alleged bully and obtain their version of events, which, of course, will be totally different to yours. If the 'grapevine' has not been working previously, it certainly will be now. You will know when your bully has been interviewed. During our research, one victim mentioned that, with her bullying manager, every time he was 'hauled over the coals' he whistled on his way back to his office. Another victim's bully returned with a bright red face, which stood out against his white hair and beard.

Of course, bullies are good actors and may *appear* to take it in their stride. Your bully may go straight to his/her office, to be joined by a follower behind closed doors. If this is a situation of 'bullying in isolation', the bully will try to gain his/her composure and continue working, leaving you to wait for the bomb to drop. No matter how composed the bully appears, however, underneath he/she will be seething and wanting someone to pay for this humiliation. You can be assured that the next few days are going to be unpleasant.

I have an interview with my manager/ the CEO and the bully — what can I expect?

You need to take a contact person or support person with you to the interview, ideally your shop steward or occupational health and safety representative. Be clear about what action you want taken — transfer to another section (for you or the bully) or a grievance hearing. In a perfect world you could expect the CEO to believe you and to sack your manager on the spot, with you being promoted to the bully's position. Unfortunately, we don't live in a perfect world.

Let's look at a possible scenario. You, the victim, are female and the bully and the CEO are male. When you enter, the bully is already there and he and the CEO are laughing together. Immediately, you feel uncomfortable and excluded. The CEO then outlines your complaint and asks the bully for a response. The bully laughs and says, 'There is absolutely no truth to these allegations. I can sympathise with her, and understand that, because she is premenstrual [or menopausal, depending on the victim's age]. She is at the mercy of her hormones. But I will try to be more understanding in future.' Or he may say, 'I deny everything. She is paranoid [or aggressive, or unapproachable], her behaviour is out of control, she won't let any other team members have their say.' Or, 'This is all a figment of her imagination; she really needs to see a psychiatrist.' Somehow the blame is cast back on you. You become defensive, you are unable to think clearly and you become tearful — thus appearing to confirm the bully's picture of you as a hysterical female.

Don't think this is exaggerated — it happens all the time when victims are unsupported. An advocate should be able to prevent the interview from following these lines.

CEOs and management, instead of taking the attitude that their managers are too valuable to lose, should respond like this.

Another scenario: Your CEO welcomes you into his office and says, 'I was very distressed to receive your memo and have started making enquiries into your allegations. I can promise you a thorough investigation will be made, with positive outcomes. I have spoken to [your bully] and I can guarantee that, if your complaints are substantiated, there will be no further instances. I will get back to you within the next few days with my findings.' He then asks if you need time off, and so on. This is an assertive, highly professional response from a CEO who does not value one worker over another.

The CEO or the board of management may suggest a workplace conference led by an external facilitator. A workplace conference is a meeting which provides a forum for those people affected by the bullying to explain how they have been affected and to contribute to discussion on how best to resolve the issue and restore good working relationships. It is our experience that such conferences rarely solve a bullying situation.

We can try to avoid making choices by doing nothing, but even that is a decision.

Gary Collins

CHAPTER 11

Unions — help
or
hindrance?

We must remember that a right lost to one is lost to all.

William Reece Smith, Jr

Unions are there to provide advice and assistance to their members on workplace issues. This assistance includes advice on grievances, mediation and conciliation, representation at any meetings or investigations at every stage of company grievance and disciplinary procedures and negotiations with employers on implementing any relevant company policies and procedures and enterprise bargaining agreements.

What can a union do if I am being bullied?

Unions can play a large and important role in any case of bullying. As said above, a union's role is to represent and advocate for their members and protect members' rights in industrial matters. Bullied employees who are union members can seek the assistance and advice of their union and request that a union representative act as a buffer between them and their employer.

Having a union representative at your side can have a beneficial psychological effect. Bullies like to isolate people and often victims internalise their feelings. Having support in the workplace, being able to discuss the mistreatment and appropriate action with someone can make you feel less alone.

> AMANDA: I really was going to try and hang in there in any case. But I was going to need a little support.

Union representatives can lead you through the various processes, starting with your initial interview with your manager or the bully's boss, and provide advice on your options. If communication with your employer breaks down or if the union believes there has been a breach of your rights, it can assist you to lodge your case at the Industrial Relations Commission so that a neutral party can intervene. Depending on the seriousness of the breach or case, union lawyers may assist you at 'mates' rates'. (You are also free to use private representation, which, of course, could be a greater cost.) If you do choose to engage a private solicitor, investigate his/her background, his/her success rate and his/her fees. In some states there are specialist community legal centres that offer free assistance to people experiencing difficulties in their workplace.

You will need to give your union representative copies of all documentation relevant to your case, for example, your position description, your contract, if any, dates and times of incidents, any written communication that you received from the alleged bully, witness statements if possible, and any relevant company policy and procedures. You should make notes at every meeting with your union representative and clarify with him the proposed course of action. The last thing you need at this very stressful time is more worry and anxiety about broken promises.

What can I expect of my union representative?

Your union representative should take your complaint seriously, give you a sympathetic and supportive response and deal with your complaint in strict confidence to avoid damaging gossip. The rep should then attempt to resolve the complaint on your behalf, using the appropriate workplace grievance procedure and the union/company disputes procedure. The representative should support you at every stage of a complaint procedure, making detailed notes of every phase. If the alleged bully is also a member of the union, the representative should not represent both parties; the union branch should be approached for an alternative representative.

Often, because of the lack of support from co-workers, victims of bullying place all their hopes on intervention by their union. Many subsequently express their disappointment in, and frustration with, the lack of professionalism and preparedness of their union representatives.

> **CASE STUDY**
>
> *Having been bullied out of my job, my union delegate completed my application to the Industrial Relations Commission and I signed and posted it. I then decided to see a lawyer and when I showed him a copy of my unfair dismissal application he advised that the union delegate had not ticked the box to say I wanted reinstatement. He said I should have applied for reinstatement, as it gives a stronger defence.*

I quickly sent an e-mail to the IRC and my ex-employer's barristers advising them of the mistake. This error on the union's part created further stress for me.

(Martin, 38, employment consultant)

Always seek advice from an experienced lawyer regarding any unfair dismissal.

Unfortunately, during the past decade, changes in the composition of the workforce and the structure of the economy have had a significant effect on union membership in Australia. Many unions lost members, causing them to become under-resourced, which in turn adversely affected their ability to meet members' needs and expectations. In the twelve months April 2000–April 2001, union membership numbers increased for the first time in over a decade — up by 23,500 members — but, even with this increase, in April 2001 only 25 per cent of Australia's 9.1 million employees were in unions.[72] This reduction in union membership may be a reason for the increase in workplace bullying: bullies feel more secure because workers are less protected, and workers put up with the bullying behaviour because they feel that there is no one to back them up.

When you lodge a grievance or instigate industrial action because of bullying, your employer will also seek representation. Unfortunately, many victims find that, compared with the high standard of the legal advice obtained by their employer, their own representation is weak. Don't let this happen to you. It is essential that you ask questions of your union representative to assess his/her ability and capacity to take on your case. If you are not happy with your representation, do not be afraid to say so. You must be able to have absolute trust in your union; after all, your future is in their hands, and you are a paying member. If they do not handle your case competently and with unconditional commitment, make an official complaint.

Unions need to act with the same professionalism you would expect from a lawyer, doctor or accountant. When you first meet such people, you expect to be greeted by a well-dressed, well-spoken professional. This first impression immediately instils confidence. Unfortunately, some union delegates lack this professionalism and, if unions are to survive and thrive in the twenty-first century, this needs to change.

I was disappointed in my union rep. He was always casually dressed, coming to meetings in jeans and a T-shirt or grubby woollen jumper. Sometimes he hadn't bothered to shave. This wouldn't have bothered me if he'd done his job properly, but he made promises, in front of my employer, stating that the union would be approaching the media and the current Minister about my case. When this didn't happen, I rang the delegate continuously but was always fobbed off. So I felt that I couldn't trust him. Not only did I lose trust in him, but worrying about what else he might not be doing put me under further stress, when I was already sick with nerves. Eventually, I just gave up. It seems to me that unions will agree to fight in the beginning, but then someone else's problem comes along and your case is literally forgotten.

(Penny, 34, welfare worker)

Your union representative must be in 'your camp', someone who will go in to bat for you strongly and who is absolutely trustworthy and honest. No one expects unions to wave a magic wand and make it all better. It is preferable for a delegate to admit that the union is understaffed and give you your options, stating which may succeed and which may fail, than promise the earth and let you down. Bullying in the workplace is still a 'new' issue and, unfortunately, most union delegates and union representatives in workplaces have not received the necessary training to deal with it.

The extent of support you actually receive will depend on the union to which you belong, which state you live in, how strong the union is at your workplace and the level of experience of the union delegate assigned to your case. Some unions have their own political agendas and some are able to wield more power than others, because of either political standing or membership size. However, it is still advisable to be a member of a union.

As said previously, in a case where one union member is pitted against another, the branch should be approached for assistance in these circumstances. No one official should represent both protagonists in a case.

What if my union says I don't have a case?

Get proper legal advice. Your case may be weak, and certainly bullying situations where it is one person's word against another's are difficult to prove. Unfortunately, there could also be the possibility that the union representative is in collusion with management, or someone higher up in the union is not in favour of tackling your case (as in one bullying case we heard about — the bully was a powerful union official at the workplace and the victim was made to understand that there would be no point in trying to obtain assistance).

If a lawyer considers that you have a case, you need to decide if you have the mental (and financial) resources to continue your fight. If a lawyer verifies the union stance, you then have major decisions to make, that is, whether to stay in your job and put up with the bully's behaviour or look for other employment.

What happens if I'm not in a union?

If you are not in a union, then we suggest that you join one. Then you can seek assistance, though it is not really the right way to go about it, as some unions have found that the new member leaves as soon as the conflict is resolved. If finances are a stumbling block to joining, most unions allow monthly or quarterly payments. Make joining a union a priority. Unions aim to achieve the best outcomes for workers and can influence what happens with workplace problems. Don't think that you are immune and that you will never need help.

You need to protect your rights, so if you cannot access union advice, you should approach a community legal service. Many legal practices offer an initial one hour of free legal advice (see Appendix C).

First they ignore you. Then they laugh at you. Then they fight you. Then you win.

Gandhi

CHAPTER 12

Legal options

LITIGATION, n: A machine which you go into as a pig and come out of as a sausage.

Ambrose Bierce

You may find that, though you tried to resolve the conflict within your workplace, nothing changed. After you complained to your employer, no real investigation was done. A 'Claytons' mediation took place, that is, the bully gave a token apology with no penalty imposed or disciplinary action taken, the bully still works there and, worst of all, the abuse has 'gone underground' and become worse. You've had enough.

What are my options?

You can either decide to leave the workplace and find alternate employment, or fight for your rights through the WorkCover system.

> AMANDA: I decided that Stella was right. I shouldn't resign. I mustn't resign. I must stay and fight. And the truth was, when I relflected soberly, I didn't have all that many options ... at my age and without a decent reference and with jobs in the charity sector very thin on the ground and having saved not nearly enough to even *begin* to think of retiring.

How do I make a WorkCover claim?

Because each state has its own WorkCover system, conditions may vary from what we have outlined below; check with your state Workcover Authority. However, the first step *of any claim* is to report your complaint. Every workplace is required to keep a register or report book, in which details of all injuries are recorded. If you can't find the book, you should put these details in writing to someone in authority, such as the company's health and safety officer. Once your complaint is reported, it is the duty of the employer to acknowledge, in writing, that your complaint has been received by the organisation.

The next step is to consult a doctor, who will provide a WorkCover medical certificate giving details of your condition. Depending on your state of health, this certificate could authorise a reduction in your hours or days of work, or put you off work altogether. (With bullying, we would recommend taking time off work to cut contact with the bully.) You need to fill in the back of this certificate, sign it and have it witnessed, and photocopy it for your records before passing on the original to your employer. (After the time covered by this first certificate has expired, your doctor or other health specialists can issue further certificates if you need more time off work.)

You must also obtain a Worker's Claim for Compensation form, obtainable from your employer, the WorkCover office or any post office. This form must be completed, signed and dated by yourself and the employer, preferably on the day of injury, or as soon as possible afterwards (as strict time limits for the making of claims may apply). You keep the worker's copy. **Note:** If this claim form is not lodged, you will not be paid.

Remember, you must keep copies of any documentation related to a WorkCover claim. We advise that you keep everything together in an easily accessible file, as this will be particularly helpful if you have to go to conciliation or to the Magistrate's or Federal Court.

How soon will I know if my claim is accepted?

Your employer can neither refuse to accept your claim nor dismiss you for lodging a claim. Even if your employer denies liability, your claim form must still be accepted, the employer section filled in and the completed form submitted to the company's insurer within a certain period (time may vary between states).

If you need time off work and are claiming weekly benefits (wages), WorkCover must advise you in writing within a certain time (usually within four weeks; time varies between states) if your claim is being accepted or refused. If your employer accepts liability, the company will usually commence paying weekly benefits on your normal pay days and wait for reimbursement from WorkCover. You must continue to submit valid medical certificates to your employer for as long as you are away from work or on reduced hours or attending any other health professional.

If your employer denies liability and you are without an income during the investigation process, you may have to use accumulated sick or holiday leave. If you have no accumulated leave, you can apply to Centrelink for sickness benefits. As an income and assets test applies to these benefits, you may not qualify if your partner is working, but it is always advisable to put in a claim. If you start to receive benefits and then your claim is accepted, WorkCover will reimburse Centrelink from your outstanding payments. Your employer must reinstate any sick or annual leave used because of your injury. The flowchart below shows the steps in the WorkCover process.

Injury/stress claim
lodged with the employer

Even if the employer denies liability, there are
3–10 days (varies between states) to lodge claim
with agent. It is then up to the agent to determine
liability. *If* employer accepts liability, the company will,
in most cases, commence weekly payments.

Claim accepted by
employer or agent. Agent has
up to 28 days (varies between
states) to respond. WorkCover
payments commence.

Claim rejected by employer
and agent. Seek legal advice.
You may need to access sick or
annual leave or, if you do not
have either, apply to Centrelink
for sickness benefits.

Return-to-work plans,
doctors' and psychologists'
reports, etc. (see page 133).

You may need to apply for a
conciliation conference (contact
WorkCover Conciliation Service)
(see page 135).

*If dispute is not resolved at conciliation, the conciliation officer must
be satisfied that you have taken all reasonable steps to resolve
dispute. The conciliation officer will then issue a certificate allowing
you to proceed to the Magistrate's Court (See page 135).*

Magistrates' Court

*Win — WorkCover
commences — any back pay
plus medical costs plus legal
costs paid.*

*Lose — No WorkCover.
You pay all the medical costs,
plus, possibly, your and other
side's costs.*

If my claim is approved, do I need legal advice?

You should obtain legal advice even if your claim is successful — take advantage of the initial free consultation offered by most lawyers. If you are a union member, contact your union for a referral to someone who specialises in the area of WorkCover. We advise that you find out the lawyer's charges at your initial appointment.

Will I be sent to a psychiatrist?

Whether your claim is accepted or denied, you will get on the merry-go-round of doctors, psychologists and psychiatrists. It is not unusual to be sent to two psychiatrists for assessment. Before your appointments, the psychiatrist would have received a report from WorkCover detailing your claim.

It is very difficult to get your 'case' across in a 35 or 40 minute appointment, but you should answer the psychiatrist's questions honestly. Explain what happened, how long the bullying had been going on, how you felt at the time of the incidents and how you are feeling now. If your self-esteem is shot to pieces, say so. If you are depressed or have had thoughts of suicide, say so. If you are on medication, take it with you or have the name(s) written down — don't rely on your memory.

After the appointment a report will be forwarded to WorkCover; your legal representative should obtain a copy. (Unfortunately, it has been known for a WorkCover insurer to use one dot point, taken out of context from a psychiatric report, to further reject a claim.)

Who pays all my medical expenses, and what am I entitled to claim?

From the time you first attended your doctor and obtained the WorkCover certificate, all accounts are sent to your employer, who then forwards them to WorkCover. WorkCover will pay all reasonable costs, including physiotherapy, pharmacy, and transport costs if you have to travel, for example, to a counsellor (train, bus, tram and taxi fares and, if you travel by car, a cost per kilometre is payable). All original receipts are forwarded to WorkCover and, if your claim is approved, you will receive a reimbursement cheque. If your claim has been refused, keep all receipts so that, if your claim is later accepted, you can submit them for reimbursement. *Remember to keep copies of all receipts.*

Unfortunately, if your claim is ultimately rejected, all bills will be returned to you and they will become your responsibility. However, you may be able to claim some of them through Medicare or your private health fund. (Costs for psychologists are not recoverable from Medicare.)

What can I do if WorkCover says I can return to work, but I'm not ready?

There may come a time, following a psychiatric assessment, when WorkCover will write to you saying that they believe you are now fit to resume work and they will be stopping payments. If you do not agree, contact your doctor and lawyer for advice. The lawyer will request a copy of the WorkCover psychiatrist's report; you should obtain a copy for your file. Your lawyer may then send you to a psychiatrist of her choice for an assessment.

Remember, *it is up to your doctor* to say if and when you are fit to resume work.

What if my claim is rejected?

Unfortunately, this happens quite often and it can be a devastating setback to your recovery and resolve to fight. You may start to ask yourself: Did I imagine it? Was it my fault? Your partner may question you about what really happened at work and say things such as, 'It's over now. You should forget it and move on.' Try not to get angry or depressed. Telephone your lawyer, who will make an application on your behalf for a WorkCover conciliation conference.

The conciliation officer will be independent and impartial and will know how WorkCover relates to all parties (victim, employer and agent).

If all parties including the conciliation officer agree, you as the victim may be able to have legal representation. (This varies depending on where you live — you need to check conditions in your own state.) This puts you at a double disadvantage — employers or agents will often refuse to allow your lawyer to attend, but employers are allowed to bring WorkCover insurers who are fully conversant with the WorkCover Act. You can, however, bring a support person such as a union delegate or an advocate/contact person and, if you are seeing a psychologist, we recommend that the psychologist attends and addresses the hearing. **Warning:** If any document or information requested from you has not been supplied to the conciliation officer, you may be unable to use it later if the dispute goes to court.

If an agreement is not reached at the conciliation meeting, the conciliation officer can direct the employer or insurer to make weekly payments to you to cover your medical expenses for a limited time. If the conciliation officer believes you have made reasonable efforts to resolve the dispute, the officer will issue a certificate to that effect, which entitles you to go to court to pursue acceptance of your WorkCover claim.

If conciliation does not work, what legal avenues are open to me?

Bear in mind that, although in theory there are legal avenues available, in practical terms there are obstacles to success as detailed below.

- **Cost.** Legal action is expensive and you will have to pay your own legal costs (union lawyers are usually cheaper). Also, if you are the only income earner in the family, you could be without income until it is resolved in court, unless you have applied for social security benefits.
- **Time.** Legal action is notoriously slow and it can take up to a year between conciliation and court.
- **Lack of resolution.** Usually, if a case of bullying has gone to court, it is because the victim has left work, either voluntarily or involuntarily. You are 'in limbo' for the time the court process takes, unable to put the traumatic experience behind you.
- **Continued trauma.** A court case involves reliving the bullying experience and revisiting the feelings of helplessness, the insecurity and stress over and over.

Bear in mind that going ahead with a legal fight will be tough and, at times, soul destroying. The prevailing culture of disbelief with WorkCover claims can have a destructive effect on an already vulnerable person. Before continuing along the legal path, you will need to decide if your mental and physical health, as well as your finances and your personal relationships, can stand the strain (see April's story, page 181-4). This is what the employer and the WorkCover insurer play on.

> The way in which compensation authorities such as ... WorkCover ... deal with injured people greatly affects claimants' psychological recovery ... i.e. the perceived negative dealings towards patients ... through claims management and psychiatric assessment can potentially cause much damage or aggravation to the lives of people endeavouring to recover from conditions such as trauma.[73]

Once you make the decision to go ahead, you will need to try to keep mentally and physically fit for the ordeal ahead. Make no mistake, it will be an ordeal. Be very careful not to seek relief from inappropriate sources such as alcohol, gambling and drugs — you will need a clear head to fight the bully and the continuing effects on you of the bully's actions. Try to manage your stress with some of the strategies covered in Chapter 14 — regular exercise, yoga or meditation. Mix with positive, motivated people and do things that make you feel happy — gardening, listening to music, sport, playing with your children or grandchildren.

What happens at the Magistrates' Court?

The waiting time between the conciliation conference and appearing at the Magistrates' Court will add to your stress, particularly if you have gone through the conciliation process and the conciliation officer believes your claim should be accepted, but your employer or WorkCover insurer refuses to accept your claim. You will feel further victimised, possibly angry and certainly depressed; the stressful experience is being dragged out even further and you are unable to attain closure and move on with your life.

Approximately six weeks beforehand, your lawyer will advise you when your case will be heard in the Magistrates' Court. At that time, if WorkCover requests further psychiatric assessments, so will your lawyer. This will be a very stressful time, particularly as the date draws near. You will have doubts and wonder if you are doing the right thing.

Your health may deteriorate, with a return of headaches or nightmares, nervous rashes and bowel problems. Your family may suffer with you and urge you to give up. 'Forget it. Let's get on with our lives. All this is doing is tearing us apart.' This may be true, as you will eat, drink and breathe the forthcoming court date. Try to relax, using some of the techniques mentioned in Chapter 14.

If you are involved in a family business, even if you receive no direct benefit in the way of wages, it is possible the company may receive a summons to produce certain documents. You could receive a summons for your tax records. This is an attempt by the 'other side' to find out if you are receiving wages and thus are 'fit for work' or illegally claiming WorkCover payments; it could also be a pressure tactic.

A vindictive employer may attempt to stretch out the court hearing. It is not unknown for a case to take two weeks and, depending on the outcome, someone has to pay. For a case of this length with costs for each side of approximately $30,000, the loser (who could be you) would have to pay up to $60,000. The aim of the game is to force the victim into giving up because of the legal costs involved (this is financial bullying; see Chapter 2, page 32). This is where the risk factor comes in. Your lawyer and barrister will know when to 'pull the pin', but it is ultimately your decision — they take instructions from you.

Unfortunately, when an insurer denies liability, the spotlight switches from the stressful workplace incidents that damaged you as the claimant to an attitude that you are claiming something to which you are not entitled. Conciliation is compulsory, but you may find that the insurer has control. Under the adversarial system, the insurer may attempt to investigate many aspects of your life under the pretext of ascertaining relevant information. There is no protection in the process for the injured party until the matter finally reaches court which, depending on the state in which you live, could be between eight and twelve months.

On the day your case is to be heard, take a support person to the court with you, perhaps your partner, a close friend or a former co-worker. Your lawyer would have briefed a barrister, who will 'run' the case. Be prepared to be bullied by 'the other side'. Try to remain calm and think about your answers to their questions. If you 'explode' you will be playing into their hands, as they will assert that the problem was caused by you and that no bullying took place. Your case may be adjourned, which means that you have to go through more stressful waiting.

If you have been 'retrenched' or 'restructured' out of your job, the financial burden will be heavy by the time you reach the Magistrates' Court, particularly if you have dependants. If there is a possibility of losing your house, seek professional help from a financial or debt counsellor; they are available in all states and offer a free, confidential service. Your local library will have numerous books on money management that could help you to cut back on spending or to rearrange your debts to minimise the impact of your lack of income.

Are any other legal avenues available for victims of bullying?

If you have been dismissed as a result of your complaint, you may be entitled to lodge a claim of unfair dismissal under the Workplace Relations Act. The Industrial Relations Commission decides whether your termination was 'harsh, unjust or unreasonable'.[74] Anyone dismissed for perpetrating bullying behaviour can also claim unfair dismissal if it can be proved that the employer tolerated such behaviour or did not have adequate procedures in place for dealing with it.

If you want to claim unfair dismissal, you first need to find out if your termination is legally classed as unfair. Consult a lawyer. (Unfortunately, some employees, such as those on three months' trial, casuals and contract employees, may be excluded from access to unfair dismissal laws.)

In theory, workplace bullying cases could be prosecuted under the Workplace Health and Safety Act, but success requires proof 'beyond a reasonable doubt'. There have been some successful cases prosecuted in Victoria, but they mostly involved acts of workplace violence (physical abuse and assault) as well as verbal bullying. We found only one case where a perpetrator was successfully prosecuted for bullying only ('an employee … was fined $1000 plus $1300 costs for verbally abusing and taunting another employee'[75]).

Taking the legal avenue to obtain redress for bullying may not be an option, given the cost of legal representation. If you do go ahead, the process will be extremely stressful. Be sure that you have the necessary personal strength, support from family or friends and financial resources before you choose this path.

Challenges are what make life interesting; overcoming them is what makes life meaningful.

Joshua J. Marine

PART 2

CHAPTER 13

The bully — is there another way?

You may fool all the people some of the time; you can even fool some of the people all of the time; but you can't fool all of the people all the time.

Abraham Lincoln

In all our interviews and discussions while researching this book, the most controversial questions were, 'Are bullies aware that they are bullying?' and 'Do you think a bully can change his behaviour?' Victims in particular had a passionate reaction; they were adamant that bullies were fully conscious of what they were doing and that their behaviour was so ingrained that change would be impossible. Health professionals were less rigid and mostly agreed that change was achievable for some bullies — those whose motivation was promotion or survival, for example — if they were given the right impetus.

It is possible that those people who are unaware that their behaviour constitutes bullying *may* be able to change the pattern of behaviour if they are willing to undertake further training in communication and management skills or if pressure from above is removed. However, we doubt that sociopathic chronic bullies can change, even with intensive counselling and therapy. Some professionals working with psychopaths agree that the condition does not respond to treatment.

> When it comes to treating psychopaths, don't waste your time. Nothing you do can make any difference at all.' One quite likely possibility is that therapy — particularly in the group setting — provides the psychopath with an opportunity 'to learn more about other people ... It improves his ability to con.' [76]

Am I a bully?

Have colleagues or employees ever accused you of bullying or intimidation? If the answer is 'yes', is it possible that the situation could have been a misunderstanding? Perhaps your communication style is too abrupt, or even brutal — you may have said or done something to someone without realising the hurt it inflicted on that person. You need to consider the sensibilities of others and their levels of self-esteem or humour before you speak or act, and realise that what one person finds acceptable could be distressing for another more sensitive individual.

If you are seriously concerned that the accusation might be true, we encourage you to answer the following questions honestly.

- Are you inflexible, moody, petulant, unwilling to change?
- Do you have problems managing your anger?

- Has your management style been described as tyrannical?
- Do you need to shout to get your message across?
- Are you overly critical of subordinates' work or constantly finding fault over minor issues?
- Are sarcasm, innuendo and put-downs your chosen method of communication?
- Do you humiliate, ridicule or belittle colleagues in front of others?
- Have you threatened or shouted abuse or obscenities at a colleague?
- Do you frequently check up on your workers or monitor their breaks?
- Do you exclude a particular worker from essential information or meetings?
- Do you set impossible objectives or timelines?
- Do you deliberately target union representatives who challenge your authority?

Read through the behaviours listed in Chapter 1 and ask yourself, 'Do I do this?'

BRYONY: Suppose I did say a few things that were ill considered, and for the life of me I can't remember doing it. But suppose I did. Most people wouldn't treat that like the end of the world was nigh.... The world is a tough place. No one was ever sweet to me when I was surviving and making the best of some of the worst schools in this country. I'd like a dollar for every time someone's said personal things to me. For God's sake, what kind of sheltered life have you led, Amanda?

Why do I behave this way?

A 'yes' response to any of the above questions may indicate that you are a bully. Can you think of a reason? Do you feel threatened by, or are you jealous of, a particular colleague? Is your colleague better looking, better qualified, more popular or more efficient than you? Intimidating others may make you feel important and powerful. You may feel threatened by people who are well liked or who are good at what they do, so you bully to protect the control you have.

Most researchers believe that the tendency to bully begins in childhood (see Chapter 3). You may have feelings of insecurity stemming from your school days, you may have had pressure put on you as a child to succeed or you may have been bullied yourself and see bullying others as a way of reclaiming your power and self-esteem.

Were you always in trouble at home and at school? Looking back, can you see a long-term pattern of aggression and disruptive behaviour? You may always have had problems with socialisation and anger management because of inadequate socialisation in childhood. You may have had domineering parents who were bad role models, abusing each other, your teachers, the umpires and referees on sports days, and whose parenting style was generally punitive.

You may just be a petty tyrant and a small amount of power has gone to your head.

CASE STUDY

I had resigned after months of constant criticisms and humiliation. On my last day I drew on all my courage and asked him, 'What did I ever do to you? Why did you do this to me?' He smirked and said, 'Because I can.'

(Glenn, 22, railway clerk)

Perhaps it's time to forgive yourself, and be who you really are. Stop pretending and putting on a false front for others. If you can understand why you bully, you may be able to adapt your behaviour and change your management approach and your interpersonal style.

What can I do to change?

The hardest and most important first step is admitting that you have been a bully. You may have denied it, even to yourself, until now, but you now know that what you have been doing is wrong. Your verbal and emotional abuse has inflicted unnecessary and probably long-term pain on your victims. You chose personal gratification over other people's rights.

Many bullies refuse to take responsibility for their actions. Before you can change, you have to acknowledge that conscious behaviour has consequences that can damage others. You can no longer make excuses for yourself — 'I was having a bad day'. 'He is the type who needs a firm hand'. Shut your eyes and think back to a time when you bullied someone. Try to put yourself in that person's shoes and imagine how you would feel if someone barked orders at you, put you down in meetings or moved you out of your office without consultation.

Does your workplace encourage bullying? Are you so pressured to work longer, harder and faster that you bully as a way of passing that pressure on to your colleagues or subordinates? If so, you may have to lessen your stress by releasing some control of the work, delegating more to others and introducing more participative decision making.

Do you have personal worries that have impacted on your working life? If so, leave them at home during working hours and take steps to sort them out as soon as possible.

You will probably never be able to change your personality but you can learn to adapt your behaviour *if your motivation is strong enough*. Exercise self-discipline. Control your next impulse to shout or threaten, remain calm and objective at all times. Move your focus from the superficial pleasure you receive from manipulating and controlling others to the deeper pleasure you will eventually gain from doing right by them. Achieving a balance in your working life, letting go of the need to abuse and intimidate, will increase your self-esteem and enhance your relationships with others.

If you are unable to do this by yourself, get help. Seek counselling from a psychologist. Enrol in management and communication courses.

You need to start treating others the way you like to be treated. However, this may not be possible for you — most researchers believe that bullies do not have the capacity to empathise or care for others.

Can I sustain this change?

We make no promises here. Realistically, it may not be possible to modify an entrenched pattern of behaviour. Where it is possible, it will take a long time, a lot of self-discipline and patience, counselling, support from forgiving colleagues, and there are certain to be occasional relapses. Your greatest challenge will be to put other people's needs first.

If you lose your job as a result of a proven bullying complaint, see this as an opportunity to make a fresh start in a new workplace with new colleagues who will accept you on face value.

What can I do to manage my anger?

Feeling anger isn't in itself a bad thing. Today's world of terrorism, war, poverty and obvious injustice causes anger and depression in most of us, but taking those feelings out on others — letting rip at colleagues, scaring them with outbursts of rage — is a bad thing. We need to let our anger out — internalising it is unhealthy and can cause physical and mental problems — but you need to control your outbursts, to express the anger in a way that doesn't hurt anyone else.

The first step in anger management is to learn, and regularly practise, physical or mental techniques that calm your nervous system, such as deep-breathing (taking a deep breath and counting to ten, or counting from fifty backwards), a walk in the fresh air, a swim, listening to music or a relaxation tape — whatever works for you. For some, this could mean locking yourself away in your bedroom and pummelling your pillow, or letting yourself cry out the anger.

It is advisable to take note of whatever stimulates your anger and avoid that situation or person as much as possible, then discuss these issues with your counsellor.

How can I communicate better in my workplace?

You need to use assertive but non-confrontational language when dealing with other people, and try to bring out the best in them.

- **Make people feel good about themselves.** Compliment them; focus on their strengths and what they are good at. This is far more likely to get the outcomes you want than commenting on their weaknesses.
- **Listen.** Train yourself to listen to what others say — listening is an important element of successful negotiation.
- **Try to understand 'where people are coming from'.** Always attempt to see things from the other person's perspective.
- **Develop your sense of humour.** Use humour to lighten potentially hostile situations and brighten your colleague's day. Learn to laugh at yourself.
- **Use 'I' language.** Instead of saying, 'You really make me angry', say, 'I feel angry when ...' Take a positive attitude. 'I'm sure we can solve this problem together.'
- **Watch your tone of voice, and avoid sarcasm and put-downs.** Don't issue ultimatums. Instead, say, 'I would like you to ...', 'If you could have that ready by ...', and so on.

- **Make eye contact, smile, and address others by name.** This personalises the interaction. Don't speak to colleagues as though they were anonymous groups, for example, by saying things like, 'You people don't seem to understand' or 'Ladies, gather around'; this creates a distance between you.
- **Don't criticise a colleague in front of others.** When you have to tackle someone, do it in private, be direct and upfront, and focus on the problem, not the person.
- **Be specific about what you want done** and give definite timelines where you can. If there is a misunderstanding, saying something like, 'Maybe I wasn't clear enough', indicates that you are willing to share the responsibility. You could then give a practical suggestion about how it could be done differently next time.

If you have to approach a difficult work situation or colleague and you are worried about relapsing into your previous confrontational style, write down what you intend to say and practise it before you tackle that problem.

The bottom line for bullies is that your behaviour could be affecting your own health. Evidence is emerging to suggest that anger can physically manifest as heart problems. 'Hate hardens the arteries ... with bullies having 2½ times the artery calcification of others.'[77] If you won't change your attitude for the benefit of others, do it for yourself.

Treat others just as you want to be treated.

Luke 6:31, *Bible for Today*

CHAPTER 14

Survivors — leaving the past behind

Experience is not what happens to you; it's what you do with what happens to you.

Aldous Huxley

You've been through the wringer and are at a low ebb. Many emotions — anger, betrayal, sadness, regret, guilt, a desire for revenge, a yearning for the life you used to have and the person you used to be, confusion — are churning inside you. You feel nauseous, need pills to get to sleep, your doctor has prescribed antidepressants and you burst into tears for no reason. You are irritable with family and friends, and have generally lost interest in their lives. Welcome to the post-bully world.

Remember, life isn't fair or equal. It is a journey, during which you will have both good and bad experiences, and one where you get to choose the paths you take. Now you are at a crossroad — which way will you go?

What choices do I have?

Though you had no choice about what happened to you or the stressful situation you found yourself in, you do have a choice about how you deal with the aftermath of those circumstances. Accept that life does not always turn out as we hope. You are probably saying, 'But I lost a year of my life and I did nothing wrong.' Yes, and it could be another year or two before you recover, particularly if you took your case to court. Realistically, you may never be totally free of the experience. What happens to many people is that they go on with their lives but have occasional relapses — rashes, migraines, panic attacks, insomnia, periods of depression and hopelessness.

You can choose to surrender to your misery and wallow in it, adopting victimhood as a lifestyle, or you can choose to accept the past, acknowledge the bullying as a learning experience and give yourself permission to move on. This will be hard for those people who enjoy the attention they are getting and are reluctant to let it go.

How do I drop the baggage and go forward?

The first step is to move away from the bully — you will not be able to commence the healing process until this happens. Also, if you have left the workplace but are pursuing legal options, closure of the experience will be postponed until all court proceedings are over.

The next step is understanding the process of healing. The loss of your job, your self-esteem, your idea of yourself as being capable and in control, is a kind of bereavement and you will go through the grieving process, which has several stages, as outlined in the table[78] below. You cannot postpone grief; it is important to give yourself time to mourn.

Stages	Thought processes during healing
Denial	The bullying is happening, but I don't see it, or don't want to see it.
Anger	I realise I am being bullied and this makes me very angry. Why did he target me?
Bargaining	I love my work and I promise to change so my manager will 'like' me and I will keep my job.
Depression	I have tried but I can't do it any more. Everything is going wrong and everyone blames me, even at home. Is life worth it?
Acceptance	I've had counselling and know it was not my fault. I know I will grow from this experience and I can put it behind me. I will survive.

You will need to reach the final stage — acceptance — before you can heal fully.

During our research we spoke to many survivors of bullying but did not find one who claimed to be totally restored to health. Many have moved on, but still carry the 'baggage'. Others, who have had support from doctors, psychologists, family, friends and co-workers, have accepted what happened, but even after one or two years are still experiencing bouts of depression, tears and 'triggers' that bring back memories of their ordeal.

Abiding by the following suggestions will give you your best chance of getting over the trauma and progressing to a full and happy life.

Don't look back

If you keep looking back, the bully has won. If you were retrenched or dismissed, think of it as a blessing. Remember, it *was* just a job that you lost and, with today's flexible employment, most of us will be retrenched or dismissed several times in our careers.

Get into a regular routine

Don't stay in bed until midday and 'slob around' in your pyjamas. Your job was as much about having a daily routine, social contact and feeling that you were making a contribution to the world as it was about income. Schedule your day so that you have things to do — volunteer at the local opportunity shop, deliver meals on wheels — anything that gives you a regular commitment and gets you up in the mornings.

Stop moaning

Don't talk about your situation obsessively. Your friends will listen sympathetically at first but, if this tunnel vision continues for too long, they will lose compassion and not look forward to seeing you. Don't allow the bully to win another victory — shutting you off from friends and family. Force yourself to visit them and take an interest in their lives. Tell them your news, then say, 'That's enough about me. What's happening with you?' — and mean it!

Be kind to yourself

It's very important that you put yourself first.

- **Learn to say NO.** Know your limitations and don't feel obliged to do whatever people ask of you.
- **Take extra care of yourself.** Your health is much more vulnerable at times of stress. Muscle tension or low immunity may cause you to suffer from ill health — cold after cold, headaches or aching back or shoulders. Go outside each day, listen to the birds, feel the sun's warmth on your face. A lack of bright light — especially in winter — triggers sadness in susceptible people.
- **Eat well.** Don't skip meals, eat for comfort or binge on junk food or caffeine. If you don't have the energy to prepare nutritious meals, take a multivitamin and mineral supplement.

Think positive

There's no way you can avoid feelings of shock, guilt, helplessness, anger and grief. You have to go through them and, although it will seem impossible at times, you *will* reach the light at the end of the tunnel. Don't focus on past bad times. Celebrate the good things in your life — your friends, your family, the peaceful country we live in. Take that frustrating negative experience and turn it into something useful. Retain a positive and resilient outlook and you will heal faster. Negative people say things like, 'It wasn't fair', or 'Where's the justice?' and consider themselves victims; positive people agree with Malcolm Fraser — 'Life wasn't meant to be easy' — and get on with doing something about the things they don't like. As soon as you have a negative thought, try to replace it with a more positive one. Think: 'The glass is half full, not half empty.'

> JACK: Like most narcissists, Bryony finally dug her own grave.
> AMANDA: I feel as if I've just come out of a long dark tunnel.

Get involved in a hobby

Find an absorbing hobby or pursue one that you already enjoy, preferably something that will so occupy your thoughts and energies that your cares will melt away.

- **Gardening.** Pottering in the garden will get you in touch with 'mother earth' and the beauty of nature.
- **Art.** Painting, sculpture, photography, pottery, woodwork can release your imagination, help you to gain confidence and prove to yourself that you can do something creative.
- **Writing.** Take a course in creative writing, put your emotions into poetry, write an article on workplace bullying or a murder mystery, modelling your villain on your bully! Even if it's just in your diary, writing can be therapeutic.

- **Shopping.** There is nothing better for the ego than buying yourself a new outfit or a treat (or ten satin cushions as one survivor did!). Be very careful that your spending does not get out of hand, however, or the benefit will be lost worrying about how to pay off your credit card.
- **Travel.** You don't need to go overseas to reap the benefits of travel. Go to the country and walk in the bush. Go to the beach and listen to the waves break, feel the sand between your toes, see the sun rise over the water. Get back in touch with nature to heal the hurt.
- **Pets.** Buy a dog, if you don't have one already. One survivor who was very lonely after losing her dog to ill health, went out and bought two Jack Russells; she enjoys their company, especially when out walking or watching the television, and they don't allow her to brood for too long. If you are not a 'dog person', buy a cat; it can be very therapeutic stroking a warm bundle of purring fur on your lap. If you don't have a partner or child, a pet is something to cuddle!

Identify your goals

Give yourself little hurdles to overcome, for example, list ten things you would like to achieve in the future. Start with something easy, for example, sorting out your wardrobe, and tick off each goal as you achieve it. This will make you proud of yourself and will be another step forward on the road to recovery.

Study

Some stimulating study will help to restore your confidence and give you a purpose. Leaving work could be the catalyst to re-think your career. Having 'time out' gives you a chance to evaluate the direction your life is taking. Though you may want to stay in your familiar field of work, this could depend on the reference you receive from your previous employer and your age. If you are still young, employment will be much easier to find than if you are over fifty. If you decide on a career change, take advantage of any offer of outplacement services for retrenched employees or ask for it to be part of the overall redundancy package. If you feel you need a career change but are unsure what area would be suitable, speak to your counsellor or a careers counsellor. The cost may be covered by WorkCover, so check with the insurer — they will be keen for you to return to full-time employment.

I was forced out of a job, yes, but that job wasn't me. I retrained under WorkCover and now I'm doing exactly what I was born to do. I have peace and serenity. I went through a horrible, humiliating, miserable downer for over a year. I wouldn't wish the experience on my own worst enemy — no, take that back — I would wish it on the woman who bullied me — but she was actually a catalyst for change in my life. So I'd tell other people going through it — it's not the end of the world. Think positive. Change is good.

(Julia, 26, medical secretary)

Learn to forgive

Do not hold on to anger and hatred. Holding a grudge can eat into you, causing long-term illness. Hate the behaviour, not the person who did it.

I felt better as soon as I was able to say, 'I forgive her.' It was obviously very cleansing for me to release the bitterness, because I slept well from then on after hardly sleeping for months, and my migraines came much less frequently. In a strange sort of way, she [the bully] made me a stronger person, and gave me a better understanding of myself.

(Billie, 24, pharmacy assistant)

Learn to relax

Relaxation can be achieved simply with deep breathing, soothing aromatherapy oils, or by putting aside at least half an hour each day to relax completely, with your feet up. For stressful occasions, use a Bach flower remedy (such as Rescue Remedy), available from pharmacies and health food shops. Other relaxants are:

- **Music.** Use music as therapy to 'soothe the savage beast'. It has a positive effect on our immune systems and brain chemistry — stimulating the brain to release endorphins (the body's natural feel-good chemicals), lowering blood pressure and stress hormones in the blood — and can enhance healing. Even our heart rate can be influenced by the pace, volume and rhythm of music.
- **T'ai chi.** T'ai chi relaxes the body through stretching and slow movements and clears your mind of negative thoughts.
- **Yoga and meditation.** With regular yoga practice, you can attain greater vitality and suppleness, relaxation, serenity and self-realisation. Meditation also clears the mind of negative thoughts, aids positive thinking, gives you back control of your life and assists in regaining a regular sleeping pattern.
- **Massage.** There are different types of massage — we recommend having one that works on the muscles to release tension or one purely for relaxation that leaves your body with a sense of wellbeing and contentment.

Laugh

Humour is still the best medicine. Even if you don't feel like it, force yourself to laugh and smile — this will make you feel more like laughing and smiling spontaneously. Putting a smile on your face will make you feel better straightaway and seeing the lighter side of setbacks can held reduce stress. Watch your favourite comedy shows on television — 'Friends' or 'Seinfeld' or 'M.A.S.H.' or 'Fawlty Towers' — whatever makes you laugh. Go to the local newsagent and look at the humorous greeting cards for an instant chuckle.

> AMANDA: It got to the point where I couldn't cope.
> STELLA: Applying for a week's compassionate leave when your cat died? Did you really expect to be taken seriously when you started doing things like that?

If you need help, ask for it

You need to work through your feelings. Don't shut yourself off from family and friends; tell them how much you are hurting and that you'd appreciate their support. If you cannot cope, your doctor may refer you to a psychologist or a psychiatrist who can help you understand whether your feelings are a normal reaction to your experience or have escalated to serious depression. Counselling can be helpful. It will help to talk about and come to terms with the fear and feelings of helplessness and anger that you've experienced, especially if you have feelings you can't share with your partner, friends or family. Your psychologist may be trained in hypnosis and may recommend it as a possible aid to recovery — it can assist in the areas of panic attacks and lack of confidence.

Exercise

Allow at least half an hour every day for vigorous exercise. A brisk walk in the fresh air, a bicycle ride or a strenuous session at the gym will boost your body's level of 'feel-good' endorphins — chemicals released by the brain to control pain threshold — and improve your mood. As one psychologist puts it, getting those endorphins 'jumping up and down' will assist in your recovery from depression. The psychological benefits of exercise include the maintenance of a sense of control, enhanced self-esteem, positive body image and a feeling of wellbeing. The martial arts — karate, kickboxing, judo — have obvious physical as well as psychological benefits — increased self-confidence, self-esteem, concentration, self-discipline, self-respect and courage. If you are on WorkCover, take advantage of whatever extra assistance your doctor feels you need for a full recovery, such as physiotherapy, massage, hydrotherapy or gym.

How can I get over my depression and regain my self-esteem and confidence?

Start with small steps, for example, by structuring your day into set tasks, then, at the end of the day, tick off the ones you have accomplished. If you haven't started a diary, start one now and write your list of daily tasks in it. Watching the ticks grow either daily or weekly will give you a sense of achievement. If it is hard to get motivated, build in a reward system — for each tick, put $2 aside to go towards a restaurant meal, a visit to the theatre or opera, a new hairstyle or new shoes, or reward yourself with a new book or a chocolate bar.

Day 1 could look like this.

Time	Activity
7.30	Get out of bed. ✓ Walk the dog. ✓ Collect milk and paper. ✓
8.30	Breakfast. ✓ Read paper. ✓ Shower. ✓
10.00	Tidy kitchen. ✓ Sweep floors. ✓ Clean toilet. ✓
11.00	Morning tea. Watch news on TV. ✓ Exercise to music tape. ✓
1.00	Meet Michael for lunch. ✓ Shopping. ✓
3.00	Weed pot plants. ✓
5.00	Prepare vegetables. ✓ Make casserole. ✓
Evening	Ironing. Watch television. ✓ Take dog out again. ✓

Writing your feelings in your diary each day can be cathartic. Was it a 'good' or 'bad' day? Did anything trigger any memories? If you know what the triggers were, resolve to avoid them in the future. If your depression is a general feeling of being down rather than a clinical condition, consider taking St John's Wort (*Hypericum*), a herbal remedy which, for some people, can be as effective as antidepressant drugs. However, be careful and monitor yourself, as even natural remedies can have side effects. If you are taking any other medication, consult your doctor first.

Clinical depression is an illness that needs chemical treatment such as antidepressants or therapy, and you will need medical assistance to combat it.

Recovering from depression will be a slow process, but it can be achieved if your motivation is strong enough. The bully's intent was to take away your dignity and destroy you. Don't let the bully win.

How do I face collecting my personal items from work?

This can be stressful and you will feel highly emotional, particularly if you have been at your workplace for a number of years. Your self-esteem will probably be at its lowest, and this humiliating experience will add to your already high levels of stress. The organisation may ask that you contact your ex-manager and arrange a time to collect these items. If you are not comfortable doing this, request another person within the organisation to arrange this for you.

CASE STUDY

I was dreading it. My sister drove me to work and waited in the car park while I went in. My friend Mia was waiting for me in reception, thank goodness, as Monica [the bully] was also there, gloating. She was still there when I came out and she watched me, smirking but not saying a word, as I carried my things out to the car.

(Lee, 24, telephone sales)

It is advisable to have someone with you for moral support and on whom you can 'offload' your feelings on the way home. If you are not comfortable with returning to the workplace, ask a colleague to collect your items.

People will tell you to forget, to 'pick up the pieces and carry on', and the optimists will tell you cheerfully, 'One door closes and another one opens'. What a wonderful world it would be if recovery were so easy! Be aware that returning to a workplace that has caused you such pain may set back your progress. However, everyone is different and will react in different ways. For some, that final departure from the workplace can be cathartic. One way to achieve some sort of closure is to arrange a farewell lunch or dinner with those co-workers with whom you are still friendly. One group of ex-employees from a particularly toxic workplace have formed their own survivors' group and meet regularly — a great way of giving and receiving support.

How do I face returning to work?

If you have not had your employment terminated and the bully is still there, it will not be possible for you to return to work without experiencing further friction and stress. Depending on the level of bullying and the time you were subjected to it, your medical advisers may feel that you are not ready to return immediately to full-time employment and may recommend that you initially work only two or three days a week. (This should be written in your return-to-work plan.) You should abide by what they say. It will be difficult to go back, and you could still suffer from 'trigger' reactions. We advise that you continue to see your psychologist until you feel that you no longer need professional support.

You may be unable to return to the kind of work you used to do. Bullying can diminish your self-confidence and your trust in others to such an extent that working for an employer is no longer an option for you. If this is the case, you may be able to start your own small business from home, depending on your past experiences and field of work. You will have to discuss this with your partner, of course, as it will impact on your family life. Any changes will also depend on your current financial position and lifestyle, as your income may be essential to cover mortgage and school costs, car payments, and so on.

Well-meaning psychologists, friends, even partners, seem to think that it's like falling from a horse, you get back on again as quickly as possible. Their attitude may make you feel that you are 'bludging' on the system and could increase your depression. The reality is that some people recover quickly after a crisis while others take longer. As in every other area of life, the degree of resilience we have depends on many factors — our emotional intelligence, our support networks, our upbringing, the cohesiveness of our families, and so on.

When someone tries to push you into returning to work before you are ready, quote the following to them: 'You know, you have been pushing me too hard and I simply cannot move at the pace of your expectations for me. I have to find my own pace, and you have to walk at my pace or you cannot help me.'[79]

Go confidently in the direction of your dreams. Live the life you have imagined.

Henry David Thoreau

CHAPTER 15

Employers — where to from here?

The successful man is the one who finds out what is the matter with his business before his competitors do.

Roy L. Smith

A bully has been revealed in your company. You've had the difficult experience of investigating a complaint and deciding what to do about the bully and, in the process, have lost a valued staff member (either the victim or the bully) — you want to make sure that you never have to go through this process again. Or perhaps you are reading this book and want to ensure that your employees never have to endure what our victims have gone through. Or maybe you have heard about of one of the recent high-profile cases and have realised that, if a member of your staff is found guilty of bullying, you are vulnerable to legal action. Remember, employers who bully or allow bullying to continue are breaching occupational health and safety regulations so, no matter who is actually doing the bullying, it is your responsibility to end it. You have a duty of care to all employees.

The bottom line is that it makes good business sense to ensure that workplace bullying is prevented, or at least identified and controlled. Therefore, you need to establish preventive measures or strengthen your existing ones.

Where do I start?

Good intentions will not be enough. Achieving a bully-free workplace is a complex task, and management at all levels of your company will need to be involved in the process and dedicated to it. A huge gap exists between the existence of a code on bullying and its practical enforcement — what is the point of having an exemplary policy on paper when it is not practised 'on the floor'?

During our many interviews with victims of bullying and professionals working to rehabilitate these victims, we found that few are satisfied with the way workplaces attempted to solve bullying.

CASE STUDY

I went through the workplace grievance procedure, but nothing changed. They seemed to feel that they'd done their job by listening to me.

(Warren, 19, electrical sales)

The first step is to set up a review committee. In large businesses, the committee should include representatives from human resources, risk management, unions, public relations, management and general staff. Smaller companies may not have representatives from these areas but, if possible, review committees should include the employer, a middle manager, union representative and staff member.

If you already have an anti-bullying or anti-harassment policy in place, the committee's first task will be to carry out an objective and unemotional appraisal of its strengths and weaknesses. Evaluate the current policy and each step of the procedure on the basis of its practicality and how it matches up to the guidelines for a new policy as outlined below. Do not be tempted to amend your current harassment policy by just adding the word 'bullying'. It is probably a good idea to scrap this policy altogether — it is almost certainly out of date — and write a new one. From our own working experiences and those of others, many organisations have policies that are outmoded, sitting on someone's shelf collecting dust, and not opened from one year to the next. *All organisational policies and procedures should be updated and reviewed regularly.*

The committee will need to assess every facet of the company's existing workplace environment, addressing the following areas: existing policies relating to harassment or inappropriate behaviours; procedures and regulations; management climate; employment patterns; stress and the work environment; skills of supervisors and managers; and training programs.

If your company has had several bullying complaints, your workplace could be 'toxic' and you will need to identify areas of the workplace where bullying behaviour has been a problem or where bullying might be a problem in the future. It may not be possible to remove the source of the bullying but you can at least ensure that your workforce is aware that any future abusive behaviour will not be tolerated.

> JACK: And he'll give Bryony a glowing reference so she'll agree to let him break her contract, and she'll be very quickly snapped up by some other outfit for her 'tough' 'hard hitting' 'no prisoners' approach, and in two or three years will have 'delivered similar results' to yet another organization.

Educate yourself. Learn all about the different types of bullying and share this knowledge with all staff. You need to know what you are dealing with. Review the management styles of your executives and supervisors — an aggressive approach can be interpreted as bullying and, when management is aggressive, that aggression can flow through to supervisors and workers. You can establish the prevailing views on management approaches with an attitude survey, completed anonymously. This assessment can be conducted by qualified in-house staff or, to ensure that the review is thorough and unbiased, the committee may prefer to bring in an independent specialised consulting team to guide the process for the planning committee (see Appendix D for one way of measuring management style).

This evaluation will allow the committee to identify areas of vulnerability with regard to potential bullying conduct by managers.

Does your policy emphasise analysis to the detriment of action? Is it technically correct, that is, it adheres to all the requirements, but is practically void? No matter how well the policy reads, if the procedure is not workable, the policy is useless. It means the company wants to be seen to be doing the right thing rather than actually doing it.

The only way to evaluate the effectiveness of your new policy before its implementation is to test it. Staff should be included in this step. Create a scenario that challenges the policy and carry out a role-play. Treat the case as if it were real. This may seem like a waste of time, but if you later encounter a really challenging case of bullying that reveals your policy to be ineffective, you will wish that you had tested it. Gain feedback from all participants and onlookers and make any appropriate changes or improvements.

Your review committee should draw up the policy after input from, and in consultation with, all levels of your company (that way the workers will feel they 'own' it and will be more likely to trust that management will ensure that it works) and it must meet union requirements.

Once a written policy is drafted, the next step is establishing a confidential method by which your employees can, anonymously and without fear of retribution, report abusive behaviour that violates the company's anti-bullying policy, for example, a suggestion box for small companies or a hotline for large business.

If you don't have an existing policy, you will need to start from scratch.

What needs to be included in an anti-bullying policy?

Generally, an anti-bullying policy should define unacceptable behaviour and contain comprehensive prevention strategies, provisions outlawing bullying, a complaints procedure and training for staff, and should designate a contact person or persons to whom workers can report behaviour. The policy must be carefully drafted to ensure that, during the investigation, the rights of neither the complainant nor the alleged bully are infringed. Essential ingredients of an effective policy are outlined below.

The policy

The policy must have a clear definition of bullying, should indicate clearly what behaviour is regarded as bullying and should state that bullying will not be tolerated. (Don't go overboard with political correctness, however, so that someone can be accused of bullying because of their 'tone of voice' — the behaviour must be ongoing, deliberately inflicting distress.)

Every member of staff must be provided with a copy.

The policy should be updated regularly.

The policy should contain clauses stipulating (a), that victims are 'reimbursed' for any holiday and sick leave they were forced to take when the bullying became too much for them, and (b), the measures to be taken against employees who make false allegations (only if the accusation is made with malicious intent).

Procedures

1 **Response.** A mandated response time should be set (for example, three working days) for the employer to respond to the complainant. There should be an immediate separation of the complainant from the alleged bully that does not punish the complainant (for example, paid leave during the investigation). This section should also specify the support, counselling and rehabilitation available for victims of bullying and for those proven bullies who are willing to accept training to change their behaviour.

2 **The complaints procedure.** The policy should set down the complaints procedure very clearly, detailing the steps bullied workers may take to obtain protection and assistance. Most current complaints resolution systems do not work in bullying cases. Perhaps because of inadequate internal guidelines, human resource people often respond to complaints by treating bullying as a personality conflict; nothing is resolved, and the victim's only options are to put up with the bully's behaviour or resign. It must be said that human resource people are often in an ambivalent position, torn between loyalty to the company that employs them and their obligation to employees.

CASE STUDY

When I complained to HR, they send down a very junior person to act as mediator. My manager [the bully] was very charming. He said that he had high expectations of his staff but that I continually failed to meet those expectations, that I wasn't tough enough to cope in the modern business world. When I tried to pin him down to specifics, he continued to waffle on about my lack of professionalism. And the HR kid bought it! After the meeting, she suggested that our conflict was most likely to do with our age difference — the 'generation gap', as she put it — and that the situation could be resolved if I was more flexible. She recommended that I do some training in communication skills and leadership.

I was stunned. When I complained to the HR manager, I was told that I must follow the plan of action that had been devised. I was given absolutely no support. I asked for a transfer but that was denied (it needed my manager's approval). I was so angry that my health became worse — migraines, and a red, itchy rash on my face and chest — so I resigned. That was two years ago, and my manager has since been promoted. It's the injustice that still gets to me.

(Martin, 48, investment analyst)

3 **Mediation processes.** Mediation should be available but should be more than a token gesture on the part of management; the process must be guided by an approachable, neutral mediator and must be capable of offering full resolutions and closure. This will enable the company to avoid expensive and potentially embarrassing litigation. However, our knowledge of bullying cases indicates that mediation rarely works.

4 **Investigation.** To be unbiased and absolutely fair to both parties, the investigation procedure should never be conducted by an internal department such as human resources because there may be a perceived conflict of loyalties. An external investigator should be called in, with the final decision being made by a panel of at least three decision makers (never one person, and never a middle manager). Critical to the success of any policy is that confidentiality must be guaranteed. A worker, if he believes the process may be unfair because of a perceived bias in favour of a bullying manager, should have the option to request that an independent, neutral party investigate the case. However, the fact that payment for such a service may be made by the employer could create a conflict of interest if there is already a perceived bias towards the bully.

5 **Sanctions.** The policy should state plainly the range of possible outcomes of a proven bullying episode and the sanctions that could be imposed against those who violate the policy (for example, a public apology by the bully, demotion or transfer of the bully, voluntary transfer of the victim, or a mutually agreeable severance package for either party). This section should also contain an antiretaliation clause specifying that any subsequent bullying after the filing of a complaint will be considered a separate infringement if done by the same perpetrator or a new violation if by a different perpetrator.

Contact person

We believe there should be contact officers, specifically for bullying complaints, chosen from a cross-section of employees willing to take on the role. The role of the contact person is to listen to the complainant, talk the complainant through the options and help to decide what action to take, if any. The contact person does not have the authority to resolve the allegation and is not expected to play an active role in challenging or disciplining the bully.

The number of contact persons will depend on the size of your organisation. It would be ideal to have one contact person for each section, department or work area.

Start by putting out a memo with a description of what the role will involve and request *volunteers* to nominate. Acting as a contact person should be voluntary — this will encourage those who have strong feelings for natural justice to apply, whereas the temptation of extra remuneration would bring an influx of unsuitable applicants and could cause friction amongst other employees.

The person/s selected for this position, once trained, will have

- a basic understanding of the organisation's policy and procedures relating to bullying

- an understanding of relevant state and federal legislation
- basic counselling and negotiating skills
- a strong commitment to diversity and natural justice
- good communication and writing skills to maintain records
- the ability to be a team player and to work without supervision
- empathy and a professional approach.

The contact persons should be supervised by the human resource manager, if you have one, or a person in a managerial role, a CEO or a member of the board of management. It should be at least one level above any middle manager with direct contact with staff.

The role of the contact person is to

- be the initial contact for any bullied worker
- listen to the worker with empathy and impartiality
- handle the allegation in a confidential, expedient and sensitive manner
- provide options, support and appropriate referrals
- expedite the resolution of any bullying complaints
- advocate for the eradication of bullying within the workplace
- assist in identifying bullying within the workplace
- discuss issues of bullying with workers in a confidential, non-threatening environment, knowing that they will not suffer any consequences to either themselves or another for 'blowing the whistle'
- maintain a confidential record of all communications, actions and options given
- ensure that the contact person's supervisor is informed of all discussions
- participate in relevant training to become a contact person, and regular training as required
- actively support management and the organisation to eliminate bullying within the workplace

- assist and actively participate in the development, implementation, yearly review and maintenance of the organisation's bullying policy and procedures
- be fully conversant with the organisation's bullying policy and have an understanding of the boundaries of this position
- continue to monitor the position to ensure that no further incidents occur
- provide feedback on any issues relating to the process not covered by the policy
- ensure that all future allegations are thoroughly investigated according to the policy.

Training and education

The policy should outline compulsory training for managers, human resource staff responsible for dealing with bullying complaints, the contact people and all general staff. Training at all levels is essential.

1 Company executives should be given an overview of workplace bullying, details of the financial and legal consequences of not having an effective prevention program in place and information about the overwhelming personal cost to victims. They also need to have a fairly detailed knowledge and understanding of the workplace anti-bullying policy.

2 Department managers and supervisors should be given the same overview of workplace bullying and how it affects the workforce, and be given training in stress management, conflict resolution and communication skills — they should also know every detail of the company's anti-bullying policy. This training should emphasise the difference between reasonable and constructive feedback on work performance and constant, negative comments that are unsubstantiated.

3 All employees should have training sessions that include discussion of the company's policy, the range of behaviours that constitute bullying, the warning signs that victimised co-workers may exhibit, an outline of the policy emphasising reporting methods and the help available to bullied workers and encouragement for them to come forward if they are being bullied. Training employees to recognise abusive or inappropriate behaviour increases the odds that this behaviour can be spotted early and appropriate action taken before the behaviour becomes too entrenched and before it has had serious consequences for the victim.

Ongoing monitoring and evaluation

Appoint someone to be responsible for keeping up with changes in legislation, Codes of Practice or Best Practice Guidelines. Your policy should be updated and improved as appropriate. Suggested methods are

- monitoring patterns of sick leave and workers' compensation data
- monitoring feedback from worker attitude surveys and exit interviews, union reps, mentors, consultative committees and the employee assistance service
- suggestion boxes to enable people to raise concerns anonymously
- keeping an annual record of staff turnover and of the number who have left each department (enabling you to relate any unusually high turnover to a particular manager).

These data will assist in risk identification and risk assessment.

How can I ensure that the policy will be effective?

Developing a company policy on workplace bullying is not enough. Don't allow it to generate a plethora of meetings, reports, hearings, more reports and pretty posters on walls — it must be enforced each time an infringement is reported, without exception. Those not in favour of a zero-tolerance policy (that is, proven transgressors are immediately 'out the door') may prefer to build in to the policy a progressive disciplinary system that allows the bully a chance to change before facing termination. However, the bully and victim should not be expected to work together again.

At the induction of new staff, emphasise that the company will not tolerate abusive behaviour in the workplace, and provide them with a copy of your policy.

What can I do to prevent or minimise further bullying in my workplace?

You will need to adopt the following pro-active approaches to control or avoid future bullying incidents.

- Look for danger signs in your workplace which might indicate a climate where bullying is likely to occur, for example, an extremely competitive environment, fear of redundancy, a culture of envy among colleagues or promoting oneself by putting colleagues down, an authoritarian style of management, organisational change and uncertainty, lack of training, poor work relationships generally with little respect for others and their points of view, no clear codes for acceptable conduct, excessive workloads, impossible targets or deadlines, or no clear procedures for resolving problems.
- After input from all levels of your organisation and after ensuring that it meets union requirements, introduce an anti-bullying policy that contains comprehensive prevention strategies, provisions outlawing bullying, a complaints procedure and training for staff. Provide each member of staff with a copy, update it regularly, and ensure that managers abide by it.
- Ensure that all future allegations are thoroughly investigated according to the policy.

- At the induction of new staff, emphasise your zero tolerance of all abusive behaviour in the workplace and provide them with a copy of your policy.
- Review the management styles of your executives and supervisors — an aggressive approach can be interpreted as bullying. Emphasise the difference between reasonable and constructive feedback on work performance and constant, negative comments that are unsubstantiated.
- Emphasise that you expect an atmosphere of cooperation and mutual support in your workplace, and that aggressive behaviour will not be tolerated.
- Increase your understanding and awareness of bullying so that you can recognise signs that it might be occurring (for example, regularly check sick leave records and note if anyone is taking regular days off, note high staff turnover in any one department, or a pattern of complaints against one person). Interview anyone who leaves and ask if any workplace issues have precipitated their departure.
- Use yearly appraisals and regular anonymous surveys to uncover any problems staff may be experiencing.
- If your company is a 'union shop', meet regularly with union representatives to discuss any contentious issues.
- Make all members of staff aware, via regular items in the departmental newsletter, memorandums or e-mails, that you have an 'open door' policy if items of concern are not resolved through the regular chain of command.
- Ensure that you meet regularly with all staff, perhaps once a month. Ask about what is happening in their areas of the company, what projects they are working on and the progress they are making, and encourage feedback on how work procedures or any other aspect of the company could be improved. Keeping your finger on the pulse in this way will help to avoid a situation where a manager takes credit for

another employee's work. If you are answerable to a board of directors, let the staff know what is happening at Board level. (Naturally some items will need to remain confidential.)

If you are a CEO and do not see the staff regularly, the following methods may help you stop bullying behaviour before it becomes established.

- Make time for the staff, for example, by walking through the office or workplace each morning, saying hello, stopping to talk to an individual or group, getting to know their names and positions within the company. This need not take more than ten or fifteen minutes of your time each day but will be enormously valuable in terms of gaining the trust and respect of your workforce. Once this becomes a regular custom, you may be able to sense anything unusual.
- If your staff and managers have regular staff or team meetings, request a copy of the agenda and any notes or minutes kept. This may help you to see if your manager is claiming an idea that belonged to another staff member.
- Ask your personal assistant, or someone you trust, to let you in on 'grapevine' reports, for example, that someone left the office abruptly or was seen in a distressed state in the toilets.
- Meet regularly with all lines of management to enquire on staff performance. If a manager continually mentions one name, particularly in the context of being 'difficult' or having 'behavioural issues', this may need further investigation.

Of course, the size of your organisation affects how you deal with bullying. Large businesses will usually have more financial resources, and access to professionals such as human resource personnel or health and safety officers. No matter how small your business or how limited its resources, you still need to implement practical strategies for dealing with bullying.

What other things can I do to keep my staff happy?

Your aim should be to look after all your employees and make boosting staff morale and keeping staff a top priority. Value your people and their expertise, and earn their loyalty.

Don't employ mediocre managers. Insist they have the right skills, as well as interpersonal skills and integrity. A good manager has to be able to communicate well and develop positive relationships with a whole range of people; be understanding and able to appreciate different perspectives; be flexible and able to handle situations as they arise; be encouraging and facilitating of staff involvement so that they feel valued and supported; be welcoming of different ideas and opinions and able to sift out the good ones without alienating the person who offered the bad one. 'To be an effective manager these days, you have to be as proficient at reading human emotion as you are at balancing the books.'[80]

If you have to retrench people, do it well. Allow them to have the dignity of time to tidy their desks, say a proper goodbye to workmates and clients and have a farewell morning tea or luncheon or drinks in the office to mark the occasion. For some, the indignity of being escorted out of the building by security guards has been the most traumatic factor of the whole bullying experience and the catalyst for severe depression.

> **CASE STUDY**
>
> The next thing, two gorillas from security escorted me out of the building. For months, it was that moment that replayed over and over in my head. People not wanting to stare turning away so as not to witness my humiliation. Made to feel like a criminal when I'd done nothing wrong. Feeling so powerless. I've left other jobs but had a proper send-off, with everyone signing a card and collecting for a gift. But this — this was just awful.
>
> (Cheryl, 33, telephone sales)

Investigate ways of changing other factors that can encourage hostile or unhappy work environments, such as ineffective or inappropriate job descriptions, inadequate communication, or a lack of stimulating and challenging tasks.

Make a commitment to flexible working arrangements that enable your workers to fit in study or family commitments — recognise that the day-to-day pressure of work is handled differently by different people.

Commit to providing staff with ongoing training in stress management and career development programs.

Introduce mentoring schemes.

Hand out booklets with a summary of the company's anti-bullying stance to workers at regular intervals. The booklets should be written in language that is clear and easy to understand, and should be available in the first languages of all employees.

If you want good employees, be a good employer.

W.G.P.

CHAPTER 16

Personal journeys

Learn from yesterday, live for today, hope for tomorrow.

Anonymous

Throughout this book we have used small excerpts from the many stories told to us, and now we let some victims tell their own stories of what happened to them, how they coped and how they are feeling now. All are at different stages. Denise has put the bullying experience behind her and has moved on. April's case is still current and she is bitter about the cost — personal and financial — to her. When Janine wrote her story, she had just found out that her contract was not being renewed and she was relieved to be leaving her bullying workplace, despite the daunting prospect of unemployment. Simon is fighting for his rights.

April's story

I had put in a claim for WorkCover after an intimidating work environment caused by an increasingly infected workplace led to discrimination and bullying, but returned to work because of my concern for my clients. On my first day back, I found that my department co-workers had been through everything on my desk, moved my photographs around and removed some of my things (very personal items such as sanitary pads and tampons). I felt devastated and violated.

My manager acknowledged my distress and sent me home. The next day I received a letter from my employer advising me that my claim had been refused. I was shocked and unsettled, wondering what was happening. This was the start of a long and distressing journey. My employer demonstrated yet again their callous attitude and bullying tactics towards their employees, and I learned how little power WorkCover has to settle matters, especially if both the insurer and employer refuse to accept the claim.

I found that the ones with the power and finance have the ability to delay and string out all processes while the employee has to somehow struggle on. It is a David and Goliath-type battle. I would not be surprised to find that many who take on these challenges quit due to the pressures brought upon them by an incompetent system — our legal system — which favours the ones with wealth and power, yet the taxpayer is forced to pay for these systems.

This came at a time when we had started to extend our home, my income being the sole wage, and we were totally dependent on it. As my employer had refused to acknowledge my claim, I was unable to return to work and had to wait for my conciliation with WorkCover. This took over three and a half months as we had to wait for the formal letter from the insurer, then make application to WorkCover. It appeared that WorkCover was there for the insurer rather than for me and I do not believe that WorkCover did the best they could for me. It took about four weeks for them to come to a decision.

During this period I was not being paid at all by my employer. Initially, we used some of our house extension money to pay bills and the mortgage, which caused more financial problems as time went on. We had to borrow money from family and friends to cope with the expenses of living.

There are simple things that have become agony, like requesting assistance from a welfare agency, not having enough money to get medication for a very sick animal, trying to organise to pay bills when you don't have the money, advising the bank and dealing with debt collectors who treat you like a leper. I have been so grief-stricken about sorting out some of these issues that I have broken down many times and had to get assistance to try to work something out. After being told what had happened, the bank agreed to wait while I found money to cover the mortgage and then, in the same breath, asked me, 'Could you pay anything today?' All these matters have become such a destructive force in my life and eroded further my attitude to my fellow human beings. It is so upsetting to have been put in such a horrible, degrading position because of an intimidating work environment that I feel as if I've left one tormenting environment for another.

We have been able to access sickness benefits from the Government but these amounts have to be paid back when the matter is settled, and are not equivalent to my wage. The pressure — emotional, mental and physical — has destroyed me further, as well as putting enormous duress on my partner and also adversely affecting my family and friends.

After waiting over four months since the first rejection of my claim, I have been informed by WorkCover that I do have a case and will need to go to court to resolve it. My solicitor advises me that it will take about another six to eight months to be heard. We are still in limbo, no wage, no one taking responsibility — just grief. It is very difficult to comprehend and I have been in a depressed state throughout this period. My employer has threatened me with the sack twice. My solicitor said they cannot be stopped from sacking me and if they do I would then need to go through an unfair dismissal case. I have worked for this company over eleven years, have never been told that my work was unsatisfactory and am the last of the long-term employees; 40 per cent of the staff were long-term until recently, when many left or were forced out because of the poisonous workplace.

My work friends were unsure what to do as they were still in the unhealthy work environment which is known to target people who did not conform to management views or who spoke out about issues affecting staff. This translated into a slow distancing between us, to protect themselves (management had made comments to staff about them speaking to me), and because of my concern not to put them in a potentially damaging situation. Thus I am deprived of friendships that mean a great deal to me.

Now I am getting letters from the insurer stating that they are returning my accounts for me to pay as they have rejected my claim — they mention nothing about waiting until it is settled in court. Each time one of these letters come, I become even more anxious and disturbed about my situation. I hate to collect the mail now because I'm afraid there will be something horrible in it.

So I have left a bullying, intimidating and discriminatory workplace only to be dealt with in the same way by a system that gives no support to victims; instead, it compounds the adversity and intensifies the tensions. It is disturbing that these systems appear to support the employer who chooses to take the denial path and chastise the employee who stands up to be counted, who does not run away from the situation, as so often happens. Unless people are willing to stand up and say, 'No, it is not okay', employers can continue to wreak havoc and destroy lives for their own selfish means. All employers today in this civilised country have access to knowledge of how to work well with people and achieve the best for their staff and their business — if they choose to ignore these guidelines and knowledge they need to be held responsible.

April, 39, accounts clerk

Janine's story

In 2000, on returning to secondary teaching as a contract teacher after a six-year break, I observed many changes in the ways schools operate. In my absence, education had been corporatised and decision making had become very 'top down'. More power was invested in senior 'management' — I have seen a deputy-principal scream at individual teachers in meetings because they dared express an alternative view — and year level coordinators, giving rise to the potential for its abuse, including favouritism to buddies. Everyone seems under more pressure than previously. Many are frightened for their careers, so are more intolerant and critical — particularly of newcomers. The potential for bullying is rife. According to one local organiser, most of the Australian Education Union organisers' time is spent following up occupational health and safety issues arising from workplace bullying — a direct reflection of poor management in schools.

Equal opportunity and occupational health and safety legislation also seem to have become less relevant. Ageism and sexism flourish. Frequent comments have been made that I, in my late forties, am 'past it'. One coordinator, in his fifties, is infamous for his discriminating ways — he will not listen to women or support them in dealings with difficult students — yet the female teachers excuse him on the grounds that 'he has poor social skills as a result of an emotionally deprived childhood'!

When I finally made a written complaint about this man's behaviour, I was advised to drop it or I would not be employed the following year. I persisted, but agreed to deal with it in-house. It was not dealt with until three months later, deliberately scheduled by this man's management friends immediately prior to my first interview for a job for the following year. I missed out on the position. I applied for a second round of jobs, only to find that the man against whom I had made the complaint was on the interview panel. Again, I did not get the position. Finally, I received a position for 2001 when the person offered a contract ahead of me withdrew.

Because, as a contract teacher, I felt vulnerable, I became a union representative in 2001. (Contracts are still offered on a twelve-month basis — or less when a short-term vacancy comes up. Because their jobs have no security, contract teachers have become a sub-class within schools. Colleagues advise that, to obtain permanency, you should either put your head down and not do anything that might upset or show others up, or identify the power brokers, get close to them and don't do anything that might be viewed as 'wrong'. In other words, protect yourself.) I found, however, that being a union representative was a double-edged sword, as the Deputy-Principal has a history of abusing union representatives.

My workplace has ongoing problems with staff absenteeism and stress claims. I personally have suffered from an accumulation of petty behaviours and abuse, resulting in major stomach upsets, diarrhoea, muscle aches and pains and two serious bouts of influenza. I have constantly felt tired, run-down and depressed about my ability to cope with the job in the face of ongoing harassment. At first I thought I might be going through menopause. Finally, I sought counselling and realised that I was experiencing a workplace culture of ongoing bullying and harassment. Some examples are:

The Deputy-Principal complained about my 'ongoing problem with lateness to class' (I had been seconds late several times but always with valid reasons — either the timetable had scheduled me to be in two places at once, or the photocopier had broken down or was out of order).

An out-of-class pass system is provided in the student diary, but the policy is that 'no students are allowed out of class for any reason'. As a result, although teachers have a duty of care to remain in front of their classes at all times, students are not permitted to fetch resources from the staffroom. Thus I have to predict emergency needs and carry extra copies of assignments or worksheets, texts, paper, pens, rulers and colouring pencils for those students who come without (all at my own expense). When I requested clarification on whether students are permitted to go to the toilet or sick bay, I was ridiculed.

I became annoyed at the expense of providing my own teaching resources as teachers are resourced on the basis of who has sufficient power, influence or support. When I asked the Coordinator if we could have a hole punch or a stapler, I was told, 'No, that's too expensive, borrow one from the general office.' Also, even though I had obtained funding for a particular project, my attempts to implement it were blocked during the ordering process. The teacher in charge wouldn't allow me to look at the catalogue — physically pulling it away from me — and I ended up with the wrong supplies.

Conflicting advice based on inconsistent perceptions of my problems, which were always preceded by the statement, 'The common perception here is that you are ...', left me confused and lacking in self-confidence. 'You are too punitive. You must be more gentle, considerate and understanding of your client. Be flexible — let them choose how to behave. Listen to your clients' needs!' (Deputy-Principal) versus 'You are not in control of your classes. You must be firm and in control, don't let them speak to you disrespectfully or disobey you. Don't let them get away with anything. Don't give them warnings about their behaviour —

which just allows them a second or third shot at you' (Year Level Coordinator nominated to be my support person). I was shadow boxing with perceptions based upon very subjective observations and individual agendas and began to feel that I had lost my ability to deal with a class.

Early in the year, on my return to work after a severe bout of influenza, the Deputy-Principal shouted at me, insisting on Interim Reports being done 'right now', without giving me time to get a mark book. I tried to explain that I needed my mark book to complete the reports accurately. When, as a result, an error occurred and a parent complained, the Deputy-Principal reprimanded me for 'having problems with assertion' — though I had very plainly stated my case.

Though one student had a history of manipulating her class against a number of teachers, this was not mentioned when she gave me a very difficult time as a newcomer. Instead, I was repeatedly told that *I* was the problem. When, at the last minute, I was invited into a very hostile meeting with her parents, a Year Level Coordinator said this in front of the parents. Without asking for my view, the Deputy-Principal stated that he wanted no more complaints from the girl's parents. This in turn started gossip that I was failing to manage my class effectively.

On several occasions, despite agreement before the local union organiser that this would not happen, the Deputy-Principal stood just outside my door. On the worst occasion, both he at the door, and the Student Welfare Coordinator pressed up against the frosted glass window of the storeroom door, watched and listened to my lesson. I was barely coherent because I was full of fear. It was also very undermining having students jeering that I was being checked up on, in turn fuelling rumours and student behaviours to expedite my dismissal, for example, comments like, 'You know, we can get you fired.'

Once, when I asked where I would find a light switch in a pitch-black corridor, the Deputy-Principal shrugged, wiggled his shoulders and described a light switch very slowly and mockingly in front of other staff — I felt annoyed and humiliated being put down over such a simple request.

Because over the year I became increasingly confused, unsure of myself and frightened of doing something wrong, on two occasions I sought union assistance. This only served to increase the Deputy-Principal's antagonism, and frequent disparaging remarks were made by him and other staff, like, 'Well, I hope this doesn't mean you're bringing in the union organiser again!'

One female staff member, far exceeding her responsibilities, has been particularly antagonistic.

She interrupted my classes on eight occasions to shout at me in a most offensive and shrill manner in front of my students about my classroom management.

She once kept me waiting for ten minutes while she finished her class, yet later commented in a staff meeting that I was 'too slow in getting out of (my) classes'.

She told me I was way behind in my coursework, yet I later found that she was, in fact, three weeks behind me.

She constantly criticised my teaching approaches in front of students and my peers.

One day I arrived at class to find her physically assaulting one of my students. The boy was in tears, yet she left the class smacking her hands together, smirking at me, saying, 'Well, Ms Smith, your class is ready for you.'

When I complained about this woman's behaviour, the Principal directed that I attend a mediation meeting with her (and three others who had signed a letter supporting her). I was dreading this meeting. The faculty head assigned to oversee the meeting began by saying that it was called to address some issues that had arisen, and that comments should be kept general, then he proceeded to address his next comments specifically at and about me. Other staff then made statements obviously directed at me.

Male staff member: 'I remember a young woman here years ago who had to leave because she couldn't manage her classes.' He smiled and swung on his typist chair, laughing and smirking with the woman who had been interrupting my classes. He was obviously implying that I could not manage my classes and enjoyed doing so. I felt humiliated, but determined not to retaliate.

Female staff member: She looked savagely at me, the body language and facial expression making it obvious that she couldn't wait to have a go. She was one of the most malicious and unfair of critics and lied outright. (I felt betrayed, as she had attested to similar bullying treatment when she had served as union representative the preceding year.)

Some staff criticised me for doing things they admitted doing themselves — although they claimed that I did it far more often and that was the issue — and made hostile comments about my personality, my teaching and my professional shortcomings.

'You're unapproachable.'

'You yell at students (which I do, for example, 'Silence!', 'Quiet please!' or 'Bums on chairs on the count of three') and I never yell — it's not necessary' (yet I had comforted a student who'd been told by this female teacher to 'Shut up, you little bitch').

'You are always late to class.'

'You are too slow to move out of your classroom.'

'You are disorganised.'

'You send students to the staffroom far more than any one else (I had rarely spent a spare period in the work staffroom when other teachers' students had not disturbed me).'

Prior to this meeting, none of those present had ever mentioned any of these issues. I felt attacked from all sides but determined to look in control. When the meeting was over, I left the school. Once I was sufficiently coherent, I phoned the Daily Organiser to say that I was in no fit state to teach. After a sleepless night, it was by sheer effort of will that I returned to work the next day.

The following Monday, I was barely functioning but kept telling myself not to let them see how low they had pushed me and to keep fighting. However, when I took my Year 7 class in the library, I suddenly found myself 'off with the fairies'. One moment I was laughing, the next I felt completely absent, like I was in a vacuum. I cannot remember sitting down — it must have been half an hour or more after I'd dismissed the class that I found myself still sitting in the library, staring out the window into space, rocking back and forth. I realised that I desperately needed time out.

Over the next few weeks, I experienced the various stages associated with deep grief or loss. It was as though I had switched off inside because I could no longer cope with life. I saw a doctor who put me on antidepressants and told me to just go through it. I confused days — I was not conscious of the daylight ending, the night or the dawn. People telephoned and I had trouble focusing on what they were saying. I had to write everything down.

I went to visit an organiser at the union head office and was an hour late because, although I had been there often before, I couldn't find the way. When I look back, I realise that I should not have been driving a car. I was becoming increasingly angry. I remember screaming at the union organiser that the ex-union representative had betrayed me. When I was with people, all I wanted to talk about was what had happened to me. I couldn't sleep.

I talked to a friend and counsellor who helped me to direct the anger into political action. I contacted the union, my doctor, understanding friends and colleagues — some were so concerned they set up a roster to call me each night. The Principal was put under a lot of pressure for mishandling the issue. However, even my colleagues' support waned as time went on — after all, as one said, 'I have been very careful to build up my own reputation whilst I have been here.' It was clear she did not wish to risk it by being seen to support me too far.

Finally, I informed the Principal, through the union, that I was not interested in mediation with the entire faculty staff. I would attend mediation with the woman who had caused me so much grief. I would not return to school prior to this mediation and would make my decision on this basis. I knew that mediation with the Deputy-Principal would get me nowhere — the school's Principal had too much invested in saving face and would defend him no matter what.

The college, fearing an ongoing WorkCover claim, cooperated. The Deputy-Principal arranged a consultant psychologist through the Department of Education to act as mediator. After an initial aggressive response, the woman finally apologised, offering as an excuse for her behaviour that she suffered from multiple personality disorder!

In my many years of teaching, I have never before experienced the extreme intolerance and pettiness that occurred at this school. I was particularly disappointed that some colleagues, though highly moral people, said little in my defence. Since then, some have told me quietly about their own similar experiences at the school. They preferred to look the other way rather than risk further bullying. Evil prevails through oppression and fear, when good people stand by and do nothing.

In conclusion, I felt empowered by taking action. I have not solved the entire problem — I have not dealt effectively with the Deputy-Principal — but I am also realistic. I need to work and jobs for mature-age, top-level teachers are hard to find. Again, I was unsuccessful at a job interview for another year's contract. The school Principal told me the decision was based upon merit and was very close. A first-year-out teacher was employed ahead of me. The current perception is that I am 'not a good team player'; that I am, according to the Faculty Head, 'a very good teacher, but no one likes you'. When I was told that I had not been granted the position, despite being unemployed after 20 December, my overwhelming response was one of relief that I would not be returning there next year. I am applying widely elsewhere. However, this time I have a clear list of criteria for the type of position I am seeking!

Meanwhile, I still experience abuse. I took a porcelain doll I am making to work to discuss my costume plans with the sewing teacher, and left it in the staffroom. When I returned at recess, someone had pulled off the glued on wig and pulled out the hair design. I put a 'Please do not touch' sign on it. When I returned at lunchtime, the wig had been completely removed again. What saddens me is the waste. I could have been a far more effective teacher had I not been caught up by mismanagement, bullying and its resultant illness.

Janine, 48, teacher

Denise's story

I was harassed, bullied and traumatised by management for two years and ten months before I left on sick leave. I suppose it could be called secondary bullying because a close colleague was the initial target and, when I supported her, I was included in their deliberate and cruel aggravation. The bullying behaviour included such things as completely demoralising me by standover tactics, confrontation, manhandling, and mental and physical abuse, as a result of which I suffered everyday occurrences of hypertension, panic attacks and depression.

Other symptoms included sleepless nights, deep depression, crying day and night, loss of weight, loss of confidence and self-esteem, not wanting to get out of bed, not wanting to eat or leave the house, headaches, nausea, faintness, extreme aches and pains, palpitations, tiredness, nightmares.

The constant bullying and harassment over a long period of time caused my blood pressure to rise dramatically. Eight months after the commencement of the bullying, I became ill at work and was taken by ambulance to hospital where I was admitted to Intensive Care. The specialist diagnosed acute hypertension (to such a degree that I was at risk of a stroke or heart attack) caused by stress. My GP, my psychologist and a psychiatrist confirmed this diagnosis. The result is lifelong medication to control my blood pressure, ongoing monitoring for life by my GP and specialist, together with counselling from a psychologist and treatment from a physiotherapist when required.

As well as affecting my physical and mental health, the bullying caused my working life to be cut short and, as a result, I suffered financial loss. Though I was approaching the end of my career, I had intended to continue working for several more years as I really enjoyed my job and felt I was doing something worthwhile. It seemed as if my control over my life had been taken away; the direction I was taking and the choices I had made were eliminated, leaving me floundering and disillusioned. I felt that my life had been a failure and I felt ashamed.

Once I had left work, with remarkable support from my psychologist, GP, specialists, colleagues, family and friends, I started to slowly come back from my private hell. I liken the recovery stage to the aftermath of bereavement, as you have to work through the same grieving processes to recover. Stage 1 is numbness, shock and depression; Stage 2 is low self esteem, the feeling of losing control of one's life — all the usual symptoms of bereavement; and Stage 3 is taking back control and working through the painful stages of recovery — a long, drawn-out process needing ongoing support from others.

It is only now, looking back, that I realise how much my family suffered as I became withdrawn and constantly rambled on about my problems. I was self-centred and self-absorbed. For example, when my daughter was being married, I found it difficult to feel anything about the event. I did work through this with the help of my psychologist, but I was robbed of the feelings of joy and happiness I should have experienced at the time.

As a result of my experience, I feel that *management must be made accountable* for their actions. They need to be made aware of the serious consequences of inadequate management, how it affects the individual and how it disadvantages the company, for example, by the loss of skills when experienced workers leave, the overall financial loss because of bullied workers taking days off, excessive sick leave, the cost of WorkCover claims and the general loss of morale when there is an unhappy and unproductive workplace. Employers should take the time to communicate with their employees and should hold workshops for their managers to gain the skills to make the workplace a happy, healthy and safe environment.

Gaining control again was like being a baby, starting to crawl and walk, falling down and getting up, and trying again and again — a long, slow, painful process. I learned that not everyone is to be trusted and that not everyone has your best interests at heart. I am now more 'aware'.

Even twelve months after leaving that toxic work environment, I still have bad days but I am getting on with living. I go out to movies and the theatre, take classes in T'ai chi and art, have joined a garden club and am once again involved in family affairs. I was determined not to allow this 'thing' to control my life but it took time, constant counselling and monitoring by my medical team, the encouragement of family and friends and, most important of all, my own will to recover.

Denise, 59, welfare worker

Simon's story

I worked in the community sector for many years and I suppose my boss had always been a bit of a bully, but I put that down to the stress of running an extremely busy agency.

One day I received a call from a co-worker's client, threatening suicide. After talking in depth with her, I approached my boss in confidence and explained my concerns over the management of this middle-aged woman. He said the client was no concern of mine, she was not a suicide risk and that I should leave it to her case manager. A few days later this woman tried to kill herself.

Maybe my boss felt insecure because my judgement had been proved right — I'm not really sure of his motives — but from then on, he made my life hell with continual invasion of my personal space, intimidation, standover tactics and discrimination. My job description was changed and it was made very clear that my contact with clients was to be drastically reduced. The boss's attitude towards me veered between condescension and outright loathing. A colleague, Gabrielle, was also intimidated and bullied because she protested about my treatment.

Gabrielle and I were extremely stressed. We felt overwhelmed and were both experiencing health problems. I was having excruciating migraines and had trouble sleeping; when I did sleep, I had nightmares about my boss. Gabrielle was also suffering from loss of sleep and was tearful for no obvious reason. We went to our doctors and were given time off work, and we both put in WorkCover claims for stress and bullying.

A week later we returned to work but only on a part-time basis. The intimidation escalated. I was put onto answering the phones and was told that I was not to have any contact with clients. I became very worried that my position was about to be terminated.

A co-worker and I shared a spacious office, which had a large window that let in a lot of light and looked out over the garden. The pettiest action of all was when he took away the coffee machine, which had been placed in our office because it was the largest and contained a small refrigerator for milk. Colleagues often wandered in when they needed a quick hit of caffeine. He took the machine to his own office, which automatically meant that the rest of us had no access to it — we were not prepared to wander into his office uninvited.

I was worried that my desk would be next to go and, sure enough, when I came in one day, my desk was in the old storeroom, which had one small window looking onto next door's brick wall. There was only room enough for me, my chair and desk. There was nowhere to interview clients and, to access my files, I had to walk almost the full width of the floor to where my filing cabinet was stored just outside my boss's office.

> AMANDA: I was shifted out of my office ... to a little hole under the stairs ... I felt totally isolated ... Then I was called into Bryony's office and she told me that my job description was going to be revamped. About two or three days of the week I used to be out of the office visiting our various program centres ... suddenly I was told that there would be no more of that. I had to stay in my office ...
> JACK: You mentioned monitoring calls?
> AMANDA: I was the only one in the office, to my knowledge, who had to account for every outside call I made.

I was devastated. I sought legal advice and was advised to lodge a complaint with the Equal Opportunity Commission. A meeting was arranged with my boss, myself and a union representative. The union rep wanted to know my main concerns, which were my client contact and my office. Under duress, my boss agreed that I could again see clients. However, I was not permitted to return to my old office.

I felt so ill the next morning that I rang in sick. I made an appointment with my general practitioner, who gave me a medical certificate for more time off. Late that afternoon, I received a telephone call from Gabrielle, saying we had both been terminated and to expect a letter.

The reason given for our termination was that, because we were only working part time, we were not supplying an adequate service to the agency.

I found out later that some of the staff had been coerced into signing a document making damaging claims about my work and behaviour. It was so obviously unfair that I decided to fight.

My WorkCover claim for bullying had been rejected so I went to WorkCover conciliation. My boss was accompanied by his insurer, who knew the WorkCover Act back to front and wouldn't let my lawyer in. The conciliation officer agreed that I had a claim and issued the necessary certificate allowing me to go to the Magistrates' Court. I also went to the Industrial Relations Commission for a hearing on my unfair dismissal. I had plenty of evidence and witnesses to my bullying and I explained how I was not consulted regarding my termination and not offered any alternative work. The agency tried to drag out the case, which was costing me a small fortune, but I was not prepared to buckle. Eventually, they agreed to a settlement, with each side paying their own costs.

I have already been once to the Magistrates' Court, but my case was postponed as the boss has decided to enter another defence. I'm sure he is hoping that my financial situation will force me to pull out, but I am determined not to let him win. I am now waiting for another hearing date to appear at the Magistrates' Court, and if I lose it will possibly cost me tens of thousands of dollars.

I have been fortunate to have received support from my partner, my children and friends. I am not the person I used to be. My confidence has been undermined and I am tending to drink too much because alcohol blurs the edges and helps me forget. At present I am in limbo. I think that, once the court case is finally over and I get the positive result I am expecting, I will be able to put this experience behind me and make a new start.

Simon, 43, unemployed youth worker

Reject your sense of injury and the injury itself disappears.

Marcus Aurelius, *Meditations*

CHAPTER 17

What the practitioners say

We are all products of the assistance we are able to accept.

I. A. Richards

The people least mentioned so far but vitally important to the rehabilitation of victims of bullying are the professionals — human resource practitioners, doctors, psychologists, therapists, lawyers — who play a part in helping sufferers to recover from or gain restitution for the damage inflicted. Here are their thoughts:

The general practitioners

1. Dr Jo-Anne Zappia, MBBS, FRACGP, DRACOG

I was once consulted by a young homosexual man, working in a professional capacity in a large city office. He was propositioned on multiple occasions by his male manager, who was older and married, and he politely declined each time. The invitations continued and became such that the young man felt extremely violated and needed to take a leave of absence. He did not receive support from his superiors and, when he returned to the workplace, he experienced a very cold reception from his co-workers, with whom he had previously enjoyed a close relationship. The bullying here had obviously occurred on many levels and he was unable to continue in his employment and has since moved interstate.

As a general practitioner I have had the opportunity to work with many people who have experienced trauma in their daily lives. Unfortunately, this trauma often arises out of interpersonal relationships. Although intimate relationships are a frequent source of angst, our association with work colleagues is an extremely important and common source of trauma.

Opportunities for bullying in the workplace are many and varied. Despite the modern drive towards political correctness, a person's age, gender, ethnicity and sexual persuasion can all be used as ammunition by a more powerful opponent seeking to retain that power.

Workplace bullying can be either *passive*, such as discrimination for employment on the basis of appearance, or *active*, such as physical bullying or requesting sexual favours in exchange for promotion and so on.

Bullying can occur at any level in the workplace. Often I will see a worker who is suffering from the symptoms of workplace bullying as a result of their perception that they have been taken advantage of in the workplace. Bullying can occur on a horizontal level (that is from a work peer) or on a vertical level (that is from a superior).

It is not difficult to see that in a workplace there will be people with varying degrees of competence and work ethic. This can lead to the more competent or diligent employee being overloaded while the less competent or diligent colleague undertakes a lighter workload. The perceived bullying can occur here on two levels. The victim may perceive the *supervisor* as distributing work unfairly or the *peer* may be perceived as freeloading. The worker's perception of being overloaded amounts to a feeling of being bullied.

Perpetrators of workplace bullying can be both the employers/supervisors and other employees. Bullying can include such simple things as unfair rostering of shift workers and consistent misuse of delegatory power.

It would seem that perpetrators can have many unrelated characteristics. In my experience, underlying factors include personality characteristics, difficulties in their home lives and mental health problems (including eating disorders and anxiety disorders), although I am sure this list is not exclusive. The perpetrator often seems to use his or her position to maintain the victim's subordination.

Victims of workplace bullying are both male and female, experienced and inexperienced, senior and junior. Sexual harassment has been a popular media topic, and we are all familiar with the history of inequalities in job opportunities and pay discrimination.

The effect of workplace bullying seems to follow a universal pattern. The victims experience job dissatisfaction, sadness, depression, anxiety and panic attacks. In some cases people present with physical illnesses (including headaches, peptic ulcer disease and irritable bowel syndrome). In addition, lifestyle habits such as smoking and alcohol intake are often adversely affected by a poor work environment.

The solution to this problem is likely to be multifaceted. It will, of course, start with developing an awareness of the concept of workplace bullying. This awareness needs to be developed at a community level so that workers, employers and health authorities are familiar with the concept. This will enable the latter to be able to develop the means to ask the necessary questions to identify this problem in an individual. Simply asking clients whether they enjoy their job and relationships at work could form a useful part of the social history essential to any thorough medical assessment.

As well as health workers, occupational health and safety workers could be instrumental in identifying problem areas and addressing them. Mentor programs might be established in large organisations in order to create a framework for identifying and solving problems before they become serious. Critical incident debriefing could be used more widely, not just in situations of major catastrophe (such as an aeroplane crash) but in seemingly less traumatic situations (such as a verbal assault occurring between peers in the workplace). Furthermore, assertiveness training could be added to the school curriculum in order to provide people with life skills to help prevent the bullying from occurring or having any real effect.

Bullying in the workplace is, unfortunately, a very common phenomenon. There are many variables, including the natures of the perpetrators and victims, as well as the causes and effects. An increased awareness of this problem is the first step in preventing this type of emotional trauma.

2. Dr Jim Glaspole, MBBS (Melb), FRACGP

GPs see many patients suffering from anxiety and, with some, there are stressors specifically related to workplace bullying. Though I have seen cases of workplace bullying throughout my years in general practice, there has not been an increase over the period of my career. I have not undertaken any specific training in dealing with workplace bullying but have learned on the job, picking up information on industrial issues and regulations as I go along. In situations related to the workplace and other compensable injuries many GPs get the feeling that their patients regard them as bush lawyers and it is often necessary to recommend that separate legal advice be sought.

When dealing with claims of bullying, the challenge is to sort out whether the bullying is genuine or if it could be based on an erroneous perception of a situation in the workplace. If a patient is suffering persecutory delusions it may not become clear to a GP until unusual features surface in the history. For example, a claim that the patient's phone is being bugged might indicate that the person is suffering from a psychosis and is in need of psychiatric help. However, regardless of whether or not the bullying is genuine, the patient who complains of workplace bullying usually needs medical treatment.

I do not routinely prescribe medication such as antidepressants unless the bullying has the effect of producing identifiable psychiatric conditions such as depression or severe anxiety. I often work in conjunction with counsellors when the patient is on WorkCover and will usually defer to a psychiatrist's opinion with regard to the best pharmacological remedies if they are needed. Patients not funded through WorkCover will have more financial limitations, though I would refer them to the local community health centre or to psychologists in the local area if such assistance is warranted.

Advice to the patient may be given on several levels, one being the industrial front. I recommend that the bullied patient keep a diary as a means of collecting evidence to present in any future court dispute. If the bullying is coming from a colleague or at peer level, I usually advise the worker to sort it out at a level above the bully. If the bullying is coming from someone at a higher level, try to sort it out at a higher level still. I can't give legal advice, but in cases where the matter is not settled early, and where it is obvious that the worker is not likely to succeed if he takes the matter further, I might advise them to leave work for the sake of their overall health.

Many bullied workers want to stand up for a principle and choose to fight. When this happens, additional stress can be caused firstly by the intimidating attitude of insurance investigators, to the extent of putting the patient under surveillance, and again when the patient receives the standard initial rejection of their WorkCover claim. There seems to be a resistance to claims being accepted as lodged and workers who don't understand this strategy by insurers are often disadvantaged. They have the option of appealing, but even if they understand the process often don't have the stamina or emotional strength to fight on. Also, the prospect of a legal battle is intimidating and can be costly in terms of the patient's health and money. Victims can be off work and out of pocket for lengthy periods, often eight months or more.

Everyone has their biases in these cases, although GPs do try to present an unbiased, balanced view. However, we're not specialists so, unfortunately, our opinions don't carry the same weight of evidence as expert witnesses in court.

On the health front, I give general advice such as: don't resort to alcohol or drugs to cover anxieties; don't take up smoking again if you are a reformed smoker; try to switch off at weekends and do other things unrelated to work; look at other aspects of your life and keep your employment in perspective.

With regard to relationships, I tell the victim not to dump too much of their burden on family members or friends. Partners, in particular, often suffer as much as the bullied person. They may feel extremely anxious and also disempowered because they are less knowledgeable about what goes on in the workplace, particularly when the bullied worker is not communicative. Partners will need help themselves, and I often see couples together for treatment or the partner will visit me separately, sometimes without the worker's knowledge.

With regard to diagnosis, signs of anxiety can be picked up quickly — pressured speech, agitation, tremors. I try to confirm the workplace as the source of stress by looking at the patient's past history and generally get some idea of how the workplace issue has arisen and whether it is reasonable for them to be stressed about the particular problem. Some people become very stressed about minor things that would not bother others who have more robust, secure personalities.

Workplace stress and bullying often result from what could be called 'seasonal hyperactivity', for example, when a worker is covering for others on leave or when staff have not been replaced after redundancies. People are often frustrated by inadequacies in the workplace that they don't know how to address and feel that their suggestions to management are ignored.

I have not experienced any malingering in bullying cases, and have found this to be more common with claims for physical injury, detected when the patient's primary goal is to get another month off. Malingering is extremely difficult to identify and I know of some GPs who have been very surprised when presented with surveillance video footage by insurance companies.

Conversely to the usual pattern of presentation for workplace bullying, I have seen cases of patients presenting in distress as a result of being accused of bullying or harassment. This can be just as stressful as being the victim of bullying. Some people are not aware of the effect of their behaviour, and have to learn to change. These situations can benefit from mediation, where an aggrieved worker, the accused bully and management, perhaps with a union representative, can sit down to work out a problem. Unfortunately, this does not happen often and, even when it does, the situation is rarely resolved to the satisfaction of the worker, as too often management backs up the senior person because of an erroneous perception that more value is invested in the senior employee.

Bullying results in psychological trauma, characterised by poor sleep and anxiety, which I would diagnose as a generalised anxiety problem. The diagnosis can be post traumatic stress disorder (PTSD), although this is usually a reaction to a specific traumatic incident, such as a car accident, rather than a prolonged campaign of intimidation as in bullying. PTSD could result where, for example, a person was abused in front of a crowd of colleagues or humiliated on a single occasion, and the person relives that dressing-down in subsequent dreams and nightmares.

Some victims will find counselling useful. Most counsellors maintain professional relationships with clients and are able to offer great benefit to stress sufferers. Counselling does not benefit everyone, and some ineffectual counsellors may indulge patients, reinforcing their view of themselves as victims rather than empowering them to move on with life or to develop a sense of mastery over their work situation.

Once a WorkCover claim is accepted, other beneficial therapies can be obtained. If a GP feels that there is an obvious, legitimate link between the injury and the proposed therapy, and that the patient will benefit from such things as massage, regular swimming, or visits to a gymnasium, then the GP will recommend that these costs be covered, usually in a letter to the insurer. However, I usually let people help themselves as much as possible, using their initiative to discover ways to relieve their anxiety.

My message to victims of bullying is: Don't feel isolated, be aware that you have rights, contact your relevant union or industrial organiser and diarise any specific incidents.

The psychologists

1. Jane Rylance, BA, DipEd, BSocWk (Hons)

(Jane Rylance is a counsellor in private practice in Brisbane who is in the final stages of her PhD, which explores workplace bullying and what individuals do to respond to it. She sees a range of people in her private practice, some of whom have experienced workplace bullying. Contact details: West End Counselling Centre — (07) 3844 5304).

The more we endeavour to learn about bullying in the workplace, the more we realise its complexity and understand that it is not a monodimensional, 'black-and-white' situation. At the heart of this complexity lies the issue of subjectivity. Individual perceptions are integral to the ways in which interactions between people are interpreted. Indeed, this workplace phenomenon is further complicated by a growing awareness of 'role reversion', where people who report themselves to be targets of bullying also engage in bullying behaviours towards the perceived offender. These issues pose dilemmas for both those attempting to respond to bullying and those trying to develop policies and procedures to address it at the organisational and state levels.

In responding to bullying on both personal and organisational levels, a number of considerations are relevant. The suggestions here stem from my experiences in private practice as a therapist and from my PhD research. The emphasis in both arenas has been on what individuals do and what they need to be able to respond to and recover from workplace bullying. Exploring these personal issues can also inform organisational policies. What follows explores first the processes involved in responding to bullying and, second, the implications of these processes for organisational policies and procedures in addressing the problem.

The impact of bullying worsens over time, due to the ongoing nature of the phenomenon which serves to grind victims down and, to differing degrees, threatens their view of themselves as being worthy, competent, good, and so on. The experience appears to challenge core assumptions and beliefs about their profession or workplaces, and this is what causes the damage. Indeed, victimisation theories are based on the premise that damage to individuals occurs via the processes where assumptions are threatened or shattered.

Consequently, individuals engage in a range of processes to re-affirm their self-concept. These processes are categorised into two groups in my research. First is the enactment of responses to deal with the phenomenon and its effects, and second is the 'creation of meaning'. The enactment of strategies involves responses implemented over time in an attempt to stop or minimise the opportunities for experiencing the phenomenon or to anaesthetise, counter or minimise its effects.

Two major factors provide the context for what strategies are enacted. The first is people's 'usual mode of response' or what they have done in past, similar situations. Accordingly, if targets of bullying have experienced abusive or conflictual behaviours in their childhood or in other settings, then the ways they behaved in those situations tend to parallel the approaches adopted subsequently. Clusters of strategies tend to comprise 'modes of response'.

The second factor appears to be people's evaluation of whether or not they can change the experience. Over time, targets continually re-assess whether or not the situation is likely to be influenced and whether or not they have the capacity to change it. This factor, named in my research as 'the degree of influential potential', ranges from low to high. If, over time, targets assess the situation as having low influential potential, then they tend to adopt more non-direct strategies aimed at dealing with the impact of the experience rather than directly aimed at trying to stop the bullying. The opposite occurs when they evaluate a high degree of influential potential. Over time, people are likely to gradually withdraw from their workplace until, if the situation appears 'unstoppable', they leave. Indeed, as indicated by my research and experiences as a therapist, it seems dangerous to attempt direct strategies where there is a low degree of influential potential. Interestingly, it seems that time away from the workplace allows for a shift in this assessment. A number of participants in my research identified that having time off or leaving resulted in a greater awareness of the debilitating effects of the experience and of the hopelessness of the situation. Many believed they should have resigned earlier.

The second process involved in responding to bullying is termed in my research the 'creation of meaning'. This complex process is connected directly with the effects of the experience on beliefs about the worthiness of the self. People attempt to engage in establishing what 'caused' their situation. The causal factors range from self-blame (*intrinsic factors* — behavioural or personality characteristics of the target) to external blame (*extrinsic factors* — personality characteristics of the perceived offender or characteristics of the organisation). Different people will hold a range of beliefs about what is responsible for their experience and can hold both intrinsic and extrinsic perspectives simultaneously. Those who hold mainly intrinsic beliefs for much of their experience appear to be the most negatively affected by it. What people seem to do is work through a process of trying to move towards more extrinsically based understandings of their situation. Consequently, a major element in healing is to develop some extrinsic understandings so that a balance of 'blame' occurs. Holding mainly or only self-blame beliefs prevents recovery.

One of the major factors for developing extrinsic meanings appears to be the concept of 'validation'. This occurs when others in the workplace are targeted, so that each target can more easily say, 'It's not just me and, therefore, some or all fault has to lie with the offender, or the organisation.' It also occurs if others support the target and name the experience as bullying, blaming it on other factors. For those who are denied such validation, it is more difficult to develop extrinsic understandings. Many of these people are likely to engage in various attempts to receive validation, such as complaining to a diversity of people, trying to get others on side or continually escalating their responses, such as moving into the legal arena. Those who keep fighting during and after an experience of bullying, even when each battle is lost, have usually had minimal validation. It appears this kind of battling becomes a means of trying to achieve self-validation.

This links directly to another of my findings, which highlights the complexity around bullying and its inherent subjectivity. Some targets will identify behaving towards the perceived offender in ways they would classify as 'abusive' or bullying (referred to earlier as 'role reversion'). Furthermore, a number of participants in my study referred to their work colleagues as perceiving that they were the 'bully', rather than the target. This complexity as to 'Who plays what role?' leads to complications when investigating a complaint. Also contributing to these difficulties is the often subtle nature of bullying behaviours that make them harder to identify and prove, ensuring that legal avenues of response do not usually have an outcome that advantages the target.

These complications are exacerbated by the fact that, generally, organisations in Australia at present are not motivated to implement procedures to address bullying. As evidenced in my research and that of others, most frequently targets have no option but to leave the workplace because of the perceived lack of competency of organisations in dealing with the phenomenon. Leaving the organisation is the most common way that the bullying ends. Most often, utilising complaint avenues prove unfruitful and can result in an intensification of the bullying.

These complexities and the understandings around response processes have implications for practitioners working with targets of bullying and for targets themselves. They also provide a foundation for some insights into organisational responses. The following are some considerations.

CONSIDERATIONS FOR COUNSELLORS

Seeking counselling is a common response of targets; this has been identified frequently in research. In my own research it was found to be a very useful strategy by many participants both during and after the experience as people tried to recover. I can, therefore, recommend it to targets of bullying. The considerations listed here are relevant for any counsellor working with individuals who want to heal from their experience of workplace bullying.

- **Prioritising healing.** As bullying causes so much damage to the self-concept, the priority of therapeutic intervention must be the safety of the target in all instances. The development of more self-affirming concepts must be the primary goal. Given the processes involved in the creation of meaning, where individuals need to be able to shift from purely self-blaming causal factors for recovery, counselling should assist in the exploration of causal factors and providing validation. This is not to say that individuals should be encouraged to blame others completely if it is evident some of their own behaviours have been inappropriate. The complexities relating to the subjectivity of the experience mean that targets should be encouraged to explore causal factors relating to both extrinsic and intrinsic factors.
- **Assessing the influential potential.** Encouraging individuals to assess the likelihood of their actions changing the situation is important. Evaluating the dynamics within the organisation and how much influential potential exists is integral to responding to the problem and any strategies adopted must not expose people to further damage. If the situation is assessed as of low influential potential, targets need to be encouraged to consider the implications of continuing in an unchangeable situation. If the situation is assessed as of high influential potential, a diversity of strategies might be employed upon careful evaluation.

This issue of influential potential and possible resignation presents an ethical dilemma. It is not desirable that an employee should leave an organisation without trying to 'fight' for their legal right to a psychologically safe working environment. Yet, as highlighted by the results of my own and other studies, the potential effects of adopting such courses of action might be detrimental to the employee. Indeed, in these situations, leaving might be the safer option.

- **Assessing the impact.** Given that, for many, the realisation as to how negatively affected they are by the bullying does not occur until taking time off or leaving, counselling should also allow for a realistic assessment of damage that has occurred to assist in determining subsequent strategies. Framing the experience as damaging to beliefs about self-worth, while also highlighting the goals of counselling and recovery to regain that sense of self, can be helpful.

- **Awareness of the process of healing.** Evidenced anecdotally, and in my research, is that recovery occurs over a period of time and that the situation must be resolved for this to begin. Awareness of this is important for targets who may enter new workplaces before they feel fully recovered.

- **Working with the usual mode of response.** If people adopt clusters of strategies they have adopted in previous similar situations, counsellors need to be aware of the target's preferred mode. The counsellor can then encourage the target to work within that mode, or perhaps work towards utilising other modes if they are assessed as potentially effective.

- **Assisting with support in new employment.** Some people who attend counselling about bullying may have moved to another employment position or may move positions while seeing a counsellor. In these instances, individuals have rarely had the time to fully recover and may enter a new workplace still 'injured' from the bullying and lacking in self worth. They may be very sensitive to dynamics between workers within their new organisation. Counsellors need to be supportive in encouraging awareness of these sensitivities and their lowered self-esteem, to ensure that individuals work at not letting these feelings become overwhelming and obvious to others in the new workplace.

The following considerations for targets of bullying are based on my research and practice. These are not exhaustive, but I do believe they are important.

- **Educating themselves regarding the dynamics of bullying.** The subtlety and subjectivity of bullying dynamics can be confusing. Consequently, individuals may find it helpful to educate themselves about the dynamics of it. This can also assist in the creation of meaning.
- **Assessing the influential potential.** Gaining clarity on the influential potential and one's own position within the organisation is an important factor in considering subsequent response approaches and the decision about whether to leave or stay. Formal or informal discussions with trusted members in the organisation, human resource staff or management bodies might assist with such an evaluation.

  If the assessment of the influential potential is low, then complaint and confrontation might not be the safest options. High influential potential may make complaint or confrontation safer options. An evaluation of low influential potential means the situation is really not changeable. In such instances, targets need to consider what might be the ongoing effects on themselves if they continue to be employed in the organisation and continue to experience bullying. Leaving may not be desirable, but neither is increasing damage to employees when they are in a hopeless situation.
- **Seeking validation.** Given the importance of validation to recovery, encouraging targets to seek validation from colleagues and others outside the workplace might be important.
- **Seeking counselling.** Counselling has been identified in research as being helpful for targets and it is, therefore,

recommended that individuals consider seeking counselling both during and after any experience of bullying.

The following considerations are not exhaustive but merely considerations that have emanated from my research and private practice. A number of quite comprehensive guidelines and recommendations exist for organisations to deal with bullying which discuss a diversity of issues (for example, Office of the Employee Ombudsman, 2000; Queensland Working Women's Service, 2000; Division of Workplace Health and Safety, Queensland, 1998a, 1998b).

- **Development of specific policies and procedures.** Having *specific* policies and procedures for bullying and processes that assist workers to understand their situation and to address it are likely to be important. Simple grievance procedures are not enough and need to be modified to specifically address bullying.
- **Training and education.** Education for employees about workplace bullying and what can be done about it is important. This could be part of employee orientation.
- **Diversity of response avenues.** Given that people are likely to adopt approaches they have previously used in other situations, a diversity of responses might be useful. This ensures that individuals can follow their usual mode of response as much as possible and that individual modes may still assist in resolving the issue. One example might be to appoint a staff liaison person trained in understanding and dealing with bullying with whom targets could discuss their concerns and the most suitable approaches. Informal avenues for discussion such as this might be important. Another example is to provide counselling through an employee assistance program which may be utilised to discuss the issues.

- **Interviewing all parties.** Issues pertaining to subjectivity, role reversion, the target being viewed by others as the offender and the subtleties of behaviours make investigation complex. Investigative procedures need to recognise the importance of gathering multiple and relevant perspectives. Interviewing all members in the team where bullying is alleged may be useful. In situations where the outcome has proven fruitful for the target, this has frequently been the strategy adopted by the organisation — an external consultant, knowledgeable in the area, has interviewed all team members. An external consultant is useful in managing alliances and can prepare recommendations for management and staff consideration.

- **Offering counselling.** The damage that can occur from bullying is an issue that organisations have a responsibility to address. Offering counselling to staff involved in any investigation might be useful.

The complexities of workplace bullying render this area a difficult one. Fortunately, most people who go through such an experience tend to come out at the other end feeling stronger. The recovery process is rather similar to that of grief and loss. Over time, people gradually come to integrate the experience and regain the 'lost self'. Importantly, many identify learning new things about themselves, changing aspects of themselves that they learned needed to change and feeling more adept at being able to handle a subsequent similar situation. In this sense, a damaging and devastating experience can, over time, potentially strengthen those involved.

2. An interview with Terry Amey, BA, BSc(Hons), MEd, MAPS, MASH, 17 October 2001

WHAT IS YOUR INTEREST IN BULLYING?

Immediately, I want to make it clear that I don't see myself as an expert in this field. Very experienced and respected writers on this topic are now emerging, for instance, Tim Field (UK), Ruth and Gary Namie (USA) and our own Melbourne-based psychologist, Evelyn Field. I am currently a semi-retired psychologist with an intensive background in Education and Educational Psychology. However, I have been increasingly drawn into the area of workplace consultancy at independent businesses, hospitals and schools.

Recently, I have worked over a two-year period with one patient who suffered a severe stress-related disorder as a result of perceived bullying at the worksite. This person chose to pursue her case through WorkCover and the court system. My interest in workplace bullying developed out of my involvement with this case. I now am noticing, however, that if the subject of workplace bullying arises at a typical Professional Development day, if you say 'Conflict resolution' it evokes considerable participant interest, especially at hospitals!

WHY HAVE WE SUDDENLY BECOME AWARE OF BULLYING AS A PROBLEM IN THE WORKPLACE?

I suppose we are starting to see the word more because of increased publicity in the press, recent highly visible grabs on television relating to various union surveys, the increasing concern of WorkCover to develop new protocols and, especially, the extensive website information. However, our 'awareness of' and 'the existence of' are two separate issues, aren't they? Our 'awareness of' has probably increased the identification of the extent of workplace bullying. Also, surely workers today are more able to articulate their own rights and also their responsibilities to colleagues. I would suspect, though, that bullying is in fact *less* frequent in the workplace than in the past because of increasing awareness at worksites of the importance of effective interpersonal and problem-solving strategies, and of increasing understanding of their correlation to increased productivity.

WHAT SORT OF BULLYING DO YOU HEAR ABOUT IN THE WORKPLACE?

Well, you'll see that definitions of workplace bullying vary enormously in the literature and range from verbal harassment to dismissal threats and violence. For the more common workplace behaviours, such as taunts, criticism, and so on, it is generally assumed that there is maliciousness and persistence over time involved. I have to say that, in my experience, bullies usually have position power and have little idea that their behaviour is perceived by workers as bullying. They probably believe that bullying is restricted to bastardisation-type behaviour and that they themselves are utilising effective management strategies.

ARE YOU SAYING THAT MOST BULLIES DON'T KNOW WHAT THEY ARE DOING?

Surely it depends on the kind of bullying. We must assume that physical harassment, which is deliberately aimed to hurt and demean, is understood by the perpetrator to be bullying and that other reinforcement, such as peer approval, makes it worthwhile. But what about bosses deliberately making life uncomfortable to force workers to resign or go onto WorkCover? What about a long-time, ingrained interpersonal style of putting down others to enhance their own self image and ego? I suspect that, in such cases, many perpetrators would be unaware that their behaviour was perceived as bullying.

Do you believe bullies can change?

Certainly, I do, at least at the type of worksites that I'm familiar with. I came across a really useful model for understanding organisational ideology a while ago (Roger Harrison). In brief, he suggests that an organisation's ideologies can be seen in terms of four orientations: Power, Role, Task and Self. A questionnaire assesses employees' perception of their organisation's ideology compared with their own preferred ideology. In many organisations, there is a difference between the worker's orientation and values (say Task or Self) and the perception of the organisation's orientation (say Role or Power). Now, if this can be seen and understood as more normal and expected than pathological, and that any resultant tensions can be seen as opportunities for effective problem-solving and growth, then we won't misread an expected tension as due to interpersonal or vested interests. It seems to me, therefore, that with awareness and acceptance, we can often pre-empt any misunderstanding that can lead to negative cycles ending in scapegoating and bullying.

I certainly believe that, with professional development programs at the workplace dealing with all the usual suspects relating to enhancing interpersonal skills and the understanding of both organisational and workers' needs, a great deal could be done. Of course, staff themselves are tremendous at generating their own ideas and procedures to enhance their workplace. I'll show you a recent brainstorm response resulting from the task set as part of a problem-solving exercise.

Task: What can be done when a staff member complains to you that they are being bullied?

Responses

- 'Offer counselling.'
- 'Develop a policy and set of procedures re bullying.'

- 'Identify communication styles of all staff, including the bully.'
- 'Identify what is bullying at our workplace.'
- 'Ask the boss to sack the bastard.'
- 'Develop an agreed statement that bullying is not to be tolerated.'
- 'It is OK to be a dobber.'
- 'Develop a protocol on the reporting of bullying.'
- 'Develop disciplinary procedures for bullying.'
- 'Provide a support mechanism for the victim.'
- 'Develop Incident Assessment Procedures. Who does this — representative, staff team or outsiders?'
- 'Ensure that all staff are aware of signs and symptoms of bullying.'
- 'If staff wants, they can seek help from the boss — make this an acceptable culture.'
- 'Install cameras.'
- 'Develop a complaints procedure.'
- 'Lynch the bastard.'
- 'Staff development/assertiveness training.'
- 'Team building — positive feedback.'
- 'Formal and informal training.'
- 'Preventative — need for cultural awareness, awareness of individual/ organisational needs'
- 'Develop a culture within the workplace that encourages courtesy, respect, honest and open communication, compliments. One that discourages negativity, such as rumour and gossip.'
- 'Reinforce importance of every staff member's role.'
- 'Make the bully aware of his style — offer support/counselling, give opportunity to change.'
- 'Place sanctions on bullying.'
- 'Nominate another staff member to support victim.'
- 'Model other positive interpersonal behaviour (set an example).'
- 'Don't ignore — improve understanding.'
- 'Affirm colleagues.'

- 'Role reversals.'
- 'If all else fails, call the police or use a length of 4" × 2"!!'

As you can see, an enjoyable twenty-minute brainstorm has provided the basis, after evaluating each idea, for the development of a set of principles and procedures that the staff will feel ownership of and commitment to. As a consequence, I suspect the chances of a staff member being harmed by bullying will be much less.

WHAT ABOUT THE VICTIMS? WHAT PROBLEMS DO THEY REVEAL?

In my experience, common symptoms include heightened pervasive and anticipatory anxiety, including panic attacks. Emotional difficulties can include ongoing anger and depression. Physical symptoms include muscle tension and pain, light-headedness, heart palpitations, severe headaches, including migraine, perpetual fatigue and digestive problems. Cognitive difficulties may include concentration and memory problems, apathy and indecisiveness. Behaviourally, victims often have sleeping difficulties and overconsume food and alcohol. Unfortunately, sometimes phobic behaviours (especially to the work situation), paranoia, poor impulse control and interpersonal difficulties may be present.

I've seen figures indicating that about half of all victims exhibit severe stress symptoms over a long period of time, and also a significant number of victims show symptoms of post traumatic stress disorder — even many years later.

WHAT IS POST TRAUMATIC STRESS DISORDER?

Well, you'll find a full definition and diagnosis in the *Diagnostic and Statistical Manual of Mental Disorders (DSM-IV, APA[81])*. However, the three major characteristics are, first, that the client re-experiences aspects of a previous trauma — for instance, a chance stimulus (a piece of music, a smell) will remind them of the event, causing them to react as if it were happening again. Second, clients avoid normal life experiences to protect themselves from perceived hurt; sometimes they feel numb and alienated; they say, 'I don't care about anything any more.' Third, increased arousal may be evidenced by flashbacks, 'waking nightmares' or sleeping difficulties.

WHAT STRATEGIES HAVE YOU FOUND USEFUL FOR VICTIMS OF BULLYING?

I've noticed that victims often think that they are weak and cowardly or at least that much of the fault is their own. Of course, this is sometimes reinforced at the worksite by the bully, such as, 'She is incompetent, erratic, and so on.' Therefore, it is essential, I think, to fit the traumatic events into a comprehensive and meaningful framework, that is, 'make sense' of it. Most importantly, victims should be led to understand that they were not totally responsible. Assertiveness training is useful.

Strategies would perhaps need to include:

- self-awareness raising — being aware of personal style
- organisational evaluation — awareness of ideology
- reaching acceptance after clarification and feedback
- relating skill training (assertiveness, deflection, humour, communication techniques, such as active listening, 'I talk', etc.)
- conflict resolution skills (including mediation)
- dealing with anger (own/others')
- rational thinking
- positive self-talk
- a cognitive behavioural approach, including making plan/action strategy, short-term/long-term goal setting, rehearse behaviours, etc.
- stress management — physical/mental strategies for regaining full physical health (relaxation training, diet, exercise, maximise recreation, regain humour, enhance relationships, etc.)

- forgiveness — let go of resentment, depersonalise the trauma (Success is the best revenge! Thank you, Leunig!)
- develop problem-solving network to deal with ongoing issues (for example, WorkCover).

HOW LONG DOES RECOVERY TAKE?

The degree and speed of recovery from a bullying experience will depend on a number of factors:

- the degree of trauma — the greater the trauma, the more likely it is to lead to symptoms we'd label PTSD
- the emotional strength and maturity of the victim
- the victim's interpersonal style — a propensity towards pessimism, low self-esteem and poor problem-solving skills — is more likely to lead to depression
- the levels of support received from colleagues, family and friends
- the importance placed on career by the victim
- the duration of the bullying experience
- whether the victim is willing to adopt counselling strategies that can make them emotionally stronger.

In some cases, trauma over time can induce biochemical changes that need the assistance of medication to restore the balance.

Because there is usually a power differentiation between bully and victim, victims often believe that they have no choice but to accept the bullying. For some people, there is even something reinforcing, almost masochistic, about being a victim and they will choose to remain so rather than decide to follow the path of recovery. Some child victims remain victims as adults; they have few life skills, a general mistrust of themselves and others, problems with negotiation and confrontation and may start a vicious cycle in which they avoid social situations and become more isolated, thus confirming their low self-esteem and 'difference'.

WHAT ABOUT REACHING CLOSURE?

To attain closure, survivors of bullying should be encouraged in the following ways:

- Leave behind the baggage, that is, the physical — the organisation and the people they cared about, and the psychological — make farewells, collect personal items. Closure is a state of mind, which basically means that you have regained control.
- Develop an action plan listing all the things you want to do and tick them off as you achieve them.
- Resolve the issues you can and accept, through rational and positive self-talk, that some issues cannot be resolved, but they are not essential to your health and happiness.

WHAT ARE THE HARDEST CHALLENGES?

The hardest challenges I have faced working with bullied clients are those listed below.

- The systemic aspect — for example, the denial of the problem by the organisation because of vested interests, refusal to acknowledge the problem exists to avoid responsibility, and so on.
- The larger systemic picture — WorkCover, the insurers and the courts are all adversarial experiences and work against the regaining of wellness of the victim, and the power distribution is inequitable, that is, the organisation and WorkCover have access to huge dollars and the best legal advice.
- Because of the above, the client is unable to really effect interpersonal changes or behaviours at the worksite.
- Perhaps accentuated by above, the client's long-term PTSD or depression may have led to biochemical changes so cognitive behavioural strategies or relaxation techniques will have only a limited effect.

- The interpersonal hurt is so severe that the desire for revenge hinders victims' ability to move forward with their recuperation, often because of no closure.
- Unfortunately, even though some employers have Codes of Practice, they are not mandatory and are not policed.

The physiotherapist

David Morarty, BA, BAppSc (Physio), GradDip (sports Physio), MAPA

THE EFFECT OF STRESS ON THE MUSCULAR SKELETAL SYSTEM

Stress, which is any environmental change that must be adapted to if health and life are to be maintained, or any event that elicits an increased cortisol secretion in physiological terms, will invariably have an effect on the muscular skeletal system. Therefore, many types of stress, particularly of a negative nature such as those encountered in work-related stress, for example, workplace bullying, can certainly have major effects on the body's physiology and muscular skeletal system. Broadly speaking, any stressful situation including physical trauma, prolonged heavy exercise, infection, shock, decreased oxygen supply, prolonged exposure to cold, pain, fright or different emotional stresses, invariably causes an increased secretion of cortisol.

'Stress' has also come to mean any event that elicits increased cortisol secretion by the adrenal cortex, or an increase in sympathetic nervous activity. In its extreme form, this body response is commonly labelled the 'fight or flight response', where the sympathetic nervous system is activated and certain physiological responses such as increased heart rate, increased tension in muscles, increased blood pressure and suppression of other systems, such as the digestive system, occur to enable danger to be confronted or avoided. Situations that may engender sufficient stress levels to have a physiological effect in people might be, for example, aircraft flights, awaiting surgical operations, final exams for students, unusual or uncomfortable situations, competitive athletics, exposure to excessive heat and cold, workdays compared to weekends and many employment experiences. Employment experiences that could produce such physiological effects are time-urgency situations, aggressive work colleagues or employers, discrepancies between levels of aspiration and achievement or even continued subtle 'put-down' situations. All these types of situations could result in a fight or flight response of different degrees.

The value of the fight or flight response in modern life, where either fight or flight is appropriate, is therefore questionable, and can have certain detrimental physiological effects, such as enhancing the development of certain diseases, particularly athro-sclerosis and hypertension, and some cancers. This path would be better investigated by a medical practitioner. As a physiotherapist, I see the manifestation of stress continually in the muscular skeletal system. This is primarily in terms of increased muscle tension, which has varying physiological effects of:

  i increased muscular pain
  ii restriction of movement of joints, ultimately resulting in restriction of joint movement and, therefore, pain
  iii around the cervical and thoracic spine, shortening of important postural muscles which result in compression of joints of the upper cervical spine (neck), often causing cervical headaches
  iv neuromeningeal restriction or tethering, via chronically shortened and tightened muscles, and/or tight and restrictive joints, where degenerative process has began in those joints. This phenomenon is commonly known as a pinched nerve; if this takes place in the upper neck, it could cause continual severe headaches or, in the lower neck, can produce arm pain, pins and needles and a range of symptoms often clustered together as repetitive strain injury (RSI).

It has been my clinical experience that people who are exposed to chronic stress, whether it be in their home life, failure to meet their own expectations, fatigue, personal relationships or employment difficulties, may be suffering these muscular skeletal effects of stress on their systems. This is often part of a diagnosis where trauma or chronic injury, in a physical or biomechanical sense, is lacking in a patient who presents with symptoms of increased muscle tension and other aftereffects. Muscles that are chronically tense or become shortened are, as a result, unable to carry out tasks, ranging from simple tasks, such as rising from a seat, to more demanding tasks such as athletic activity. Therefore, muscles of increased tension are more likely to be torn or injured or purely to go into spasm, which is an uncontrolled contraction much like a cramp, causing intense pain. This can happen to the muscles of the body as a result of prolonged stress.

Psychological stress can also exacerbate already pre-existing physical injuries or physical weaknesses, such as tight muscles, neck pain, back pain and a predisposition to headaches. A person might, therefore, present with exacerbations of their physical symptoms when stress is encountered, particularly on a long-term basis. A relevant example might be someone who has a family history of headaches, muscle spasms or back pain, who then might report an increased frequency, intensity or duration of these symptoms when exposed to stress, such as that which may be encountered in their occupational setting. It is, therefore, plausible, and I have seen this clinically on a repeated basis, that people will come in complaining of more severe symptoms after an episode of stress, confrontation, criticism or disciplining in their work setting.

This picture is often seen in the industrial injury patients who, because of their decreased capacity at work due to their injuries, are either overtly or subtly criticised, sanctioned or ostracised in some manner. They will then often present for treatment in a worse condition than they have on previous visits, complaining of an increased severity of symptoms, with clinical findings to support what they are saying, for example, similar muscles are more tender on palpation, active movements are performed with more restriction and more obvious pain is demonstrated with a lower level of function. It is quite conceivable that such deterioration of a person's physical condition could be caused in the event of workplace bullying, to the extent that the effects of such activity were perceived as a stress by the person and had subsequent effects on the person's muscular skeletal system. The longer the duration or the further frequency of such a stress, the more likely the person would be to suffer symptoms such as muscle tension for a prolonged period, which results in muscle shortening, affecting posture, joints and nerves.

Poor posture or pain-avoiding posture (antalgic posture) can quickly become habit for a person who is suffering these symptoms on a daily or continuing basis. Therefore, stressful events such as bullying in the workplace can have a very real and often lasting effect on muscular skeletal pain and dysfunction, particularly in more susceptible type people.

Great opportunities to help others seldom come, but small ones surround us every day.

Sally Koch

CHAPTER 18

The employer view

A business that makes nothing but money is a poor kind of business.

Henry Ford

Small business owners — Elizabeth and Gene

We have owned and worked in a variety of businesses within the hospitality industry for the past twenty-six years. We've had a reception centre, motels and now a bed and breakfast.

Over that time we've employed a lot of staff and have had very little problem with bullying. People who lack management and communication skills tend to bully their subordinates or equals — they appear to have a 'survival of the fittest' mentality. Some of our chefs were bullies, in that they'd hound or threaten or be particularly sarcastic towards the waiting staff. Again, this was due to poor interpersonal skills.

We get the occasional bullying attitude from customers, usually fuelled by alcohol at wedding receptions or dinner dances. Once I [Gene] was grabbed by the throat and rammed up against the wall by a wedding guest. Elizabeth was abused and threatened by a motel guest, a 'celebrity' whose show had been cancelled because of lack of interest; he took out his rage on the first person he saw — 'chewed me up and spat me out'. We've been accused of stealing property belonging to guests, for example, cameras left behind, but the bluster soon disappears when we stand up to them.

Bullying starts at school. These days there is a lack of respect for teachers and for discipline, children model their behaviour on their peers, who are often out of control, rather than their parents. They then carry on this idea that they can act as they like in the workplace and can't modify their behaviour. We don't think that the usual three-month trial is long enough; it's easy to be on your best behaviour for a short time. Six months would be better.

There was one occasion when a young male apprentice pulled a knife on a female chef. He had had a bad role model — his father was a very domineering man and his mother very cowed — so he brought his background to the work environment and could not cope with being given orders by a woman.

Our only real bullying experience was between staff at our motel/restaurant. Because we were travelling between two businesses in two different states at that time, we had to delegate a lot of the managerial work. We had a young man, Graham, managing the restaurant and a young woman, Lara, managing the motel. Lara was having a relationship with another staff member, Ruth, who was our receptionist and sometimes waitress in the restaurant. Graham was very good looking and very professional. Despite our absences, we began to notice that the till wasn't balanced, that alcohol and food were missing. We had no foolproof systems in place for checking dockets, and sometimes the register would be one or two hundred dollars out. You had to accept the excuse that someone had pushed the wrong button. Lara and Ruth said it was Graham, that he was rarely at work when we were away, that he fiddled the accounts, and helped himself to half a lobster here, a bottle of whisky there. He denied it, of course, and certainly there were many legitimate reasons for his absence, such as banking or shopping for the restaurant. We gave him chance after chance, but eventually, when the pilfering continued, we had to tell him to go. He just looked at us, shook his head and said quietly, 'You just can't see it, can you?' That was when the doubt set in, but it took us almost eighteen months before we found out that Lara and Ruth had plotted to get rid of him — they'd undermined him, lied about him and set him up — and we were so gullible that we fell for it. Graham was just the fall guy. Our biggest regret is that we were never able to apologise to him. In hindsight, it should have been obvious who the culprits were. We hate to think how much those two stole from us; we estimate at least $7000 worth of alcohol and goodness knows how much in food and other stock. We trusted them and they took advantage of that. I suppose we were more inclined to believe them because it was two against one.

The hardest part is judging who is telling the truth. Who do you believe? Dominant personalities get away with murder. Lara was confident and outgoing, whereas Graham was quiet and got trodden on.

Small-business operators have to play many roles, work long hours and have to delegate, therefore, a lot of aspects of the business are out of your control and there are ample opportunities for employees to abuse that trust. We have to say that the vast majority of our staff have been really honest and hard working. There will always be the occasional one who thinks he is hard done by and should be paid more, but small businesses like ours can only offer the minimum wage.

We are not interested in 'baby-sitting' staff any more. We've always been good employers, fair, but perhaps too friendly with our staff. With some people familiarity breeds contempt, and we were seen as too soft, too generous. Some staff thought they were owed something and believed we wouldn't miss the odd bottle of spirits or bottle of wine.

We expected loyalty in return for good treatment, but they knew we'd always pick up the slack — that was the problem. Our motel cleaners, mostly middle-aged women, were reliable, the salt of the earth, and did what was expected of them and more, but the vast majority of casuals — mostly younger people — do not turn up on time or work right through. All workplaces should have some sort of agreement or contract with every employee — like a position description, but more detailed — that says, 'In return for $X, I agree to do this', with the work set out in specific steps.

Tough management and bullying are two totally different things. There is a big difference between firm control and unreasonable demands. When we take on new employees, we tell them very specifically what the job involves and what is expected of them, but we are not autocrats. We don't say, 'Do it our way or else.' We give them freedom to think for themselves and to use their initiatives, and say, 'This is the way we do it, but if you think of a quicker, smarter way, that's fine — as long as the job is 100 per cent.'

The lawyer

Patsy Toop (Patsy is a partner in Clark and Toop Lawyers, Melbourne. Tel: (03) 9347 7177)

I now see a lot more cases than previously of workplace bullying and of bullying in schools, most of which relate to stress-induced trauma rather than physical violence. It is very hard to decide which is worse, because the person who is physically abused is also mentally abused but, whether the damage is physical or psychological, it is disgraceful that people are being attacked in their workplaces. Employers are negligent in allowing bullying to happen — and to continue to happen.

The rise in the number of bullying claims means either that intimidation and abusive behaviour is on the increase or that people are more aware that legal redress is available to them. Bullying has always existed but it is now discussed more substantially in the media and at government level.

We have all experienced bullying in the school playground but we don't expect it to follow us into our working lives and so are not prepared for it. When it does start, it takes a lot of strength for an individual to complain because the bully tends to be in a position of power in the organisation. With most of my clients, their workplaces have policies in place (usually anti-harassment rather than anti-bullying) but these policies are not followed. Most employers relate bullying to harassment and do not accept bullying as a separate entity (of course, harassment is a form of bullying).

Some organisations investigate bullying internally through their Human Resources Departments. However, because the focus tends to be on the WorkCover aspect of the situation, this encourages a kind of 'hip-pocket' approach where the goal is the minimisation of premium payments rather than the best outcome for the worker concerned.

By the time I see victims of bullying, they are at their wits' end and quite unwell, they have exhausted their holiday leave or sick leave, their doctor considers that they need more time off work and so they come to me to find out what more they can do. This is a big step because it usually requires them to formalise the complaint and put in a claim. Stress cases are investigated very extensively by the accident compensation insurer and most are not accepted first up but, once the investigation has taken place and the extent of the issue is aired by the independent party, that is, the insurer or investigator, usually the claims are accepted. The ones that aren't accepted end up having to go to court.

I have a number of court cases coming up where, as a consequence of a negligent employer allowing harassment and bullying, the victims have become so unwell that they probably will not work again. These become common law claims. With workers' compensation cases, you have to establish through independent witnesses that the abuse has happened and some cases fall down because the co-workers are not prepared to support the victim for fear of reprisal by the bully. Usually, we get disaffected witnesses, in other words, people who had the same experience but left the workplace before the behaviour caused major damage to their health; they are able to testify that they experienced the same kind of behaviour from the bully when they were at the workplace.

Often, bullying starts because there is a change of direction within the workplace and the individual is deemed to be 'surplus to requirements'. Rather than reskilling or making the individual part of the process, systematic bullying begins as a tactic to 'encourage' this person to leave. The individual often is not aware of the change of direction or that his job is at risk, and when he starts to be treated badly he is at a loss to understand why.

Once the bullying has happened, the next step is going through the WorkCover process, which requires medical confirmation that the person's sudden deterioration in behaviour or mental stress is a result of some significant contributing factor from the employment. Because bullying is spread over a period of time, formulating a complaint is difficult because usually the victim is unable to pinpoint one event and, in isolation, so much of the behaviour sounds petty. For example, it can be as subtle as intimidating body language or receiving a particular look from the bully that pierces you, an 'I'm going to get you' kind of look.

Usually, a bully is very successful at securing support from other people. He starts to complain about the person's work performance and, eventually, these complaints become legitimate because the bullying causes the victim's work performance to deteriorate. Constant attacks and harassment diminish their self-confidence, shatter their self-esteem and they become exactly what the bully has complained about — inadequate in the workplace. Ultimately, the crunch comes. Management says, 'You are not performing', and they are given 'counsellings' (which are, in effect, warnings — one, two, three and you're out). And so victims are left destitute, without a claim or a job, unless they have been seeing a doctor who can say, 'See a lawyer.' They have two options, either to try in their depressed state to find other employment (which is hard because they have the black mark of being 'let go' against them) or to do something drastic, such as attempt suicide or suicide. Unfortunately, I have had some cases where this has happened.

I once spoke to a lawyer who said he was so browbeaten by a bully that he could not compose a basic letter without fear of reprisal; he felt that he had lost the capacity to complete such a simple task. That is what happens. The target of the bullying becomes so cowed, so intimidated, that they can't stand up for themselves.

Many victims do not seek legal assistance. They take their long-service leave and then resign, or quit and try to get another job (with poor references, usually). The bullying experience leaves a permanent scar and it takes them a long time to get their confidence back.

The outcome of most bullying scenarios is that the bully stays and the victim goes, though I have had one case where the reverse happened. This was unusual in that the victim had enormous strength of character, and other workers and management also had issues with the bully. Management could see what was happening and, though it wasn't affecting them directly, eventually had to do something about it.

Those who do seek legal assistance must be warned of the risks of litigation, making it unlikely that those in financially strained circumstances will pursue it. Those who decide to take action must have very strong support from their lawyers, doctors and families.

A victim may begin a legal case but stop pursuing the complaint because of the cost. Sometimes employers will 'string out' a case, forcing the victim to withdraw because he simply cannot afford to continue. The insurer takes instruction from the employer, who may have other agendas, such as not wanting the victim to achieve compensation, or not wanting to recognise that bullying occurred, even after the event. If a case goes to the Magistrates' Court, the employer's legal costs are covered by WorkCover, and if the victim loses the case he has to pay both the WorkCover fees and his own. This possibility is frightening and deters many claimants. (If the victim wins, there is a scale of fees charged and WorkCover will pick up the majority of the cost.)

The financial implications for most victims of bullying are terrible. They leave their jobs, are encouraged by their doctors to find other employment (often one of less responsibility because they do not feel capable of working in a position equal to the one they left) and so less remuneration, possibly for the rest of their working lives. There is no legal redress for this loss.

Only severely affected people are in a position to take action through common law claims. For example, in Victoria, to obtain a lump sum for mental impairment you must have a 30 per cent whole person impairment, judged by American Medical Association guidelines. It is extremely difficult to reach 30 per cent impairment. I have had only one case that got to 30 per cent but the doctors said that it was secondary to the injury, in other words, *because of the injury* rather than *because of the event that caused the injury*, so there was no entitlement to a lump sum payment. It is quite discriminatory to have such a high impairment requirement for people with stress-related illness when the requirement for bodily impairment is 10 per cent. If we are talking whole-person impairment, what is the difference? One injury you cannot see, the other you can, but the hurt is probably deeper with the first. People with mental illness or disability or behavioural disturbance should be treated exactly the same way as people with physical injury.

In order to pursue a common law claim, you have to show negligence on the part of the employer. This is very difficult in stress cases because, usually, the victim is ill, is not at the workplace and does not necessarily have the support of the other people who work there because the bully has managed to get them on side. For common law purposes there has to be a severe injury — the 30 per cent is one way of actually achieving that. There is also the requirement to establish negligence on the part of the employer. There is the ability to sue but, again, it is at a significant cost at a time when a worker has few financial resources. If a case of bullying has been proven, then there is a great possibility that the person would be able to establish negligent conduct on the part of the employer.

Cases of psychological bullying might not necessarily get off the ground in terms of a complaint because they require WorkCover inspectors to come in and ask questions about the workplace, and most people are not prepared to say how toxic it is or acknowledge that a colleague is being bullied. Often, people don't understand mental stress or emotional disturbance and view it as a sign of weakness.

When a WorkCover claim is lodged, the worker has to attend a psychiatric examination. WorkCover psychiatrists base their judgements on only one interview lasting between 35 and 60 minutes, which is not enough time to assess the worker properly. It is difficult for victims to get across their case within the allotted time. They may be unable to pinpoint where the bullying started and finished and incidents that were of major significance to them may sound trivial, but it is the repetition of such incidents, day after day, that wears individuals down.

The psychiatrists are given information (usually employer generated and insurer generated, such as WorkCover investigation statements) and required to answer certain questions, for example, whether employment was a significant contributing factor to the person's illness and whether the person really is sick. I often see reports from insurers that say something like, 'This person has a significant depression. If you believe the worker, employment is a considerable contributory factor. However, amongst the material given to me there is a substantial number of statements from people within the organisation stating that what the worker is complaining about did not happen. If that is the case, employment would not be a significant contributory factor.'

Other times a person may have a background of emotional problems, and the psychiatrist tries to blame those earlier life experiences, rather than any employment-related contributing factor, for the worker's current poor state of health. A psychiatrist, psychologist or GP who has had many sessions with the victim is in a much better position to evaluate the effect of bullying and harassment on that person, particularly if there has been a sudden deterioration in their mental, emotional or physical health. It may take them some time to understand the cause because victims are often reluctant to divulge the cause of their poor health.

What I tell people who consult me early in the process is to put everything in writing — for example, if a person makes an unreasonable demand during the day, make sure you confirm that in writing and send it back to them. Record every incident and keep a file. Unfortunately, most victims do not make notes in the early stages of bullying because they may not understand *why* the abuse is happening, or may be in denial. Bullies have difficulty with paper trails because their abuse can be easily exposed if accurate records are kept.

Education and training are the keys to preventing bullying, and this education should include awareness that people can be pushed over the edge very easily. I don't think bullies expect really poor outcomes. They have no scruples about making the person sick to get rid of them but I am sure they would have a great deal of guilt and remorse if that person took his own life or abandoned his wife and three children as a direct result of the bullying. Some of my cases have ended in suicide or attempted suicide, which I think may have been cries for help, desperate attempts to jolt people into awareness of their suffering, to teach the bully a lesson, because the only power they had left was to make the bully suffer. That is the ultimate revenge, leaving the bully with lifelong guilt.

I do not understand how bullies survive as long as they do in workplaces. Unfortunately, they are often managing directors of companies, people in positions of substantial authority, who are seen as aggressive, achieving go-getters and, because organisations have gone from strength to strength under their management, no one stands in their way.

There should be substantial education in workplaces that alerts individuals to outcomes of bullying. At a minimum, bullies should be retrained and given an understanding that their behaviour is totally unacceptable, and mechanisms put in place to prevent them from doing what they have been doing. I think that bullies (and here I am taking the stance of clients who have been badly affected) ought to be punished, perhaps by taking away some of their power or responsibility, or some of their direct supervision of, or interaction with, other staff, so that neither they nor other individuals are exposed again to the kind of situation that could instigate further bullying. Such actions on the part of employers will make victims feel as though their injury has been recognised.

Employers must be vicariously responsible for bullying in their workplaces, particularly if they have a bully who has not been counselled once the bullying becomes apparent. I find it difficult to believe that bullying can be so subtle that employers are unaware of it. Education is necessary at all levels of employment to ensure that people are aware of certain behaviours that may indicate bullying, for example, a manager repeatedly complaining about one particular employee may need investigating to check the validity of the complaints.

Workplace bullying has become a very significant cost to government. Perhaps there should be some kind of independent bullying board or authority that protects victims so that, in making a complaint and having their situation investigated, there can be no reprisal on the part of the employer to terminate. I realise this is an ideal, and probably not practical, because there will be cases where a person's job performance really is inadequate, with termination the only solution.

In bullying cases you have to demonstrate that the systems in place in the organisation are such that they are likely to be abused and likely to engender bullying. Mostly, there is a written workplace policy and procedure guide on bullying and harassment stating that workers will not do this or that, this behaviour is not acceptable, and so on, but nobody reads it or even knows where the policy is. If procedures have been broken, it is interesting how it suddenly becomes a tool for management to use to threaten or intimidate or counsel an individual. They say to a worker, 'You should have understood this, it's on page 32', or 'This was e-mailed to you on 23 July last year. Why in the world did you do this when you knew it was against company policy?' Again, it comes back to education and training. Of course, if a victim quotes the policy to management or points out where management has failed to follow proper procedure, they don't like the fact that you are standing up for yourself.

Victims want acknowledgment that the bullying did take place. They want the bullying to stop, the bully to be punished and the bully to understand what they went through. This does not usually happen unless there is some kind of legal redress, where the toxicity of the workplace and the whole pattern of abuse is revealed. That is a kind of acknowledgment and, though we can't know what the bully is thinking, at a minimum he or she would be very unsettled.

Escaping with dignity is the issue. I think the best outcome is to fight and win. For people who have been victimised, the most significant thing in terms of getting on with their lives is to be proved right, to have it acknowledged that they have been abused. The best form of treatment for most victims of bullying is to get back to work, obviously not in the same work environment but in an environment that is less pressured or intimidating.

Equity and justice professional

Jill Wood, Acting Superintendent, Equity and Diversity Unit, Victoria Police

We are certainly more aware of bullying behaviour in the Force. This does not necessarily mean that there has been an increase in bullying but is more likely because increased education, such as our push on equal opportunity, has increased awareness of what constitutes unacceptable behaviour. Our Human Resources area is currently working on a draft policy to cover bullying and occupational violence, with an anticipated commencement in 2002. We are aiming at a preventative rather than a complaints-based model, that is, one that protects our employees (including supervisors and managers) from bullying and foreseeable occupational violence from fellow employees, employers, clients and customers.

I'd interpret workplace bullying as repeated, unreasonable behaviour creating risk to employees. There is always a power imbalance, for example, lower ranks bullied by higher ranks. Workplace cultures can certainly encourage bullying, particularly where there are big power imbalances.

Although sexual harassment and racial discrimination should be treated as separate issues, there is some element of harassment in bullying. Some examples are:

- a person is picked on because he is different — he may be overweight or perhaps dresses differently — by work colleagues or his boss
- an unsworn staff member in the lowest ranks is continuously expected to do work not appropriate to their level
- a person is given a time-consuming job at 4.30 p.m. on a Friday afternoon and told to do it by the end of the day.

An example of psychological bullying is where a manager makes life difficult for subordinates on a daily basis. Though not necessarily a high-level manager, this person's area is critical to the running of the force; staff are seen as subordinates and the manager behaves like an absolute dictator. He knows he won't get any further in the organisation but has a certain degree of power at his current level and uses it inappropriately 'because he can'. Or the bullying may start because someone new and more competent starts work in his area.

Most of our bullying cases occur with the unsworn staff. Those that have occurred among sworn staff are caused by obvious differences, for example, a male officer with feminine characteristics will stand out in the macho police environment.

Bullying can occur between a probationary constable and a more senior officer. Younger recruits have grown up in a diverse population — it has always been part of their lives — so their attitudes represent a challenge for the entrenched culture. This younger mind-set is not yet a true reflection of the prevailing police culture, however, and can be threatening to police members who prefer the old ways. We receive some complaints from younger police officers about inappropriate name-calling and racial slurs by other police officers.

There should be separate procedures for dealing with psychological bullying cases. There is definitely a need for an anti-bullying policy, though it will only work if all levels are committed to stamping it out. Certainly there will be instances when, because of the 'mate' factor, the bully will merely receive a mild admonishment from a senior officer, such as, 'It might be a good idea to stop, mate.' Often, pressure will just cause the bullying to become more underhand and worse. There is an ingrained attitude in some managers. They will toe the party line but their attitudes remain unchanged.

There definitely needs to be more education to increase awareness of inappropriate bullying behaviours. At present unsworn managers are not really conscious of bullying as a concern. Because of Equal Opportunity and Equity and Diversity training, they are more aware of the need to treat people properly, and of possible problems with power imbalances. I think the really important thing with bullying training is to show *how it affects people*. One way to do this could be to use actors as part of the training process, to role-play the traumatic emotional impact.

By the time bullying is reported, the victim has usually been pushed to the absolute limit, has been victimised for a year or more and is at the end of their tether. They try to resolve it themselves, talk to colleagues, access strategies from the Internet, before they complain. They may be on sick leave, ready to quit the force and try to pick up the pieces.

Unsworn members have a code of practice that imposes warnings — one, two, three and out the door. Sworn members can be disciplined under the Police Regulation Act. They might be admonished and put on a two-year good behaviour bond. If there is a disciplinary hearing, the member could be fined, put on a bond or dismissed.

I am not sure that conciliation works in bullying situations. Bullies lack empathy, and often you can see from their defensive body language — folded arms, for example — that they do not accept that their actions were wrong.

There is no offence of bullying, no statute as there is with assault or indecent assault. We may be able to charge bullies with 'improper conduct' or 'likely to bring the force into disrepute', which is an offence under the Police Regulation Act. We are looking at ways of dealing with these issues.

We have not kept records of bullying incidents, so I can't give any statistics. However, we have noticed a definite increase in discrimination complaints over the past two years: 28 in 1999/00, 50 in 2000/01, and 23 in the short period from July to October 2001. This increase can be seen as positive as the message is getting across that any form of discrimination is totally unacceptable within the Victoria Police.

With our draft code, our Human Resources section, the Equity and Diversity Unit, and the Police Association will have input. We may circulate the draft for comment and ask for interested parties to form focus groups. The policy will cover both sworn and unsworn staff, though disciplinary measures will be dealt with separately.

I very much doubt if bullies can be re-educated. 'Once a bully, always a bully.' It is my experience that they have serious personality problems. They may be able to change on the surface, but underneath they have not altered at all. I tell staff, 'When you put on the blue uniform, leave your prejudices in the locker,' but how many are able to really do that?

I do not know personally of any incidents of pair bullying, though I am aware of cases where co-workers have ganged up on a victim — sometimes one very isolated person against twenty others — a soul-destroying situation.

Psychological bullying is very hard to prove because it often comes down to one person's word against another's. As soon as they become aware of what is happening, workers being victimised should document every occurrence, thinking back to the very first incident.

With regard to disciplinary measures, members who infringe the rules can be put on a Performance Improvement Plan, with provisos that they undergo training, show awareness of their misbehaviour and demonstrate that nothing similar will happen again. The problem is, of course, that they will be on their best behaviour for the required time and then revert to old behaviours as soon as their time is up.

We have a website where members are able to report problems. Ethical Standards has a members' hotline, and some reports are made to the Diversity Unit. We sometimes receive anonymous letters, and we always investigate the contents of these. Unsworn staff have the opportunity to report problems at their annual appraisals. Sworn staff have performance enhancement programs and individual workplaces/stations have local action plans and regional action plans. All managers now have to demonstrate a commitment to equal opportunity, and the same commitment will be expected with regard to bullying.

The Victoria Police is a unique organisation. The Equity and Diversity Unit conducts some investigations and others are conducted by the Ethical Standards Department. There is a review being done on the Unit and we are considering more use of external consultants for investigations. We have always found external conciliators to be very professional, with both parties ending up very happy with the result and, because the issues are dealt with immediately, there is no 'festering' of wounds.

The major focus of the code will be to encourage a healthy and functional workplace that provides a fair go for all. We want flexible work practices that impact on people, making them happy to come to work. To do this successfully will require wide-ranging education and commitment throughout the organisation. If it is to work, it must be embraced by all managers and have sanctions in place for non-compliance.

How we resolve a bullying complaint depends on what the complainant wants to do. If the accused is the person's manager, we would have to go above that manager to try to resolve the issue. We would interview all parties — the complainant, the accused and colleagues. Once the accusation has been proved, depending on the seriousness of the problem, the bullying manager might be removed. Most of these situations can be resolved quickly by local managers. If the behaviour is identified and continuing, we will take all steps possible to appropriately deal with the bully.

Human resource professional

Sophie, 33, Manager, Human Resources (manufacturing)

Our manufacturing company has a large and diverse workforce comprised of many different cultures and religions. We don't have a problem with psychological bullying. Any complaints we receive mostly relate to horseplay type behaviour on the shop floor, such as workers pushing, shoving or perhaps throwing parts at each other.

We don't have a specific bullying policy, but believe bullying is covered under our Diversity program, which promotes equal opportunity and aims to eliminate any form of harassment and discrimination, including any behaviour or conduct that is unwanted or unwelcome, such as jokes, threats, e-mail messages, embarrassing comments or approaches. We stress the importance of understanding that behaviour that one person finds acceptable could offend, humiliate or intimidate someone else. We also encourage staff who overhear or observe incidents of harassment to point out the unacceptable behaviour to the perpetrator or to report it.

We have a pro-active approach in that our aim is to eliminate harassment and bullying before it takes hold. The message, constantly reinforced, is: *If someone asks you to stop, you must stop.* Initially, we encourage the victim to challenge the bully, ask him or her to stop the behaviour, and warn the bully that, if the bullying does not stop, the victim can make a complaint.

We have enlisted staff on a voluntary basis to act as contact officers for harassed staff. Their role is purely to be the 'first points of contact', providing resource information and support; they are sounding boards only and do not try to resolve the problems or make decisions about disciplinary measures or work changes. Contact officers have to apply for the positions and we have specific selection criteria that include communication skills, empathy, sensitivity, an understanding of natural justice principles and a basic understanding of the appropriate legislation. We have regular network sessions with the contact officers.

Our Diversity program has a high profile in the company. We build up awareness through multilanguage messages in our in-house newsletters, posters displayed on noticeboards and discussion at team meetings. We distribute booklets that outline our policies and give the names of the contact officers who can give them confidential help regarding the company's complaints and resolution process.

We also conduct an annual anonymous employee survey that monitors such things as workload, stress and leadership. Once results are compiled, all supervisors, managers and heads receive specific feedback on their particular areas. This enables managers to compare results and measure them against previous years' surveys to note any obvious changes.

Complaints regarding employees paid on an hourly basis are handled in accordance with the collective bargaining agreement. Complaints regarding our salaried employees are handled by Human Resources in strict confidence, though it is never easy to contain these cases. We remind all interviewees that the conversation must remain confidential and that any breach may lead to disciplinary action.

Initially, if the behaviour continues after the worker complains, we will discuss the concern with the accused person, taking care not to make any judgements at that stage. If the situation is serious, or if the accuser requests it, we will separate the two people involved. We handle the investigation internally, ensuring that all the legislative guidelines are adhered to and everyone is treated fairly. We have very good relationships with the several unions that operate here and they are fully involved in complaints processes.

We genuinely believe our company is the best it can be. It is a very inclusive environment and our employees feel valued.

An investment in knowledge pays the best interest.

Benjamin Franklin

CONCLUSION

The main goal of the future is to stop violence. The world is addicted to it.

Bill Cosby

We issue a challenge to you, the reader, to evaluate your own behaviour at work. It doesn't matter whether you are a worker or in management. When you read Chapter 1, did you recognise any of the subtle abusive techniques used by bullies? Are they practised in your workplace, either by others or by you? Does your business exert pressure to work longer and harder?

Australia needs to get serious about stamping out workplace bullying. We must stop encouraging harsh management techniques and outlaw all abusive behaviours. Government needs to look at causal factors — deregulation, economic rationalism, the increase in casual and contract jobs, the downgrading of hospitals, universities and schools, and so on — then balance economic management against the needs of its citizens and commit to changes which would build a more cohesive, productive and compassionate society.

The flow-on effects of the cataclysmic terrorist attacks in the USA and the ensuing war have caused the already sluggish global economy to slow down even further. Australia now has to cope with the resultant major loss to tourism, the consequences of the Ansett collapse, the cost of asylum seekers. Overall, this will mean more company losses, more cost-reduction programs, more mass redundancies, more pressure on retained employees — the perfect climate for bullying to thrive — and so the cycle continues.

We acknowledge that employers are confronted with many issues and problems in this age of economic downturn, but they need to prioritise the wellbeing of their employees and rethink their costing strategies — when people have to do more with fewer resources, abusive behaviour escalates. Retrenchment, though effective as an immediate 'cost cutter', may cost more in the long term due to stress claims, increased WorkCover costs, and so on.

Both employers and workers need to change their attitudes and stop considering bullying to be a normal and acceptable behaviour in the workplace. Large businesses need to ensure that the competencies and ethics of their managers are above reproach.

Some Australian employers are doing their best to tackle this issue. Many, because there are few complaints, do not believe that they have a problem. Workplace harmony can be an illusion, however, with all sorts of problems bubbling beneath the surface.

We believe that psychological bullying should be treated separately and not 'lumped in' with violence, harassment and other diversity issues; it should be taken just as seriously as workplace violence and other occupational health and safety policies. Ideally, it should be stopped early with effective conciliation, with both bullies and victims treated with compassion. Every workplace should have an anti-bullying policy and demonstrate strict adherence to it. Where possible, there must be contact people appointed within the organisation who are available to give advice and support to victims. Reputations and businesses can be ruined by a false accusation, so investigators need to be consultative, flexible and non-judgemental to ensure that there are no misunderstandings; those accused of bullying must be considered innocent until proven guilty. The introduction by the Federal Government of Medicare rebates for therapy with psychologists, as there is for psychiatric therapy, would be of significant assistance to victims of bullying and other workplace stressors.

The bullying experience is different for everyone. Many factors shape the way we respond to trauma — our personalities, the degree of support received from families, friends and colleagues, cultural background, gender, age, emotional maturity and the amount of adversity life has thrown at us so far — and there is no perfect way to deal with it.

A concerted national awareness campaign would be a good start, with education implemented at both government and company levels to encourage reporting. The more workers — victims or witnesses — prepared to expose bullies, the more chance there is of action being taken and the abusive behaviour stopped.

Our politicians, sporting heroes and parents must set the standard and be prepared to act as role models, thus influencing children and the general public to consider bullying as unacceptable behaviour. Awareness is growing — SAINTS, a joint venture between the Victorian government and seven St Kilda footballers, is a program where the footballers visit schools to discuss bullying, using classroom activities and role-playing scenarios[82] — but there is so much more that could be done.

In an ideal world, we would love going to work. Our workplaces would be stimulating and exciting, our colleagues friendly and supportive. At worst, our workplaces would be tolerable because they are safe and we receive a regular salary. We should *never* be terrified of going to work, every day should *not* be an endurance test and we should not be left crippled emotionally, psychologically or physically by events that occur there.

The Australian workplace is going through a period of profound turmoil and change. In such a climate, workplace bullying will continue to rise and the cost, both financial and social, will be significant to Australian industry, workplaces, individuals, families and the general community. Our aims are to raise awareness of the magnitude of the problem, provide others with the necessary empowerment and survival skills to minimise the resultant stress and regain control of their lives, and encourage all workplaces in Australia to have specific and *workable* anti-bullying processes in place to protect both workers and employers. What Australia is facing now is an epidemic but, like AIDS, it is an epidemic we can control if the right measures are put in place.

I expect to pass through this life but once. If, therefore, there can be any kindness I can show, or any good thing that I can do to any fellow being, let me do it now as I shall not pass this way again.

William Penn

APPENDIX A

Australia: tackling workplace bullying

Australian States and Territories are obviously aware of the escalating problem and are at different levels in dealing with it. Research has been done at various universities, by unions and by government agencies. Community groups (such as the Queensland Working Women's Service and Victoria's Job Watch Inc.) are also working to address the problem. The Beyond Bullying Association promotes this issue through academic research, publications and conferences. Two State governments, Victoria and Queensland, require schools to have anti-bullying policies and to take appropriate action if bullying occurs. The ACTU campaign 'Being bossed around is bad for your health — the workplace is no place for bullying' in October 2000 attempted to raise awareness of the dangers of workplace bullying and its effects on individuals as well as businesses.

Under Australian Occupational Health and Safety legislation, employers have a duty of care to their employees to ensure their health, safety and welfare at work, which includes the necessity to protect them from harm from others. However, proving bullying under this legislation can be difficult.

Australian Capital Territory

In 2000, ACT WorkCover released *Guidance on Workplace Violence* and *Code of Practice for the ACT Sex Industry* (which has a small section on occupational violence).

Queensland

In 1998, the Division of Workplace Health and Safety (DETIR, Queensland) (with the ACTU, Queensland Chamber of Commerce and Industry, Queensland Working Women's Service) developed guidelines on workplace bullying entitled *An Employer's Guide — Workplace Bullying* and *A Worker's Guide — Workplace Bullying*. DETIR has also published *Violence at Work* (1999); *Bullying at Work* (1998); *Workplace Bullying: a Worker's Guide* (1998) and *Workplace Bullying: an Employer's Guide* (1998).

Griffith University's School of Management has a Workplace Bullying Project Team that has researched and published extensively on workplace bullying, organised international conferences in this area, been involved in the development of Queensland anti-bullying strategies and currently has a number of research projects in progress; they are able to assist with implementing and evaluating workplace anti-bullying policies on a collaborative basis.

In April 1999, Workplace Consulting Queensland held a conference, *A Practice You Can't Afford*, which included addresses from employers, unionists, psychologists, the Deptartment of Industrial Relations and the Anti-Discrimination Commission.

In 2000, the Queensland Working Women's Service produced *Risky Business*, a guide for employers on managing the risk of workplace bullying. In 2001 the Premier, Peter Beattie, announced the appointment of a Workplace Bullying Task Force to examine the issue, develop strategies to help prevent bullying in the workplace and make recommendations to government. This is the first initiative of this type in Australia.

New South Wales

WorkCover NSW has produced *Intervention Strategies for Your Business*; *Drugs, Alcohol and the Workplace* (1995), *Preventing Violence in the Accommodation Services of the Social and Community Services Industry* (1996) and *Violence Prevention for Taxi Drivers* (1996). With the National Children's and Youth Law Centre, they have developed fact sheets, some targeted at young people or apprentices, others developed for employers. *Workplace Violence Awareness: A Secure Workplace for Young Australians*; *Workplace Bullying: A Secure Workplace for Young Australians*; *Awareness; Legal Consequences* (for both employees and employers); *Intervention* (when occupational violence is identified or suspected); *Intervention Strategies for Your Business* (assistance in developing an occupational violence policy, model protocol and a model interview protocol); *Prevention* (practical steps) and *Prevention Strategies For Your Business* (provides assistance in developing an occupational violence policy). The National Children's and Youth Law Centre's website also provides legal information on various issues, including workplace bullying.

Also, NSW has drafted *OHS Regulation 2001*, the first regulation requiring employers to identify hazards associated with the potential for workplace violence, rather than relying on the general duty of care.

Northern Territory

The Northern Territory Work Health Authority has produced the following checklists for violence management and bullying for employers and workers: *Working From Home*; *A Violence Management Checklist*; *Violence in the Workplace*; *Bullying — Employer's Guide* and *Bullying — Worker's Guide*.

South Australia

The WorkCover Corporation, South Australia, provides a number of fact sheets, including *Guidelines for Reducing the Risk of Violence at Work*, which covers bullying; *Managing the Risks of Violence at Work in Aged Care Facilities* (1998); *Managing the Risks of Violence at Work in the Education Sector* (1998); *Managing the Risk of Violence at Work in Home and Community Based Care* (1998) and *Managing the Risks of Violence at Work in the Hospitality Industry*. In 1998, the Working Women's Centre of SA Inc published an 80 page report on Workplace Bullying.

South Australia's Employee Ombudsman was introduced as a means of handing employee grievances independent of government. The Ombudsman's functions include advising employees on their rights and obligations, and avenues for enforcing their rights under awards and enterprise agreements; the Ombudsman can investigate workplace bullying matters at the invitation of an employee. In 2000 the Office of the Employee Ombudsman produced a substantial guide to workplace bullying — *Bullies Not Wanted: A Guide to Recognising and Eliminating Bullying in the Workplace*.

In February 2002, the WorkCover Corporation and the South Australian Working Women's Centre held an international conference on workplace bullying, *Skills for Survival, Solutions and Strategies*.

Tasmania

Workplace Standards Tasmania has produced *Violence at the Workplace* (1998) and *Workplace Harassment* (1998), which are available on their website. They are also working on guidelines for developing a workplace bullying policy for employers and a publication for employees on dealing with workplace bullying.

The Tasmanian Anti-Discrimination Act of 1998 led the way in addressing bullying, with section 17(1) stating:

A person must not engage in any conduct which offends, humiliates, intimidates, insults or ridicules another person … in circumstances in which a reasonable person, having regard to all the circumstances, would have anticipated that the other person would be offended, humiliated, intimidated, insulted or ridiculed.

Victoria

The Victorian WorkCover Authority has produced a 'Workplace Bullies' poster and 'Help us Prosecute Workplace Bullies'. In 1998 an anti-bullying campaign was run.

In March 2001 the Victorian WorkCover Authority issued 'Issues Paper: Code of Practice for Prevention of Workplace Bullying', requesting comment from interested parties. After analysis of responses, a Code of Practice will be developed. The Code will provide guidance on the duties of employers and employees under the *Occupational Health and Safety Act 1985 (Vic.)* in relation to the prevention of bullying; it is to be launched in 2002.

Western Australia

In November 1999, Worksafe Western Australia introduced a Code of Practice on Workplace Violence that covers the concept of bullying. They have also produced *Work-Related Stress — Different Meanings To Different People* (has a section on workplace violence); *Code of Practice: The Safety and Health of Children and Young People in Workplaces*; *Violence in the Workplace* (1999); *Safety Essentials: A Guide to Work-Related Stress* (1996); *Safety and Health Solutions: Violence in the Workplace* (1996); *Violence in the Workplace: Information for Workplaces Where People may be Exposed to Physical Assault, Verbal Abuse, Threats or Intimidation* (pamphlet).

APPENDIX B

Australian laws relevant to workplace violence, harassment and discrimination

Commonwealth

Crimes (Family Violence) Act 1987

Human Rights and Equal Opportunities Commission Act 1986

Racial Discrimination Act 1975 (includes the *Racial Hatred Act 1995*)

Sex Discrimination Act 1984

Disability Discrimination Act 1992

Workplace Relations Act 1996

Occupational Health and Safety (Commonwealth Employment) Act 1991

Australian Capital Territory

Discrimination Act 1991

New South Wales

Anti Discrimination Act 1977

Northern Territory

Anti Discrimination Act 1992

Queensland

Queensland Criminal Code
Anti Discrimination Act 1991
WorkCover Queensland Act 1996
Workplace Health and Safety Act 1995
Industrial Relations Act 1999
Training and Employment Act 2000

South Australia

Sex Discrimination Act 1975
Handicapped Person Equal Opportunity Act 1981
Equal Opportunity Act 1984
Occupational Health and Safety Act 1994
Industrial and Employee Relations Act 1994

Tasmania

Sex Discrimination Act 1994
Anti Discrimination Act 1998

Victoria

Equal Opportunity Act 1977
Equal Opportunity Act 1995

Western Australia

Equal Opportunities Act 1984

APPENDIX C

Where to get help

Australia-wide

ACTU MEMBER CONNECT
(for referral to a union)
1300 362 223
1300 365 205 — Ansett hotline

ACTU WEBSITE
www.actu.asn.au

AUSTRALIAN INDUSTRIAL RELATIONS COMMISSION
(for unfair dismissal applications)
(03) 8661 7777

CENTRELINK
www.centrelink.gov.au

DEPARTMENT OF EMPLOYMENT, WORKPLACE RELATIONS & SMALL BUSINESS
www.dewrsb.gov.au

FEDERATION OF COMMUNITY LEGAL CENTRES
(for referral to your closest community legal centre)
1st Floor, 212 King Street
(03) 9602 4949

HUMAN RIGHTS AND EQUAL OPPORTUNITY COMMISSION
GPO Box 5218, Sydney 1042
Complaints line: 1300 656 419
General enquiries and publications:
1300 369 711

NATIONAL ASSOCIATION OF COMMUNITY LEGAL CENTRES
(02) 9264 9595

NATIONAL OCCUPATIONAL HEALTH AND SAFETY COMMISSION
www.nohsc.gov.au

AUSTRALIAN COUNCIL OF TRADE UNIONS
ACTU helpline 1300 362 223
www.actu.asn.au

WHISTLEBLOWERS AUSTRALIA INC.
www.whistleblowers.org.au

WORKING WOMEN'S CENTRES
www.wwc.org.au

Australian Capital Territory

ACT WorkCover
www.workcover.act.gov.au

Care Financial Counselling Service
(02) 6257 1788

Women's Legal Service (ACT and region)
GPO Box 1726, Canberra 2601
Advice line Monday to Friday 9.30–12 noon
(02) 6257 4499 or
toll-free: 1800 634 669

Queensland

Financial Counsellors Association (Qld)
(07) 3029 3622

Financial Counselling Services (Qld)
(07) 3257 1957

Griffith University School of Management
Workplace Bullying Project Team
e-mail: M.Sheehan@mailbox.qu.edu.au or
P.McCarthy@mailbox.qu.edu.au

Queensland Association of Independent Legal Service (QAILS)
(07) 3229 8749

Queensland Division of Workplace Health and Safety
GPO Box 69, Brisbane 4001
www.detir.qld.gov.au/hs/hs.htm

Queensland Equal Opportunity Commission
www.adcq.qld.gov.au

Queensland Working Women's Service Inc.
www.2.eis.net.au/~qwws

West End Counselling Centre
(07) 3844 5304

Women's Legal Centre
(07) 3392 0670 or
1800 677 278 (country freecall)

WorkCover Queensland
GPO Box 2459, Brisbane 4001
e-mail:info@workcoverqld.com.au
www.workcover.qld.gov.au

Working Women's Service
Suite 104, Level 1, 303 Adelaide Street,
Brisbane 4000
(07) 3224 6115
toll-free: 1800 621 458
fax: (07) 3224 6111
e-mail: qwwc@eis.net.au

New South Wales

Credit Line
(02) 9951 5544 or 1800 808 488
(country freecall)

Financial Counselling Association (NSW)
(02) 9858 1377

Legal Services Commissioner
(02) 9377 1800

NSW Department of Industrial Relations
www.lawlink.nsw.gov.au/adb

NSW Equal Opportunity Commission
www.dir.nsw.gov.au

Women's Legal Resources Centre
(02) 9637 4597 or
1800 801 501 (country freecall)

WorkCover NSW
GPO Box 5364, Sydney 2001
(02) 9370 5000
e-mail: contact@workcover.nsw.gov.au
www.workcover.nsw.gov.au

Working Women's Centre
Suites 1–4, 1 Barrack Lane, Parramatta 2150
(02) 9689 2233, toll-free: 1800 062 166
fax: (02) 9689 2841
e-mail: working_womens@fcl.fl.asn.au

Northern Territory

ANGLICARE
(08) 8948 2700

CENTRAL AUSTRALIAN WOMEN'S
LEGAL SERVICE
(08) 8952 4055

DARWIN COMMUNITY LEGAL SERVICE
(08) 8941 3394

NORTHERN TERRITORY EQUAL OPPORTUNITY
COMMISSION
www.nt.gov.au/adc

TOP END WOMEN'S LEGAL SERVICE
(08) 8941 9989

WORK HEALTH AUTHORITY
Minerals House, 66 The Esplanade, Darwin 2600
1800 019 115

WORKING WOMEN'S CENTRE
GPO Box 403, Darwin 0801
(08) 8981 0655
toll-free: 1800 817 055
fax: (08) 8981 0433
e-mail: wwcnt@octa4.net.au

South Australia

COMMISSION FOR EQUAL OPPORTUNITY (SA)
e-mail: eocsa@dove.net.au
www/eoc.sa.gov.au

EMPLOYEE ADVOCATE UNIT (WORKCOVER SA)
www.workcover.com/workers/woreau.html

OFFICE OF THE EMPLOYEE OMBUDSMAN, SA
www.employeeombudsman.sa.gov.au

SOUTH AUSTRALIAN COUNCIL OF COMMUNITY
LEGAL CENTRES
(08) 8362 1199

SOUTH AUSTRALIAN FINANCIAL COUNSELLING
ASSOCIATION
(08) 8362 1199

WOMEN'S LEGAL SERVICE
(08) 8221 5553 or 1800 816 349

WORKCOVER CORPORATION
GPO Box 2668, Adelaide 5001
13 18 55
e-mail: info@workcover.com
www.workcover.sa.gov.au

WORKING WOMEN'S CENTRE
PO Box 8066, Station Arcade, Adelaide 5000
(08) 8410 6499, toll-free: 1800 652 697
fax: (08) 8410 6770
e-mail: wwcsa@camtech.net.au
www.wwc.org.au

WORKPLACE INFORMATION SERVICE
1300 365 255
e-mail: wisinfo@eric.sa.gov.au

Tasmania

ANGLICARE FINANCIAL COUNSELLING SERVICE
(HOBART)
(03) 6224 3510

ANGLICARE FINANCIAL COUNSELLING SERVICE
(LAUNCESTON)
(03) 6223 4595

HOBART COMMUNITY LEGAL SERVICE/WOMEN'S
LEGAL SERVICE
(03) 6223 2500 or 1800 682 468
(country freecall)

LAUNCESTON COMMUNITY LEGAL CENTRE
(03) 6334 1577 or 1800 066 019
(country freecall)

WORKING WOMEN'S CENTRE
160 Harrington Street, Hobart 7000
(03) 6234 7007, toll-free: 1800 644 589
fax: (03) 6234 3219
e-mail: wwctas@trump.net.au

WORKPLACE STANDARDS TASMANIA
30 Gordons Hill Road, Rosny Park 7018
1300 366 322
e-mail: info@wsa.tas.gov.au
www.wsa.tas.gov.au

Victoria

CREDIT HELPLINE (VIC) LTD
(03) 9602 3800 or 1800 803 800

EQUAL OPPORTUNITY COMMISSION OF VICTORIA
(03) 9281 7111 (9281 7100?) or 1800 134 142;
for hearing impaired (03) 9281 7110

FEDERATION OF COMMUNITY LEGAL SERVICES
(03) 9602 4949

INDUSTRIAL RELATIONS COMMISSION
(03) 8661 7777

JOB WATCH
(for free advice on workplace bullying and violence)
(03) 9662 1933 or 1800 331 617
fax (03) 9633 2024 or
www.job-watch.org.au
(Job Watch is a legal advice centre helping
employees with issues at work, including unfair
dismissal, bullying, workplace violence, sexual
harassment and discrimination.)

LEGAL AID COMMISSION OF VICTORIA
(03) 9269 0234

VICTORIAN EQUAL OPPORTUNITY COMMISSION
www.eoc.vic.gov.au

VICTORIAN STATE GOVERNMENT
www.eduweb.vic.gov.au/bullying

**VICTORIAN EMPLOYERS' CHAMBER OF COMMERCE
AND INDUSTRY**
(for advice and assistance regarding workplace
bullying, harassment, violence and OHS)
(03) 9251 4333

VICTORIAN TRADES HALL COUNCIL
www.vthc.org.au/workcover/index.html —
for issues related to WorkCover in Victoria

WORKCOVER AUTHORITY
222 Exhibition Street, Melbourne 3000
(03) 9641 1444
toll-free 1800 136 089
fax: (03) 9641 1353
e-mail: info@workcover.vic.gov.au
website: www.workcover.vic.gov.au

WORKCOVER CONCILIATION SERVICE
(03) 9628 1111
toll-free 1800 810 071
fax: (03) 9628 1000

WOMEN'S LEGAL RESOURCE GROUP
(03) 9642 0343 or 1800 133 302

Western Australia

CONCILIATION AND REVIEW DIRECTORATE
15 Rheola Street, West Perth 6005
(08) 9324 6666
country calls 1800 633 108
fax: (08) 9324 6600

**FINANCIAL COUNSELLORS RESOURCE PROJECT OF
WESTERN AUSTRALIA**
(08) 9221 2411

GOSNELLS COMMUNITY LEGAL SERVICE
(08) 9398 1466

LEGAL AID
(09) 261 6200 (1–5 p.m. weekdays),
country calls: 1800 809 616

**WESTERN AUSTRALIAN EQUAL
OPPORTUNITY COMMISSION**
www.equalopportunity.wa.gov.au

WORKCOVER WA
2 Bedbrook Place, Shenton Park 6008
(08) 9388 5603, country calls 1800 670 055,
hearing impaired: TTY (08) 9388 5537
fax: (08) 9388 5550
e-mail: postmaster@workcover.wa.gov.au
www.workcover.wa.gov.au

WORKING WOMEN'S CENTRE
PO Box 25380, St Georges Terrace, Perth 6831
(08) 9221 5122
toll-free: 1800 625 122
fax: (08) 9221 5922
TTY: (08) 9221 5410
e-mail: wls@panorama.net.au

WORKSAFE WA
1260 Hay Street, West Perth 6005
www.safetyline.wa.gov.au

Other websites

BEYOND BULLYING ASSOCIATION INC.
P.O. Box 196, Nathan 4111
www.davdig.com/bba

BULLIES DOWN UNDER
www.caitrin.mtx.net
Website of (SAEBOW) South Australian
Employees Bullied Out of Work
P.O. Box 488, Salisbury 5108
phone and fax: 61 8 8250 0388
e-mail: caitrin@dove.net.au

BULLYBUSTERS
www.bullybusters.org

BULLYDISSOLVER
www.bullydissolver.com
UK website providing information and support
for teachers and spouses of bullied workers.

BULLY ONLINE
www.successunlimited.co.uk
Website of the UK National Workplace Bullying
Advice Line

FOUNDATION FOR THE STUDY OF WORK TRAUMA
www.cw.co.za/tammun/foundation/default.htm

THE BUSINESS RESEARCH LAB
www.busreslab.com/policies/badpol7.htm
Advice for employers who wish to ensure a bully-
free work culture.

WORKPLACE BULLYING, STRESS, EMPLOYMENT
LAW AND YOU
www.workplacebullying.co.uk/index.html

WORK SHOULDN'T HURT
www.stop-the-violence.netfirms.com/about.html

APPENDIX D

Human Synergistics information sheet

For more than 25 years Human Synergistics Integrated Development System has produced well-documented growth in individuals, groups and whole organisations. Human behaviour is caused as surely as is any natural phenomenon. Identifying the cause of behaviour goes beyond simply describing behaviour. Changing the cause of behaviour is far more impactful than trying to deal with the effects.

The Integrated Development System is comprised of diagnostic assessment instruments designed to identify causes for behaviour among individuals, groups and organisations in order to improve the way they think, interact and work together.

The heart of the system is the Circumplex, a circular graph that measures twelve distinctive styles of thinking and behaviour. Some styles are positive and supportive of constructive interpersonal relationships, effective problem solving and personal growth, while others are dysfunctional and can lead to unnecessary conflict, dissatisfaction and symptoms of strain.

This common language and theme links all organisational levels by tying individual and team performance to organisational effectiveness in a measureable way.

'Figure A' provides a summary of the characteristics of the twelve behavioural styles measured on the Circumplex. The manner in which people believe they are expected to behave and actually behave in organisations has a significant impact on the way they think, interact and work together.

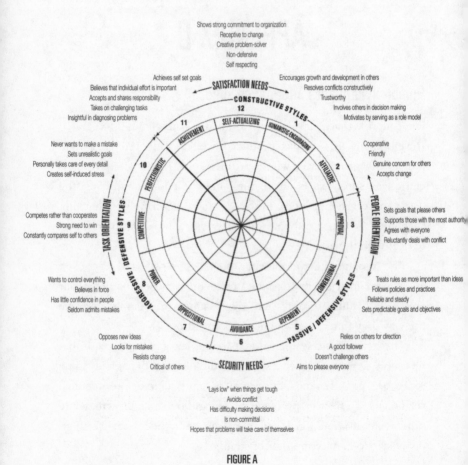

FIGURE A

Example A: Harassment and defensive behaviour

Using the Organisational Culture Inventory to measure their current behavioral expectations one organisation asked the following question: *To what extent does harassment occur in this organisation?* Sixty-seven per cent of respondents believed that harassment occurs to a great or very great extent. The behavioural expectations of these respondents are shown on the Circumplex in 'Figure B'.

The respondents experience an organisation characterised by arrogance, bullying and punitive actions, one where people are inactive and fearful. They believe they are expected to do whatever it takes to please others, stay unseen and avoid conflict. At the same time, they believe that they are expected to be critical and negative or risk being perceived as incompetent or weak. There is little expectation that people enjoy their work, achieve good results, cooperate with each other or help and support one another.

For this organisation addressing and changing the behavioral expectations is the most effective means to address the issue of harassment.

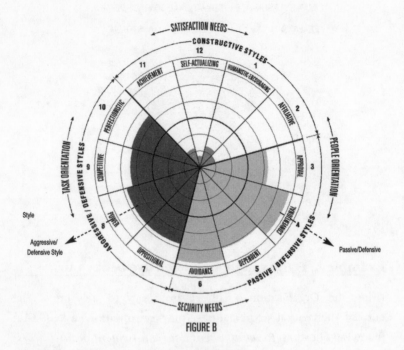

FIGURE B

Example B: individual assessment

Human Synergistics research demonstrates that the behaviour of leaders in an organisation are the key drivers of the way that people interact and work together.

The Circumplex in Figure C shows the behaviours of an individual manager. Using the Lifestyles Inventory to measure the impact of an individual's behavior on others this manager's results show a highly constructive style of effective leadership.

In summary, this manager works with people to deliver excellent results, supports and encourages others' growth and development, maintains their integrity and promotes and encourages diversity.

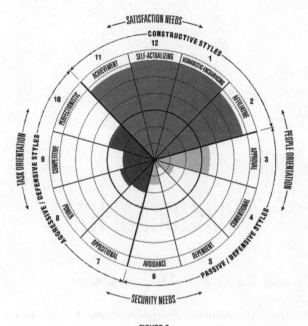

FIGURE C

BIBLIOGRAPHY

ACTU worksite: http://worksite.actu.asn.au. Fact Sheets Article No: 27 —
   'Stress'.

Allen, Felicity. 1998. *Health Psychology: Theory and Practice*. Allen &
   Unwin: Sydney.

Auw, André. 1991. *Gentle Roads to Survival: Making Self-Healing Choices
   in Difficult Circumstances*. Asian Publishing: Lower Lake, CA.

Beyond Bullying Association Inc. Homepage http://www.davdig.com/bba/

Bird, Stephen and McClure, B. Joan. 2000. *Junior Drug Awareness: Prozac
   & Other Antidepressants*. Chelsea House Publishers, Philadelphia.

Bully Down Under: Website of SAEBOW (South Australian Employees
   Bullied Out of Work) Help/Information Line.

Bully OnLine: Website of the UK National Workplace Bullying Advice Line.

Cotton, Peter (ed.). 1996. *Psychological Health In the Workplace:
   Understanding & Managing Occupational Stress*. Australian
   Psychological Society.

Department of the Premier and Cabinet (Qld). Ministerial Media Statement,
   3 June 2001, The Hon. Peter Beattie MP, 'New taskforce to examine
   workplace bullying'.

Division of Workplace Health and Safety (Qld). 1998a. 'Workplace bullying:
   An employer's guide.' Brisbane, Australia: Department of
   Employment, Training and Industrial Relations.

Division of Workplace Health and Safety (Qld). 1998b. 'Workplace bullying:
   A worker's guide.' Brisbane, Australia: Department of Employment,
   Training and Industrial Relations.

Field, Evelyn M. 1999. *Bully Busting: How to help children deal with teasing and bullying*. Finch Publishing: Sydney.

Goleman, Daniel. 1995. *Emotional Intelligence*. Bloomsbury: London.

Job Watch Discussion Paper. 'Bullies, media and the law'. http://home.vicnet.net.au/~jobwatch/

Kieseker, R. and Marchant, T. 1998. 'Workplace Bullying in Australia: A review of current conceptualisations and existing research.' Review Paper, Queensland State Government (Queensland Treasury).

Kirner, Joan and Raynor, Moira. 1999. *The Women's Power Handbook*. Viking: Melbourne.

Linn, Dennis and Linn, Matthew. 1978. *Healing Life's Hurts: Healing Memories Through Five Stages of Forgiveness*. Paulist Press: New York.

Marais, S. and Herman, M. 1997. *Corporate Hyenas at Work: How to Spot and Outwit Them by Being Hyenawise*. Pretoria, South Africa: Kasigo.

Marcus, Norman J. and Arbeiter, Jean S. 1995. *Freedom from Pain*. Fireside: Simon and Schuster.

McPhee, Cosima (ed.). 2000. *The Law Handbook 2000: Your Practical Guide to the Law in Victoria*. Fitzroy Legal Service.

Namie, Gary and Namie, Ruth. 2000. *The Bully at Work*. Sourcebooks: Naperville, Illinois.

Office of the Employee Ombudsman. 2000. *Bullies Not Wanted: Recognising and Eliminating Bullying in the Workplace*. Adelaide, South Australia.

Peiffer, Vera. 1996. *Principles of Hypnotherapy*. Thorsons: HarperCollins.

Pocock, B., van Wanrooy, B., Strazzari, S. and Bridge, K. 2001. 'Fifty Families: What unreasonable hours do to Australians, their families and their communities.' A report commissioned by the Australian Council of Trade Unions (ACTU).

Queensland Government. 2001. Workplace Bullying Issues Paper, Queensland Workplace Bullying Taskforce.

Queensland Working Women's Service (QWWS). (2000). 'Risky business: A useful publication for employers preventing and resolving workplace bullying'. Brisbane.

Sripathy, V. and Ogle, L. (eds). 1998. *The Law Handbook: Your Practical Guide to the Law in New South Wales* (6th edn). Redfern Legal Centre.

Swede, Shirley and Jaffe, Seymour Sheppard. 2000. *The Panic Attack Recovery Book*. New American Library: Penguin Books.

Victoria Legal Aid, Villamanta Legal Service and Disability Discrimination Legal Service. 2000. *Using Disability Discrimination Law: A Booklet for People Who Have a Disability*.

Victorian Government website www.eduweb.vic.gov.au/bullying/index.htm

Victorian Government. November 2000. Restoring Common Law Rights, Legislative Information Kit.

Victorian WorkCover Authority. 1999. 'All about WorkCover for Employers'.

Victorian WorkCover Authority. 1999. 'All about WorkCover for Workers'.

Victorian WorkCover Authority. March 2001. Issues Paper: Code of Practice for Prevention of Workplace Bullying.

Yeates, Nigel. 'Bullying in the Workplace: A Study of Victimisation'. http://www.sufpolfed.co.uk

Yogendra, Vijayadev. 1994. *Overcoming Negative Feelings: A Way Out of Poor Self-Esteem Guilt Anger Fear and Tiredness.* Foundation Press: Brisbane.

ENDNOTES

1   Morgan poll. 9 June 1998.
2   Source: Victorian WorkCover Authority Issues Paper: *Code of Practice for Prevention of Workplace Bullying*, March 2001, p. 8.
3   Chloe Saltau. 'Australia's "entrenched" bullying declared a health risk', *Age*, 27 September 2001.
4   Source: Victorian WorkCover Authority Issues Paper: *Code of Practice for Prevention of Workplace Bullying*, March 2001, p. 5.
5   Katie Lapthorne. 'In a rush to rage', *Sunday Herald-Sun*, 22 July 2001.
6   M. Rayner 'Considering the issues — practical solutions for the workplace'. Paper presented at Monash University seminar: *Workplace Equity and the New Millennium*. 1999.
7   'Staff set fire to apprentice', *Herald–Sun,* 28 June 1996; 'Sentence sets the tortured apprentice free for life', *Sunday Age*, 9 February 1997.
8   See Appendix B for outline of relevant Commonwealth and State legislation.
9   International Labor Organization, 'Violence on the job — a global problem.' Press release. Geneva: 20 July 1998. Quoted in Discussion Paper, 'The Distinction Between Workplace Bullying and Workplace Violence and the Ramifications for Occupational Health and Safety,' November 1998.
10 Hon. Peter Beattie MP, Queensland Government Ministerial Media Statement, 'New taskforce to examine workplace bullying', 3 June 2001.
11 'Youth fights back against bullies', *Herald–Sun* 10 March 1997; 'Work-prank terror', *Herald–Sun*, 7 April 1998; 'Hospital workers fear for their safety', *Age*, 14 July 2001; 'Blackboard jungle: help for teachers under attack', *Sunday Age*, 4 November 2001.
12 Bullying Facts and Figures, Beyond Bullying Association Inc., http://cwpp.siq.qld.gov.au/bba/
13 'Issues Paper: Code of Practice for Prevention of Workplace Bullying', Victorian WorkCover Authority, March 2001, p. 5.

14 Pamela Harris. 'Cruelty Amid the Caring', *Advertiser*, 18 October 2000.

15 Steve Dow and Larry Schwartz. 'Crisis of faith', *Age*, 28 October 2001.

16 'Issues Paper: Code of Practice for Prevention of Workplace Bullying', Victorian WorkCover Authority, March 2001, p. 25.

17 'Ignoring bullies does nothing for their victims says Jocelynne Scutt, Tasmania's Anti-Discrimination Commissioner.' *Australian*, 16 May 2000.

18 Erica Cervini. 'Blackboard jungle: help for teachers under attack', *Sunday Age*, 4 November 2001.

19 Don Woolford and Emily Osborne, 'Nurses tell of Hospital Bullying', *Advertiser*, 17 October 2000; 'Troubled nurses' (report of ACTU survey results), Health watch, 22 October 2000. (http://healthcare.monster.com.au/healthwatch)

20 'Issues Paper: Code of Practice for Prevention of Workplace Bullying', Victorian WorkCover Authority, March 2001, p. 9.

21 K. Blenner-Hassett v. Murray Goulburn Co-operative Ltd & Ors, County Court Victoria, 2651/96 (currently subject to appeal), cited in 'Issues Paper: Code of Practice for Prevention of Workplace Bullying', Victorian WorkCover Authority, March 2001, p. 1.

22 Midwest Radio Ltd v. M.A. Arnold (1999) Queensland Court of Appeal, QCA 20, cited in 'Issues Paper: Code of Practice for Prevention of Workplace Bullying', Victorian WorkCover Authority, March 2001, p. 1.

23 Carlisle v. Council of the Shire of Kilkvan and Breitkreutz, Queensland District Court, 12 of 1992, cited in 'Issues Paper: Code of Practice for Prevention of Workplace Bullying', Victorian WorkCover Authority, March 2001, p. 1.

24 Gary and Ruth Namie. *The Bully at Work.* Sourcebooks: Naperville, Illinois, 2000, p. 23.

25 ibid, p. 30.

26 S. Marais, S. and M. Herman. *Corporate Hyenas at Work: How to Spot and Outwit Them by Being Hyenawise.* Kasigo: Pretoria, South Africa, 1997.

27 Tim Field. *Bully OnLine,* website of the UK National Workplace Bullying Advice Line.

28 Tim Field, quoted in Hilary Freeman. 'Psycho bosses on the loose.' *Guardian,* 10 March 2001.

29 Melissa Fyfe. 'Spot the Psycho: A game all the office can play.' *Age,* 25 August 2000.

30 Freeman, Hilary, op.cit.

31 Jennifer Verrall. 'Laying down the law on long hours,' *Age,* 20 October 2001.

32 Michael Winkler. 'The downside of up-selling in today's market', *Age,* 17 November 2001.

33 This can, of course, be a legitimate management tool to monitor performance if done with the knowledge and agreement of the worker.

34 'Call Centre Staff Under Extraordinary Pressure.' http://www.actu.asn.au/national/media/media00/20000727call.htm. 27 July 2000.

35 'Facing the Music'. ABC 2, 15 September 2001.

36 Bully OnLine, website of the UK National Workplace Bullying Advice Line.

37 Simon English. 'Course softens up bully women,' *Age,* 7 August 2001.

38 Nigel Yeates. 'Bullying in the Workplace: A Study of Victimisation'. http://www.sufpolfed.co.uk

39 Melissa Fyfe. 'The devil's disciples: inside the mind of a serial killer'. *Sunday Age*, 29 July 2001.

40 Stephanie Dowrick. 'Empathy saves lives', 'Good Weekend', *Age*, 21 July 2001.

41 Evelyn M. Field. *Bully Busting: How to help children deal with teasing and bullying*. Finch Publishing: Sydney, 1999, p. 9.

42 ibid.

43 Daniel Goleman. *Emotional Intelligence*. Bloomsbury: London, 1995.

44 Nigel Yeates. op.cit.

45 Kathy Evans. 'The source of all evil', 'Sunday Life', *Sunday Age*, 21 October 2001.

46 ibid.

47 Mary Macleod of the UK's National Family and Parenting Association, quoted in Kate Figes, 'Slap Happy', 'Sunday Life', *Sunday Age*, 7 October 2001.

48 ibid.

49 Kathy Evans. 'The source of all evil', 'Sunday Life', *Sunday Age*, 21 October 2001.

50 Peter O'Connor. 'Workplace woes', 'Good Weekend', *Age*, 6 October 2001.

51 Kim Treasure. 'Bullying of councillors 'worse than in the playground'', *Illawarra Mercury*, 9 April 2001.

52 R. Kieseker, R. and T. Marchant. 'Workplace Bullying in Australia: A Review of Current Conceptualisations and Existing Research', Review Paper, Queensland State Government (Queensland Treasury), 1998, p. 5, using data from Alderman 1997; Beasley & Rayner 1997; Hindell 1997; MacLeod 1996; Mendelson 1990; Overell 1995; *Queensland Nurse* 1998; Spiers 1996.

53 Bullying Facts & Figures, p. 1, Beyond Bullying Association Inc. Homepage: http://www.davdig.com/bba/

54 Paul Robinson. 'A Tale of Torment by "Toxic Management"', *Age*, 17 October 2000.

55 Hon. Peter Beattie MP, Queensland Government Ministerial Media Statement, 'New taskforce to examine workplace bullying', 3 June 2001.

56 Dr Michael Sheehan, Griffith University management researcher, quoted in *Age*, 4 September 2001.

57 Hon. Peter Beattie MP, Queensland Government Ministerial Media Statement, 'New taskforce to examine workplace bullying', 3 June 2001.

58 Queensland Government. 2001. *Workplace Bullying Issues Paper*, Queensland Workplace Bullying Taskforce, p. 14.

59 http://psychiatry.medscape.com/IMNG/ClinPsychNews/2000/v28.n05/cpn2805.38.01.html

60 Mark Phillips. 'Casual work a trap', *Herald-Sun*, 22 August 2001.

61 Melbourne Institute and the Committee for Economic Development of Australia report, 'Downsizing: is it working for Australia?', quoted in Editorial, *Sunday Age*, 5 August 2001.

62 *Age* magazine 'Good Weekend', 27 October 2001 (statistic obtained from John S. Croucher, Professor of Statistics, Macquarie University).

63 *Australian*, 16 February 2001, p. 31, quoted in 'Issues Paper: Code of Practice for Prevention of Workplace Bullying', Victorian WorkCover Authority, March 2001.

64 Pamela Harris. 'Cruelty Amid the Caring', *Advertiser*, 18 October 2000.

65 M. Brown. Letter to *Education Age*, August 2001.

66 Amanda Dunn. 'Welfare concerns', *Education Age*, 22 August 2001.

67 Kim Treasure. 'Bullying of councillors "worse than in playground"', *Illawarra Mercury*, 9 April 2001.

68 Carl Marsich. Submission by Community and Public Sector Union — SPSF Group Victorian Branch, on the Victorian WorkCover Authority Issues Paper for the 'Code of Practice for Prevention of Workplace Bullying'.

69   Gary and Ruth Namie. *The Bully at Work*. Sourcebooks: Naperville, Illinois, 2000, p. 85.

70   s.170CE of the Workplace Relations Act.

71   Anti-Discrimination Commissioner for Tasmania, Dr Jocelynne Scutt, 'Definitive Moments — Capturing the Politics of Bullying', opening paper at conference 'It's Time to Make a Stand — Workplace Bullying, Schoolyard Bullying, Unacceptable Behaviour', Hobart, 16–18 October 2000.

72   ACTU website, 'Union Membership and the Workforce', 9 May 2001.

73   Michael Burge. Chair's Report, The Australian Psychological Society, *Victorian State Newsletter*, March 2001.

74   s.170CE of the Workplace Relations Act.

75   Queensland Government, *Workplace Bullying Issues Paper*, Queensland Workplace Bullying Taskforce, September 2001, p. 34.

76   Robert Hare, PhD, 'Treatment for psychopaths is likely to make them worse'. http://psychiatry.medscape.com/IMNG/ClinPsych/News/2000/v28.n05/cpn280 5.38.02.html

77   VicHealth chief executive officer Dr Rob Moodie quoted in 'Words can carry a punch' by Tanya Taylor, *Herald-Sun*, 11 July 2001.

78   Table based on the Elisabeth Kubler-Ross's five stages of dying, p. 11 of Dennis and Matthew Linn. 1978. *Healing Life's Hurts: Healing Memories through Five Stages of Forgiveness*. Paulist Press: New York.

79   Auw, Andre. *Gentle Roads to Survival: Making Self-Healing Choices in Difficult Circumstances*. Asian Publishing, Lower Lake, CA, 1991, p. 82.

80   Rosemarie Milson. 'Hold Me Now.' 'Sunday Life', *Sunday Age*, 25 November 2001.

81   A.P.A. 'American Psychiatric Association'.

82   Dunn, Amanda. 'SAINTS on the ball tackling bullies', *Age*, 25 July 2001.